# We Are in This Dance Together

# We Are in This Dance Together

*Gender, Power, and Globalization*

*at a Mexican Garment Firm*

NANCY PLANKEY-VIDELA

RUTGERS UNIVERSITY PRESS

NEW BRUNSWICK, NEW JERSEY, AND LONDON

Library of Congress Cataloging-in-Publication Data

Plankey-Videla, Nancy.
    We are in this dance together : gender, power, and globalization at a Mexican
garment firm / Nancy Plankey-Videla.
        p. cm.
    Includes bibliographical references and index.
    ISBN 978–0–8135–5301–6 (hbk. : alk. paper) — ISBN 978–0–8135–5302–3
(pbk. : alk. paper) — ISBN 978–0–8135–5315–3 (e-book)
    1. Women clothing workers—Mexico.   2. Clothing workers—Labor unions—Mexico.
3. Strikes and lockouts—Clothing trade—Mexico.   4. Clothing trade—Mexico.
I. Title.
    HD6073.C62M6596   2012
    331.4'8870972—dc23

                                                            2011037602

A British Cataloging-in-Publication record for this book is available from the British Library.

Excerpts from the following articles by the author are reprinted in this book, in modified
form, with permission from the publishers:

"Following Suit: An Examination of Structural Constraints to Industrial Upgrading in the
    Third World." *Competition and Change* 9 (4): 307–327. Copyright © 2005 by the Maney
    Publishing, www.maney.co.uk/journals/com.
"Gendered Contradictions: Managers and Women Workers in Self-Managed Teams."
    *Research in the Sociology of Work* 16: 85–116. Copyright © 2006 by the Emerald Group
    Publishing, www.emeraldinsight.com.
"It Cuts Both Ways: Workers, Management, and the Construction of a 'Community of
    Fate' on the Shop Floor in a Mexican Garment Factory." *Social Forces* 84 (4): 2099–2120.
    Copyright © 2006 by the University of North Carolina Press, www.uncpress.edu.

Visit our website: http://rutgerspress.rutgers.edu

Manufactured in the United States of America

*For the women workers of Moctezuma,*
*who taught me so much about life, work, and*
*standing up for yourself and what is just.*
*Para las compañeras de Moctezuma, que me enseñaron*
*tanto sobre la vida, el trabajo, y la defensa de uno mismo y todo lo*
*que es justo.*

*For Rob, my compañero in life*
*For Pancho and Sofía,*
*my sunshine today, whose kindness, brilliance, and*
*laughter give me hope for the future*

# Contents

# Figures and Tables

# Acknowledgments

This book would not have been possible without the support and generosity of so many people. I am thankful for the kindness and openness with which workers and managers received me at Moctezuma. I am especially grateful for my teammates, who welcomed me into their workspace, shared their daily work routines, showed me the ropes, laughed at my mistakes, invited me to their homes, and demonstrated the courage and guts it takes to stand up to injustice. *¡Gracias compañeras!* I will never forget the friendships we forged as we complained how much our feet hurt, ate lunch at the cafeteria, kept warm by piling in the car the night we took over the factory, and celebrated birthdays and Mother's Day. I owe a special debt of gratitude to Idolina whose fierce spirit, generosity to a fault, and optimism still amaze me. I thank Tere, who has remained a close friend, purveyor of information, and inspiration for her hard work and courage. I also thank the Independent Human Rights Commission, whose members shared their perspectives on the labor dispute, and especially Juliana Quintanilla, who helped me locate the labor movement leaders. Alfredo Domínguez from the Authentic Labor Front was also a great resource and friend. Their persistent and tenacious commitment to social justice is an example to follow.

At the University of Wisconsin–Madison, I thank the friendship and assistance of Patrick Brenzel, Tony Schulze, Barbara Schoerder, and especially Sandy Ramer. I have also been fortunate to have found a community of scholars and activists in Madison, Wisconsin. I benefited greatly from the friendship with Kelly Beseske, Jorge Cadena-Roa, Scott Frickel, Beth Fussell, Jody Knauss, Vicki Mayer, Steve McKay, Brian Obach, Andrea Robles, Jeff Rothstein, Andrew Schrank, and Theresa Thompson-Colon, among others. I learned how to be a sociologist—and engaged scholar—from Steve Bunker, Jane Collins, Allen Hunter, Florencia Mallon, Gay Seidman, Steve Stern, Leanne Tigges, and Erick Olin Wright. I am most appreciative for the unyielding support of Gay Seidman, my mentor and friend, who modeled how to combine incisive scholarship with committed activism. I still turn to her for guidance and to share my best and worst news.

At Texas A&M I have found a collegial home. Thanks go to the administrative staff, whose competence, patience, and kindness make my work possible: Barbara Becvar, Brenda Bernal, Mary Pendleton, Virgil Martinez, Christi Ramirez, and Allison Schertz. I am especially grateful for the support of my colleagues Paul Almeida, Ashley Currier, Nadia Flores, Joe Feagin, Mark Fossett, Sarah Gatson, Joseph Jewell, Rob Mackin, David McWhirter, Wendy Moore, Harland Prechel, Jim Rosenheim, Rebecca Hartkopf Schloss, Jane Sell, Zulema Valdez, and Neha Vora. I have been especially lucky to have shared the tenure experience with my colleague and friend Stuart Hysom until his untimely death in 2011. His sense of humor and commitment to the sociological imagination were inspirational.

I owe a tremendous debt of gratitude to my church family at Friends for providing encouragement and much needed babysitting services to complete my work. A special thank-you to the Dudo and Williamson families, Dan DeLeon, Kathy Slater, Kate Lucchese, and Ruth Schemmer.

Throughout the years I have received support from the University of Wisconsin–Madison Sociology Department, MacArthur Foundation, the Social Science Research Center and the Alfred P. Sloan Foundation Program on the Corporation as a Social Institution, Texas A&M College of Liberal Arts, Melbern G. Glasscock Center for Humanities Research, and the Mexican American and U.S. Latino Research Center, without whom my research would not have been possible. Research assistance from Brittany Cleveland, Maria Lazo, Chung-pei Pien, Gigi Trebatowski, and Kate Qian Xiong is also much appreciated. I am most grateful for Lise Creurer's amazing editorial assistance. Thanks go to Jaime Brito, Adrián Carrasco Zanini, Enrique Torres Agatón, and Glen Vigus for assistance with photographic materials.

My family has been indispensable in this journey. *¡Un millón de gracias!* to my mother Gabriela Videla, father Ray Plankey, and sister Ivonne for all their support big and small. My dad drove me to the bus station at 6 A.M. while it was still dark; my mom contacted every newspaper and freelance photographer to find photos that bring to life the courageous women of Moctezuma, both in 1972 and 2001, in the pages of this book. My sister helped to care for my baby as I set off to do fieldwork. They have doubled as research assistants, photocopying newspaper articles, tracking down workers, extending hospitality to my newfound friends. Thank you! I also appreciate the support from my in-laws, Jeanne and Thomas Mackin, who always encouraged my work.

Present in each page of this book and step of the research is my partner Rob Mackin. Not only has he debated the merits of the ideas and conclusions of this book with me, but he has also provided incisive comments on every draft. This book belongs to both of us. Our wonderful children, Pancho and Sofía, have also grown up with this project. I thank them for letting me steal away to work long into the night, miss soccer games, and fun trips. They are my inspiration. Thank you.

# Abbreviations

| | |
|---|---|
| AMLO | Andres Manuel López Obrador |
| CANACINTRA | National Chamber of Manufacturing Industry (Cámara Nacional de la Industria de Transformación) |
| CCE | Entrepreneurial Coordinating Council (Consejo Coordinador Empresarial) |
| CEREAL | Reflection and Labor Action Center (Centro de Reflexión y Acción Laboral) |
| CMO | Mexican Classification of Occupations (Clasificación Mexicana de Ocupaciones) |
| COPARMEX | Mexican Employers' Confederation (Confederación Patronal de la República Mexicana) |
| CROC | Revolutionary Confederation of Workers and Peasants (Confederación Revolucionaria de Obreros y Campesinos) |
| CTC | Confederation of Workers and Peasants (Confederación de Trabajadores y Campesinos) |
| CTM | Confederation of Mexican Workers (Confederación de Trabajadores de México) |
| FAT | Authentic Labor Front (Frente Auténtico del Trabajo) |
| FCAB | federal conciliation and arbitration board (junta federal de conciliación y arbitraje) |
| FDI | foreign direct investment |
| FSCNT | National Coordinating Union of Workers (Federación Sindical Coordinadora Nacional de Trabajadores) |
| GATT | General Agreement on Tariffs and Trade |
| GDP | gross domestic product |
| GM | general manager |
| HR | human resources |
| ILO | International Labor Organization |

| ILOGB | International Labor Office Governing Body |
| IMF | International Monetary Fund |
| IMSS | Mexican Social Security System (Instituto Mexicano del Seguro Social) |
| INEGI | National Institute of Statistics, Geography, and Information (Instituto Nacional de Estadística, Geografía e Informática) |
| INFONAVIT | National Workers' Housing Fund (Instituto del Fondo Nacional de la Vivienda para los Trabajadores) |
| IRB | institutional review board |
| ISCO-88 | International Standard Classification of Occupations-[19]88 |
| ISO | International Organization for Standardization |
| ISPT | payroll tax (Impuesto Sobre Productos del Trabajo) |
| J-1 | jackets one (production line) |
| J-2 | jackets two (production line) |
| JIT | just-in-time |
| LCAB | local conciliation and arbitration board (junta local de conciliación y arbitraje) |
| MFA | Multi-Fibre Arrangement |
| MNR1 | *Major Regional Newspaper One* (center-left perspective) |
| MORENA | Movement for National Renovation (Movimiento de la Regeneración Nacional) |
| MRN2 | *Major Regional Newspaper Two* (center-right perspective) |
| NAFTA | North American Free Trade Agreement |
| NGO | nongovernmental organization |
| OAS | Organization of American States |
| PAN | National Action Party (Partido Acción Nacional) |
| PNR | National Revolutionary Party (Partido Revolucionario Nacional) |
| PRD | Democratic Revolution Party (Partido de la Revolución Democrática) |
| PRI | Institutional Revolutionary Party (Partido Revolucionario Institucional) |
| SAMs | standard allotted minutes |
| SAR | Savings for Retirement System (Sistemas de Ahorro para el Retiro) |
| SPC | statistical process control |
| UNT | National Workers' Union (Unión Nacional de Trabajadores) |
| WTO | World Trade Organization |

# We Are in This Dance Together

# Introduction

## "WE ARE IN THIS DANCE TOGETHER"

On March 15, 2001, at 3 P.M. sharp, women workers at Moctezuma, located in central Mexico, walked out on strike.[1] I was one of them. The Mexican-owned high-end men's suit factory, part of an industrial group that included two textile firms and an international distribution center, was considered a model to follow by local entrepreneurs and state agents. In fact, the state government envisioned Moctezuma as the anchor of an industrial garment and textile district premised on cutting-edge technology and organizational innovations that would compete in the global economy. The internationally renowned firm had operated for thirty-two years under the traditional piecework system, where predominantly women workers labored individually to produce preset quotas. In 1996, Moctezuma reorganized around participatory team systems to respond more quickly to changing international markets through increased efficiency. With these changes, 80 percent of the workforce—mostly women—were reassigned into teams, while the considerably smaller cutting department—mostly male—still worked on the individual piece-rate system. The firm provided stable employment, secured by paying the highest wages available to women in the region. As such, I thought it was a perfect place to study gender, labor, and globalization.

When the strike occurred, it had only been three months since I had begun my ethnographic study of a global factory. I had joined the firm's month-long training program with the permission of management and the union. There, I learned to sew on an industrial machine and, together with other young women who made up the dominant workforce, was socialized into the benefits of participatory team systems that had been in place for five years. Under teamwork, women workers were given the chance to become multiskilled, experiencing greater autonomy and opportunity to use their ingenuity and knowledge to coordinate production. Granted greater responsibility, team leaders freely moved around the shop floor, troubleshooting problems with other team leaders, technicians, and managers. Thus, women workers under teamwork received enhanced wages and benefits in exchange for this increased effort.

For the first two and a half months on the shop floor, I was impressed with how deeply my teammates had internalized their responsibility to ensure that production ran smoothly, even though pressuring each other to do high-quality work often resulted in interpersonal conflicts. Teamwork seemed to work for both workers and the firm. Yet on February 15, our team leader called a meeting where deeper cleavages became evident. Team leader Luisa—a twenty-something, mild-mannered, young, single woman—shared a message from management. Through her, the firm announced that, in order to compete with labor costs in China and Central America and with the expected decrease in sales caused by the U.S. recession, management would cut wages and cancel all bonuses.

The news was not well received by the workers. Immediately, the eighteen women and one man in my team protested: "They want us to work at 100 percent but they don't give us the materials to do so! They broke the contract!" Another woman voiced a common sentiment: "I cannot feed my family on what they want to pay us." An older woman who had been at the factory for ten years exclaimed, "They pay us like a maquiladora. We are *not* a maquiladora!"[2] Another replied: "Well, with this union, there is nothing we can do." The team leader responded, "When I'm kicked out, I'm taking my machine with me." Everyone laughed. Unlike the majority who labored on old industrial sewing equipment, she operated a modern computerized machine. After the laughter subsided, my teammates expressed fear of losing their jobs. Rumors abounded for months that management would fire workers. It was no secret that the firm was financially stressed. In fact, women workers had voted a year ago to forgo a series of benefits to help capitalize the firm and had recently agreed to increase their effort to get special orders out on time. But this more recent news confirmed their worst fears. Five days later, management canceled the second shift and fired 400 workers, a little less than one-third of the workforce.

One month later, workers prepared to strike. I was so nervous that day, I lost track of time. Lupe, my teammate, tapped me on the shoulder. "It's time to go," she said in a calm voice. Around us machines stopped as women and men got up and walked outside to a loading dock for a union general assembly. Even though the union had not supported the work stoppage, the workers had overruled them and formed a strike committee. As workers gathered outside, the words of one strike committee member pierced the air: "I'm a single mother just like most of you, and I am not afraid of losing my job. The company has fired the entire second shift, failed to restore benefits we froze last year to help *them* out [of a financial crisis], and now they want to renege on wage increases. Let's declare ourselves on strike, *compañeros y compañeras*.[3] We are in this dance together."

Workers stood in the hot sun for what seemed an eternity debating whether to put up the red-and-black strike flag. The cutting department, composed predominantly of male workers earning a higher wage, did not want to go on strike. The women yelled at the men, "You better back us up! Teamwork got us in this mess. And cutting is next." The men conceded reluctantly; they knew that conditions at work had changed in the last year.

Meanwhile, management urged strikers to consider the ramifications of their actions. As they put it, striking would endanger "the livelihood of so many single mothers who depend on this job to feed their families." Unmoved, the strike committee, accompanied by the unpopular union leadership who were still the legal representatives of the workers, bargained with labor authorities. Word spread that if workers put up the flag without state officials witnessing it, the state would declare the strike illegal. Others yelled, "But without the flag we are illegal!" No one knew what to do. Although Moctezuma had been the site of a successful thirty-five-day strike in 1972, there seemed to be no institutional memory of this event among workers. And the labor authorities did not provide much assistance, supplying contradictory information on the steps required to declare a strike. Thus, the strike committee decided workers would guard the facilities so management could not sneak out products or machinery while the strike delegation negotiated with company representatives and state labor authorities.

In the end, the state arbiter convinced the delegation to postpone declaring a strike because doing so would "officially and unilaterally end negotiations." If the contract negotiations failed, he argued, the strike flag could go up immediately. However, after seventy-two hours of wrenching and intimidating discussion, the discredited union and company signed a contract without the consent of workers. Then, the same arbiter who brokered the deal declared the strike officially illegal; workers had to return to work or risk being fired.[4] A few weeks later, the women learned that several local conciliation and arbitration boards used this delaying strategy to break strikes around the country.

Workers reluctantly returned to the production line. However, they continued to fight the collusion between the state, company, and corrupt union in almost daily marches in the streets and meetings outside the factory gates. Dissenting workers established an independent union, but the state and company refused to accept its legality. In protest, these women shut down a major city avenue on April 4. Although this was a peaceful sit-in, the governor sent in the military police with dogs, batons, and tear gas. When we returned to work the next morning, over thirty military police in riot gear lined the company entrance. Workers pretended not to be afraid while walking through the outside gates. Confused and humiliated, the women lined up, showed identification cards, and entered the factory gates as top managers stared each one down.

After three months of protest inside and outside the factory gates, workers struggled to remain united. Workers staged slowdowns to sabotage the lines, but the costs of organizing were too high. Management threatened leaders, or anyone suspected of being one, with termination. Managers at all levels pressured workers to turn in "troublemakers." In the end, it was "your job or your neighbor's job." Company spies were said to be everywhere. What had once been one of the highest-paying and most cutting-edge factories in Mexico had become a war zone.

The case of Moctezuma, a nationally and internationally recognized firm operating at the same location for thirty-seven years, provides a unique opportunity to understand how organizational change affects the ability and inclination of workers—and, women, in particular—to consent to or resist managerial dictates. Comparing the organization of work under piecework and teamwork and the factors and outcomes of the 1972 strike with those of 2001, it becomes clear that, although workers did not remember the previous strike, management did. Teamwork was set up, in part, to assure compliance from the workforce and prevent worker contentiousness. So, why did a shop floor that was carefully reorganized to manufacture consent instead manufacture militancy? And why did women workers, recruited for their apparent docility, risk their livelihoods during a time of global economic crisis? The answer lies, I argue, in the interaction of internal factors (the contradictory gendered effects of teams) and external factors (the constraining and enabling dynamics of globalization). The convergence of these shaped, on the one hand, the objective conditions of work and, on the other hand, how women subjectively experienced work and the meanings they attached to their role as workers.

To answer the questions driving this study, I look at scholarly debates on the conditions under which women workers identify primarily as workers, how shop floor organization facilitates (or impedes) the development of that consciousness, and how recent efforts at retooling production (namely through teamwork) yield contradictory outcomes. Last, I examine how globalization—understood as a combination of economic, social, and political processes—affects relations on the shop floor.

## MANUFACTURING CONSENT AND MILITANCY

How does shop floor organization facilitate or impede worker consciousness? Much of the work on militancy is rooted in Karl Marx's distinction of class-in-itself and class-for-itself. According to Marx, the capitalist system creates a working class by treating labor as a commodity, where (implicitly male) workers sell their labor power or capacity to work in order to survive. However, in order to extract effort, and thus profit, capitalists must coerce and control workers, resulting in mounting misery and resistance. These objective conditions of exploitation create a class-in-itself, a class experiencing similar circumstances. It is not until workers advance a sense of themselves as sharing a common interest that they form a collective consciousness and transform into a revolutionary class-for-itself.

Most workers throughout history, however, have not risen up against their employers. This has spurred scholars to ask, "Why haven't workers revolted?" Antonio Gramsci provides a nuanced understanding of why workers do not defend their own class interests: hegemonic power (1971). Hegemony operates by diffusing the dominant classes' interests through social institutions to the point where the ideas and interests of dominant classes become "normative, inevitable, and even natural" for subordinate classes (Lentriccia in Barker 1993). Yet hegemonic power is not a totalizing force; rather, it is a dynamic process that neutralizes opposition by providing brief spaces of resistance that then serve to legitimize dominant rule (Thompson 1978; Williams 1977).

Workplace scholars tend to focus on either how organizational structures foster worker consent or how conflictive social dynamics influence the likelihood of worker resistance (Roscigno and Hodson 2004). The first approach, illustrated by labor process theorists, offers a more structuralist view, concentrating on how managerial hegemony follows from the organization of the shop floor. The second, more relational approach, represented by sociologists of work, focuses on the agency of workers and their social interactions with management. While not mutually exclusive, these two camps—the structuralist and relational schools of thought—privilege different aspects of the workplace, although they converge in one important area of inquiry: work cultures. I build on both models to explain the radicalization of women at Moctezuma.

Structuralist labor process scholars explain how, on the shop floor, hegemony replaces coercion with mechanisms that foster consent. They argue that workers' interests are shaped by internal labor markets, unions, and state regulations. Internal labor markets structure workplace interactions by encouraging workers to follow company rules to obtain promotions, unions to establish grievance procedures that channel worker discontent individually, and state regulations to eliminate the most egregious forms of oppression (Burawoy 1985; Edwards 1979). These mechanisms obscure the antagonistic relations between workers and capitalists theorized by Marx.

Labor process theorists thus have to explain how worker quiescence materializes from factory hegemonic control rather than militant worker consciousness. In his influential ethnography of a machine parts company in Chicago, Michael Burawoy reveals how workers devise the game of "making out" to give meaning to routine and repetitive jobs (1979). In doing so, workers regularly deliver above the required quota, securing extra effort for the company and masking relations of exploitation. Burawoy argues that workplaces manufacture consent "independent of the *particular* people who come to work, [or] of the particular agents of production" (1985, 39; emphasis in original). Differences between workplaces and worker consciousness are thus derived from technical and organizational elements.

Feminist theorists build on Burawoy's conception of hegemonic control but challenge the notion that the subjectivities and characteristics workers import into the workplace do not matter. Ching Kwan Lee compared two Chinese electronic assembly plants that are owned by the same parent company but operate in two distinct labor markets (1998). Her study demonstrates the importance not only of class but also of ethnic relations and gendered conditions of dependence in shaping workers' interests and, thus, the mechanism through which firms secure control (1998). The Shenzhen factory exercised coercive control by hiring young migrant women workers and building on their local ethnic networks and single status to extract work effort. The Hong Kong firm, in contrast, hired older women workers. Factory managers established a familial hegemonic regime in which company discourses highlighted family interests and rules provided workers with limited spaces to fulfill their roles as mothers. Loyalty emerged when the company hired a particular kind of woman and then, unlike most other workplaces, allowed her to balance work and family. Like the management at Moctezuma, these factories secured women's consent to factory structures by exploiting the workers' traditional family roles.

Gender also organizes shop floor relations through managers' image of the ideal worker. In her comparative study of four maquiladoras on the U.S.-Mexico border, Leslie Salzinger argues that managers construct multiple images of women as the ideal worker, according to their specific production imperatives and the labor supply available. Managerial tropes and strategies "name, describe and create workers' shop floor subjectivities" (2003, 10). For example, in Anarchomex, an automobile harness firm, managers preferred to hire young women workers, but, since they were in short supply locally, managers had to hire men workers. Nevertheless, managers treated all workers as if they were all young women, producing a recalcitrant and conflictive response from the men. Hence, Salzinger argues that how managers imagine workers structures the workplace and constrains worker responses.

Hegemonic control thus emerges from the organization of work and recruitment strategies, which are informed by women workers' particular characteristics and managers' construction of the ideal worker. The focus is on how managers minimize the likelihood of struggle by deploying gendered and racialized ideologies that obscure workers' class interests. How women workers resist such control, however, is less clear. Resistance tends to be confined to dispersed actions by individuals such as breaking company rules like eating on the line or, ultimately, just quitting.

The second approach to how workplace organization affects worker consciousness, the relational camp, focuses not on management control but on shop floor social dynamics. A prime example of this perspective is the Workplace Ethnography Project led by Randy Hodson, which examines eighty-two book-length organizational ethnographies to tease out the key characteristics and patterned social relations at work (2001). The comparison of many different fine-grained studies of workplaces reveals that an array of social relations and responses to managerial control are possible, challenging the hegemonic powers of management often claimed by labor process theorists.

One of the most consistent findings by sociologists of work is that lack of organizational coherence leads to worker resistance. Workers hold a normative expectation that management will provide the conditions for them to do their jobs through effective organizational structure, consistent materials, and reasonable leadership. Incoherent organization often leads to deteriorating working conditions, employment insecurity, and poor management-worker relations. Within this context, managerial abuse is more likely to develop and to generate worker resistance (Juravich 1985; Roscigno and Hodson 2004; Vallas 1987, 2003a).

A focus on workplace relations also allows for an examination of worker agency, that is, "the objective capacity of individuals to act collectively or individually in a manner that either reinforces or undermines prevalent social relations and organizational structure" (Roscigno and Hodson 2004, 18). In a comparative study of five pulp and paper mills that adopted flexible team-based practices to varying degrees, Steven Vallas contends that worker agency played an important role in organizational transformations (2003a, 2006). He argues that the multiple worker responses derived from the inherently contradictory process of organizational change. Increased worker expectation resulted in decreased managerial legitimacy, which often strengthened solidarity among workers.

I draw on both the structuralist and relational camps to understand the dialogical relationship between structure and agency at Moctezuma. While the organization of the shop floor (such as recruitment, hiring preferences, training, supervision, payment, incentives, and the character of unions and state regulations) under piecework and teamwork provided powerful inducements for consent, securing cooperation was more contradictory and conditional than labor process theorists suggest.

Focusing on the conflicting nature of social interactions, like the relational approach, reveals that management-worker relations at Moctezuma were negotiated and that women workers enacted agency when they both consented to and resisted managerial controls. It was management's ineffective response to global pressures that set the stage for worker mobilization. While managers asked women to invest in the firm's future by relinquishing benefits, management did not provide them, in turn, with the conditions needed to work at their expected levels. To make matters worse, managers then accused workers of not working hard enough, which transformed individual complaints into shared moral indignation. At this point Moctezuma's workers effectively repurposed management's symbols and language to their advantage. While managers utilized the trope of vulnerable single mothers to urge its workers to accept decreasing wages, workers appropriated the discourse to highlight management's failure as a patriarch and women's strength, courage, and resolve in the face of injustice.

The mechanism by which grievances were catalyzed into worker consciousness was through new identities that emerged from the shop floor culture. Identity is an ongoing process of self-perception produced in interaction with surrounding individuals and social structures. It was through group processes that women workers' identities changed from that of primarily mothers to workers who were also mothers. Only after this shift in identity did women workers decide to resist collectively by subverting team rules and using management's paternalistic discourse of the firm as family as a mobilizing tool.

## CREATING MEANING THROUGH WORK CULTURES

Elton Mayo and his colleagues stumbled onto an important insight in the 1930s Western Electric studies at the Chicago Hawthorne plant: workers often form informal work groups, and it is loyalty to the group that determines whether productivity increases or output is restricted. While Frederick Winslow Taylor, father of scientific management, believed workers were self-interested individuals who only responded to economic incentives, Mayo concluded that workers formed social ties of mutual interests. By providing spaces of relative autonomy from management supervision, management could foster values and rules—or cultures—that promoted cooperation and feelings of enhanced meaning at work (Mayo 1933; Roethlisberger and Dickson 1939; Vallas, Finlay, and Wharton 2009). This insight launched the human relations school of management and, later, influenced quality circle, employee involvement, and teamwork-management practices (Smith 1997).

Building on research on gender and work culture, I show how work cultures at Moctezuma provided a crucial site of identity construction that shaped whether and how women could resist managerial control. Unlike most studies of male-dominated workplaces, feminist scholars have focused on how work cultures in female-dominated industries, such as the apparel industry, build on women's family and gender roles in ways that simultaneously generate resistance, adaptation, and consent (Shapiro-Perl in Lamphere 1985; Lamphere 1987). In an ethnography of a clothing factory in England, Sallie Westwood highlights how women forged friendships across racial and ethnic divides and gave meaning to their work by celebrating life-cycle rituals like weddings and births (1985). According to Westwood, celebrations endorsed traditional gender roles, while, at the same time, carving out spaces of autonomy and resistance to managerial control. While managers disapproved of the distractions from work, they realized that prohibiting the social events could prompt women to walk off the line. Similarly, managers at an electronics Hong Kong plant allowed matron workers to take extended breaks to deal with family obligations in a tacit exchange for cheap wages. Women workers' identities as mothers shaped group interactions and relations with managers (Lee 1998).

Thus, the organization of work affects how women construct spaces to link their family and work lives in meaningful ways. Work cultures facilitate interactions between workers, shape identities around shared characteristics, and are thus crucial in both manufacturing consent and militancy.

## TEAMWORK AND ORGANIZATIONAL CHANGE

How manufacturing firms are organized affects how both women and men experience work.[5] For most of the twentieth century, factories have been organized around the theory of Taylorism, which separates conception (intellectual labor) from execution (manual labor), leaving industrial engineers to devise one correct method for workers to follow. The underpinning philosophy held workers to be naturally lazy, needing incentives and direct supervisory control to be optimally productive (Braverman 1974; Taylor [1911] 1947). Taylorist organization, then, relies on an antagonistic worker-management relationship, where there exists no mutual obligation or binding commitment to the firm. Individual workers are easily replaced cogs in a system. The labor-intensive apparel industry uses Taylorist techniques to break down production into precise, standardized, perpetually repetitive operations. Fordism, a practice of Taylorist mass production, tied higher wages to mass consumption and prevailed in firms located in the primary labor market.

Since the 1970s, increased economic competition and falling corporate profits led to a shift from Fordist large-volume, standardized runs to small-batch, demand-driven, and higher value-added manufacturing. These technical changes were often accompanied by flexible participatory work arrangements (like teamwork, employee involvement, quality circles, and lean production) premised on cooperative rather than conflictive industrial relations practices.

The debate to date has focused on whether teamwork and other participatory work arrangements are good or bad for workers. However, there is increasingly a call for research on the uneven and contradictory nature and effects of such work systems. Vallas persuasively argues that teamwork is based on conflicting normative *and* competitive logics (2006). On the one hand, organizational change calls for an enhancement of worker autonomy and loyalty to teams and the firm (normative logic). On the other hand, uncertain market conditions press workers and managers to turn production around as quickly as possible, converting workers back into cogs in the system (competitive logic). Rather than a linear, predetermined outcome, Vallas finds that competing logics result in the incomplete adoption of participatory techniques and differing levels of commitment (and resistance) to teamwork from both managers and workers.

By moving beyond a dualistic treatment of participatory group arrangements, individual and collective agency becomes visible. Thus, selective adoption of teamwork results from a negotiation between managers and workers, where neither group necessarily has unitary interests. In this context, the contradictory, intended, and unintended consequences of participatory work systems make sense. Teamwork becomes a convenient way to bundle workers' interests with those of management as well as a process that fosters worker solidarity and mutual defense. Theorizing teamwork as composed of competing logics illuminates how its implementation at Moctezuma resulted in managerial incoherence and provided both constraints and opportunities for individual and collective agency.

## WORKER STRUGGLES AND GLOBALIZATION

Labor process theorists argue that the organization of production shapes working-class struggles. More specifically, Burawoy's theory of production regimes links the organization of work with the institutions that regulate production through a typology of historical regimes that have shaped working-class struggles (1985). In a despotic regime, the factory overseer of the industrial revolution coerced labor from workers without any state intervention. However, this resulted in a backlash of working-class movements, ushering in the hegemonic regime characterized by welfare policies and workplace protections. Consent, rather than coercion, predominates in the hegemonic regime since workers' and capitalists' interests are coordinated, providing a degree of worker autonomy that normalizes and obscures exploitation and dampens collective resistance. Instead of organized struggle such as strikes, individual resistance in the form of sabotage, slowdowns, absenteeism, and turnover prevails (Hirschman 1970; Roscigno and Hodson 2004; Vallas 2003a).

Hegemonic control, however, is only viable as long as profits expand. Under conditions of increased international competitiveness, Burawoy argues that capitalist firms will seek cheaper costs of production in new regions or countries. Hegemonic despotism, then, "is the 'rational' tyranny of capital mobility over the *collective* worker. . . . The fear of being fired is replaced by the fear of capital flight, plant closure, transfer of operations, and plant disinvestment" (1985, 150; emphasis in original). Many scholars characterize globalization as hegemonic despotism. Intensified international competition—made possible by technological innovations, geographic fragmentation of production, proliferation of regional trade agreements, and neoliberal ideologies promoting deregulation and limiting state involvement in social welfare policies—has led transnational corporations to take advantage of cheap labor and lax state regulations to increase profits (Dicken 2007; Schaeffer 2009).

Capital's hypermobility drives the "race to the bottom," with falling wages and deteriorating working conditions. Workers—who are generally not as mobile—are disciplined by an increasingly mobile employer that pits them in different locations against each other; this drives concession bargaining and undermines workers' movements (Bronfenbrenner 1996; Collins 2003; Hirst and Thompson 2001; Lipietz 1987; Silver 2003). Women workers are especially disadvantaged since capitalists interpret their reproductive role and subordinate position in the family as being supplementary earners and, thus, the cheapest form of labor available (Elson and Pearson 1986; Kessler-Harris 1982). It is not surprising that under these conditions women in a developing country, such as Mexico, fear the loss of their jobs to lower-cost sites like China and Central America, just as the women at Moctezuma did. Understood from an economic perspective, however, the 2001 strike at Moctezuma is puzzling: Why would workers jeopardize their jobs in an environment of rapidly disappearing opportunities?

The case of Moctezuma demonstrates how conceptualizing globalization as a purely economic phenomenon limits its explanatory power. Capital mobility has been accompanied by increased international migration as workers search for better life opportunities for themselves and their families (Massey and Sánchez 2010). Migrants form transnational networks, which in turn facilitate political, social, and cultural exchanges that foster transnational social movements and labor networks (Evans 2000; Keck and Sikkink 1998). In addition, information technologies have widened working-class access to mass media and, with that, participation in new cultural "images, scripts, and sensations" (Appadurai 1996, 4; Castells 2000). As such, new ways of interpreting the world—as a space of imagination and contestation—and the multiplication of public spheres, of "counter-hegemonic imagined worlds," emerge (Appadurai 1996, 166; Evans 2008; Smith 2007). Thus, for the women of Moctezuma globalization was more than a race to the bottom; it also entailed social and political opportunities that shaped their subjectivity in unexpected ways, leading to a strike during a period of economic crisis.

## Understanding the Mobilization of Women Workers at Moctezuma

The case study of Moctezuma demonstrates how women workers' subjectivities and interests are shaped not only at the point of production but also by the larger economic and social context. Managerial beliefs and practices did structure social relations on the shop floor, but so did the values, beliefs, and practices that women brought with them to work from outside the factory. Management's gendered understandings of who was an appropriate employee organized the shop floor. That is, its perception that certain femininities (and masculinities) were more appropriate for particular jobs shaped the division of labor, recruitment, payment structures, and shop floor interactions.

At the same time, workers also drew from larger gender ideologies that influenced how they understood themselves and their work; this, in turn, determined how they interacted with management. The roles these workers played in their families as single mothers, junior partners in dual-earner households, and unmarried daughters were especially important in shaping their identities. They also brought into the factory class and racial understandings that mediated relationships with coworkers and managers.

Work cultures proved an important way in which women's identities were shaped. These provided a space where managers negotiated their goals of control with respect to the need for women to give meaning to their work and social relations. Under the piecework system, a *familial* work culture developed.

Following Lee, I understand a culture of familialism as "characterized by the pervasive use of familial relations as metaphor for shop floor relations, [with] . . . institutionalized practices that recognized and facilitated women's familial responsibilities" (1998, 143). Management discourses, hiring practices, and payment systems stressed women's primary commitment to the family and work as a way for women to further their family's interests. High turnover, atomized work arrangements, and a slack labor market dampened mobilization. While a strike did take place in 1972, it is better explained by the larger social movement unionism of the time than by internal politicization caused by the work organization. The familial work culture prevalent in 1972, which continued until reorganization of production in 1996, structured women workers' interests as individuals, shaping how they navigated managerial supervision and rules to fulfill their particular familial goals. Thus, individual competition for easy work to increase one's production and take-home pay prevailed, eliciting consent from workers.

Under self-managed teams, however, production quotas and bonuses were based first on teams and, later, on the department. This organizational change, I argue, resulted in a *motherist* work culture developing under teamwork, just as a motherist culture developed in human rights groups in Latin America who "transform[ed] mothering and transfer[ed] it from the private to the public sphere . . . using traditional expectations of mothers to get away with conducting political protest in times and places where no one else could" (Stephen 1997, 273). In a similar way, workers' main identity as mothers shaped how they pushed the boundaries of self-managed teams. They changed the rules to grant team members special permits to miss work to care for sick children or attend school and, in the process, built a collective identity as working mothers.

Although unified around a shared identity of motherhood that focused on women's traditional roles, the motherist work culture also provided the space for solidary ties to emerge around work issues. Women workers organized the 2001 strike through the motherist work culture and self-managed teams. Their agency and sense of urgency, however, developed through a combination of changed social relations inside and outside the factory. It was the interaction of internal and external factors that convinced these workers to mobilize.

The most important internal factor that led to mobilization was the effect of self-managed teams on women workers' identity. Teamwork as implemented at Moctezuma resulted in a contradictory process that increased both the supervision of workers and their autonomy. Management executed a consultant-led reorganization to increase productivity and quality crucial for international competitiveness. Self-managed teams employed multiskilled workers so they could more quickly respond to market or product changes by reallocating labor within teams and making workers responsible for checking each other's production and quality levels. That is, workers assumed supervisory roles previously reserved for management; this resulted in an increased experience of surveillance as team members controlled each other's expenditure of effort to attain group bonuses. Thus, antagonisms traditionally experienced between managers and workers shifted laterally between workers.

At the same time, self-managed teams allowed women workers some autonomy in moving around the shop floor so they could communicate within and between teams and consult with managers to make production-related decisions. This process required workers who had been hired for their docility to take leadership roles, speak in group settings, and relate to managers on more egalitarian terms. A motherist work culture developed in this contradictory location of increased worker conflict and augmented leadership roles for women. This work culture united workers as mothers, providing a mechanism to push the boundaries of management control in the name of motherhood.[6]

Women workers at Moctezuma drew on larger gender ideologies that stressed their appropriate roles as mothers and wives along with class understandings (closely tied with racial categories) that located poor (darker) Mexicans at the bottom of social and economic hierarchies. In the factory, darker women were assumed to be indigenous, uneducated, and of lower status. Women obtained employment to help their families, which enabled them to fulfill their motherly duties. Most women at Moctezuma spoke of themselves as primarily mothers, not workers. Even single mothers who were by their own accounts the main or sole provider for their families saw their work at the factory as fulfilling the dutiful mother role. Thus women's identities as primarily mothers meant most were loath to protest deteriorating work conditions because voicing their discontent could cost them their jobs.

Motherist ideology reinforced women workers' identity as mothers above all else. Moreover, the work culture complemented management's discourses of the firm as an extension of the home and the need to preserve jobs to protect vulnerable single mothers. Thus, while management disapproved of the extended permits provided to mothers by team members, it was in their interest to support the motherist work culture and allow such practices to continue. Tapping into Mexican traditions that exalted the values of motherhood (held dear by both mothers and nonmothers at the factory) manufactured consent. The enhanced autonomy of self-managed teams promoted solidarity rooted in women's collective identity as mothers, and this created shop floor communication and decision-making mechanisms. At Moctezuma, women used the tools of self-management to make decisions not only about production but also about their rights as mothers. Only when women workers perceived themselves and their work differently did they use these tools to organize a strike.

Deciding to strike did not emerge from an experience of exploitation. While workers complained of an oppressive feeling of continual supervision from coworkers and managers, they also acknowledged that the firm paid above-average wages and provided extensive benefits, which allowed them to fulfill their family responsibilities. A social pact where workers traded increased surveillance and effort for augmented wages and benefits ensured stability. But although flexible, workers' consent had limits.

When Moctezuma experienced the financial crisis in 2000 that affected bonuses and wages, workers continued to express loyalty to the firm and its organizational practices by forfeiting benefits (such as Christmas baskets, uniforms, and gifts of cloth for marriages and births) for a year to free up capital for reinvestment in the firm. At the end of the year, however, not only were the benefits not returned, but the firm petitioned the courts to break the collective-bargaining agreement to lower wages, thereby breaking the social pact that sustained workers' consent. At that point, managers utilized the trope of vulnerable single mothers to urge women workers to accept decreasing wages to defend the firm's viability. Women workers, however, appropriated this discourse to highlight management's failure as a patriarch and women's resilience and fortitude in the face of injustice. Moral outrage at the perceived injustice ensued although it was tempered by workers' appraisal of the local labor market. Thus the communication network that developed through self-managed teams became crucial as workers decided whether to accept deteriorating conditions of work or strike.

The key factor in shaping women workers' consciousness and their decision to strike was how they interpreted changes inside the firm in light of larger external social, political, and economic processes—specifically globalization and local democratization—that impinged on their lives and the firm's viability. For workers at Moctezuma, globalization provided real constraints *and* new possibilities. They noticed declining orders for men's suits, and management keenly reminded them that clients could take their business to cheaper sites. Moreover, media attention repeatedly linked plant closures, deepening agricultural crises, and escalating migration to globalization. Yet increasing immigration of women and men to the United States from central Mexico multiplied local networks workers could use to travel north. More than ever before, migration provided an option (albeit a dangerous and unreliable one) to bad jobs. In addition, extensive media coverage of social movements occurred during this time; the Zapatista peasant uprising in southern Mexico and the National Autonomous University student strikes in Mexico City amplified the message that collective action offered an alternative to subjugation. Together, the increased migration and ongoing social movements presented a new social imaginary of class, racial, and gendered relations.

Important changes were also occurring at the state level, which workers interpreted as favorable for them. For the first time in over seventy years, a party other than the PRI (Institutional Revolutionary Party) had won the governor's race. The business and family values–oriented PAN (National Action Party) promised change and transparency, a shift away from previous corrupt practices of government, business, and union collusion. Workers had voted overwhelmingly for the PAN in the past elections and expected support for the strike.

The convergence of these events—declining wages and benefits, management's breach of their social pact with workers, threats of capital mobility to cheaper countries, media's portrayal of globalization as a race to the bottom, increased opportunities to migrate to the United States, local democratization, and heightened awareness of collective resistance—shaped women workers' identities and proved a powerful catalyst for change.

Deteriorating working conditions and perceived unjust treatment from management empowered women workers to transcend gender and class-based expectations promoted by Moctezuma and Mexican culture. Turning management's own gendered discourse against them, workers' framed the strike as a defense of the most vulnerable workers—single mothers. In this way, workers used beliefs around motherhood to challenge the firm's authority as benevolent patriarch. Although women still identified as mothers, they increasingly interpreted their interests as also class-based and antithetical to management's interests. That is, the meaning of work was redefined as women saw themselves not merely as mothers—and thus willing to accept worsening conditions of work for the sake of family income—but also as workers who deserved jobs with dignity and living wages that could no longer be obtained at Moctezuma. At this point, when new avenues for action became possible, open contestation in the form of a strike made sense. Work became more than a way to support one's family; it transformed into a source of newfound independence, authority, self-esteem, and meaning.

As management and labor authorities blocked workers' attempts to elect a democratic union, the women increasingly forged alliances with other social movements. Interaction with other groups, coupled with the state's support of the firm rather than the workers, further changed movement participants' identities. At the 2001 yearly May Day parade, the striking women rallied eight thousand workers to demand justice for the working class and state accountability to voters. A newspaper article referred to the women as "modern-day Adelitas," alluding to the historic female revolutionary fighter. For many, working on the shop floor transformed them into citizens.

## Unpacking Social Relations on the Shop Floor with Feminist Ethnography

Principles of feminist ethnography guide this study. By this, I mean research methods that explicitly recognize and address as much as possible the power differentials between researcher and researched, seek to understand the world from the vantage point of oppressed groups, hope to improve the lives of women (and girls) by contributing to the remediation of gender inequalities, and build a more just and egalitarian society. It is also important to be reflexive about the research process, acknowledging that we bring our own biases and assumptions to the field and that knowledge is filtered through our lens. For this reason, it is important to make public not only research results but also the research process: how we arrived at the topic, maneuvered ethical and personal dilemmas in the field, and arrived at our conclusions (Mohanty, Russo, and Torres 1991; Naples 2003; Smith 1987).

As a feminist ethnographer, I aim to link macro processes and micro practices and to see how larger power dynamics affect the everyday lives of workers—especially those of women. In this study, that translated into being overt about my study, reflexive about my knowledge and position, and straightforward about what I would do with the results. Furthermore, it meant allowing others to choose whether to participate in the study, although I recognize that power relations at times made such a choice nearly impossible. Despite being uncomfortable, my being reflexive also meant naming the privileges of class, ethnicity, and nationality that set me apart from workers and at times placed me closer to management. Although my worldview and sympathies were with the workers, the fact that my son went to the same school and saw the same doctor as several of the children of management highlighted my privilege. Furthermore, I could leave the factory at any time, choose not to go to work when I was sick, and take a break when my partner needed me to stay home to care for our child.

One of the main issues confronting any ethnographer is how to gain access. How a researcher enters the field decides who can be observed and questioned and thus affects the resulting analysis. My case is no different. In fact, I believe that how I secured access was key to my being able to participate fully in the manifold and contradictory experiences of workers and managers at Moctezuma. Like other ethnographies, the study at Moctezuma came about in a roundabout way. I had originally prepared for fieldwork at a factory owned by a U.S. textile giant that had moved to the region to avoid high levels of turnover at the U.S.-Mexico border. After initial permission was granted, a representative from U.S. headquarters requested I wait for the company to examine the study. Eight months later, the transnational corporation decided to close its Mexican plant and I had to seek a new research site.

My mother, then director of a local nongovernmental organization trying to promote business-government-community linkages to fund grassroots development projects, offered to use her contacts to line up a possible new research site. She called a government official she had met through this effort, who suggested I call a friend of his in the finance office of a local garment factory and say that he had recommended that I call. Although skeptical, I made the call. As soon as the finance officer heard my institutional affiliation, why I was calling, and who told me to call, he forwarded my call to the company's director of human resources (HR). In this brief telephone interview, I learned that the director had spent a summer studying English at my university, the University of Wisconsin–Madison. We joked about drinking beers on the lakefront terrace and agreed to meet the following week.

When I met the director, a tall and light-skinned man in his fifties, at the end of September 2000, he just smiled, introduced me to his assistant, and said that she would take care of anything that I needed. I asked the assistant, a well-manicured, dark-skinned young woman in her twenties, to whom I should speak to get permission to carry out a study at the factory. This woman, Belinda, who became my main liaison with management and an important source of information, said: "Tell me what you need. It has already been authorized." Thus authorization was provided informally and behind closed doors, without discussing the project, the methodology, or the institutional review board protocol. I am sure the door had been opened through my introduction by an important state agent and by the fact that the director of HR and I shared the connection of an elite educational institution.

A week later I returned to the factory, met with the director, and participated in a four-hour tour of the plant with a young male industrial engineer. Toward the end of the tour, the director of HR approached us, saying that someone wanted to meet me. I followed him to the company's medical clinic and conference room, where I was introduced to the doctor, who also happened to be the father of the firm's majority owner. What followed was an interrogation: Why a dissertation on turnover? Why this firm? What methods would I use? I explained the circuitous route by which I had landed there, the fact that turnover was just a way to look at the possibilities and challenges for national development, which was what really interested me. I said I would like to interview workers and managers and, perhaps, if possible, be able to work on the shop floor for a while. The doctor listened intently to me and then began to speak about his own efforts to lower turnover rates. He had spearheaded, both at this factory and others owned by his family, dental and medical programs to improve the workers' quality of life. In fact, he was an academic, writing books on industrial medicine. He believed this was the best way to lower turnover at Moctezuma since wages were already the highest in the region. The doctor then turned to the director of HR, who had been standing behind me and listening the whole time, and said, "Help her with whatever she requires." Then we left. I surmised that the doctor approved my study because he valued academic research and agreed with the importance of the topic. No matter what the reason, I believe his endorsement allowed me greater access to both managers and workers. I can find no other explanation for why the firm let me stay on the shop floor during and after the strike.

The next day, I returned to the company grounds to learn more about the other two textile mills that together with Moctezuma formed an industrial group. It was a stark contrast to the previous day's tour of the garment factory just a few yards away. While the garment factory was hot, cramped, and filled with women's bodies maneuvering thousands of small machines, the textile mill contained only a few huge machines that hummed, manipulated by a scattering of men in blue uniforms. There was only one area where women worked: darning. Only women were allowed in this labor-intensive department, where they carefully repaired defective cloth by hand. The industrial engineer explained to me that men were needed for most jobs since they were "better with machines,

stronger to move heavy rolls of cloth, and more tolerant of the noise and heat."
"Girls," he continued, "have greater dexterity, patience, and are more meticulous in their work." I bit my tongue; it was only my second day, but already it was
clear that gender was an important component of how management constructed
workers and, thus, of the study. The following day, I visited the second textile
mill, located a few miles away, where fifty men made acetate lining to be used by
the garment plant. I spent the rest of October interviewing managers from HR
and waiting for a new cohort of workers to begin training. On November 6,
I began a month-long training session with nine other new workers in an area
that everyone in the factory called *la escuelita* (the little school).

The nine months I spent on the shop floor were crucial in building rapport
with both workers and managers, overcoming the differences that separated us
and feeling more comfortable expressing our opinions. A few months after
working in the pants department, a young woman came up to me and said: "You
know that time that you asked if you could interview me, and I said 'yes'? I did
not really mean it. But now, if you want, we can talk." In this book, I hope to
provide a voice for the workers, especially the women, on the shop floor at
Moctezuma. But I use their words to reconstruct a picture of the power relations
expressed on the shop floor as I understand them.

Women workers are the focus of this book for two reasons. First, my scholarly interests center on how factory work was both liberating and oppressive for
women in Mexico. Eighty-eight percent of workers at Moctezuma were female.
Second, I did not have good access to the few men on the shop floor. Although
there were five men in the two teams that I worked with, I had a close working
relationship with only two of them. I sat at the men's table during lunch once,
turning many heads and raising eyebrows. Thus, my analysis deals mostly with
how women experienced work, organizational change, and social activism.

The methods I used were participant observation, semistructured and
unstructured interviews, archival research, and statistical analyses gleaned from
information compiled on workers. After initial interviews with top management
in October 2000, I carried out nine months of participant observation at
Moctezuma (from November 2000 through August 2001). I conducted all
research with the consent of managers, the union, and workers with whom I
labored, who knew that I was a researcher and that I was not receiving a wage for
my work on the shop floor.[7] I assisted two teams as an extra hand to be used as
they deemed best. I ironed, followed the flow, organized bundles, ripped seams
of deficient pieces so that others could fix them, and assisted pressers by placing
and removing jackets on machines.

Besides the nine months of participant observation, I continued to conduct
semistructured interviews. All thirty-eight worker interviews in 2001 took place
away from the factory at a place of their choosing, usually their home or a restaurant, and lasted between one and two hours. However, most of the twenty-seven
managers I interviewed were available only during work hours; our interviews

ranged from twenty minutes to an hour in length. I returned in 2003, 2004, 2006, and 2009 to reinterview managers and workers and collect archival data. Moreover, a research assistant conducted further interviews in 2009, and I conducted phone interviews in 2010 and 2011. Each year it was progressively harder to locate workers and managers as addresses and phone numbers changed. In total, I conducted ninety-eight interviews with sixty-eight individuals. By using an interview schedule with a core group of thirty-eight of the workers with whom I had labored, I compiled a comparative database of worker characteristics and attitudes toward teamwork and the strike.

Interviews complemented participant observation by providing me the opportunity to further question workers and managers about the actions, views, and the meanings that I was attributing to them. Through interviews I was able to understand the connections between the lives of workers inside and outside the factory, how the worker's role in the family economy helped shape how each experienced work, teamwork, and resistance. Moreover, by interviewing managers at all levels and from different departments, I was able to see how differential location in the organization led to varying degrees of support for teamwork.

Anticipating problems with data collected at different periods, I asked questions in a variety of ways, and I conducted follow-up interviews with a sample of subjects to see if their recollections had changed. One third of the in-depth worker interviews took place before the March 15, 2001, strike, with the rest occurring in August, September, and mostly October of the same year. All should be regarded as having taken place in an emotionally and politically charged atmosphere; as such, critiques of teamwork in themselves are not surprising. To compensate for some of this bias, I asked multiple questions about the advantages and disadvantages of piecework and teamwork throughout each interview, requesting specific explanations and reasons for the answers, and I returned in later years to see if an individual's opinions had changed. Moreover, to overcome issues of nostalgia that can creep into recollections of both workers and managers about past organizational forms, I interviewed six workers in 2009 who had only labored under Taylorist assembly. Their recollections matched those who were present during the change to teamwork in 1996. Workers provided consistent answers and explanations for how piecework and teams functioned and did not function.

Field notes were another rich source of information. They include my careful and extensive recollection of conversations and events made on the day they occurred (or as soon as possible) as well as my reactions and sociological insights. When possible, I jotted down words on a piece of paper to remind me to put issues into my field notes. This occurred at my workstation, during a break, or in a bathroom stall. Field notes were dictated into a tape recorder and, given the length of my workday, later transcribed. I awoke at 5 A.M. to make the 6 A.M. company bus and arrived home at 6 P.M. when I took the bus or later if I conducted interviews that day. It is important to clarify that field notes are my recollection of the conversations and events that occurred on the shop floor.[8]

Another valuable source of information was the data set of over one thousand workers provided by the HR office. I was given Excel files with all workers' names along with their respective company identification numbers, dates of hire, birth dates, marital status, and levels of educational attainment. In August and September 2001, I visited the offices with a laptop and examined every worker file individually, adding information on previous work experience as well as the number, type, and date of reprimands. I constructed a database I used to compare worker characteristics and management concerns during piecework, teamwork, and flexible Taylorism (see Appendix A). Moreover, I contrasted this database of 1,046 workers with the thirty core in-depth interviews, finding no statistical difference in terms of age, educational attainment, or marital status.[9] Given the reduced number of interviews, this does not mean my findings are representative; rather, they are suggestive of broader attitudes and concerns of the workforce.

Last, I constructed a newspaper database of 415 articles on the firm, local apparel industry, and state migration processes between the years 1999 and 2009. I selected two major regional newspapers from which to sample newspaper articles, one providing a center-left perspective, the other center-right. The newspaper articles allowed me to better understand where the firm fit into local economic and political contexts and to follow worker and firm trajectories after the 2001 strike. These proved invaluable in the construction of a narrative for the years after I was at the firm. Further interviews with managers, workers, and social movement activists complemented this account.

In sum, I believe the range of methods utilized and the length of close contact with workers and managers provide a rich and unique source of data. Through daily interaction with workers at the bus stop, shop floor, cafeteria, and outside the factory gates, I was accepted as a friend by workers despite my privileged status as a middle-class, highly educated Chilean American Latina. At the same time, managers welcomed me because of our shared privileges, although they did not understand why I had to labor as a worker without pay. My ambiguous location between workers and managers allowed me to both observe and ask frank questions about the changes occurring on the shop floor and in the front offices. Moreover, through participant observation, I was able to understand situations and meanings that had been invisible to me before, such as how production structures directly led to conflicts between workers and alignment of the team leader with management. Therein lies the strength of participant observation: not having to rely on what individuals say about themselves and the situation, often in culturally sanctioned ways but, rather, by grasping, through long-term contact, the ways people interact and create meanings (Lichterman 1996).

## Roadmap to the Book

In chapter 1, I provide a historical examination of Moctezuma, the apparel industry, and women's labor force participation in Mexico, highlighting the political and economic changes that affected its development. Then, in chapter 2, I discuss the 1972 strike and describe the labor process under Taylorist assembly as it existed from 1964 to 1996. I demonstrate how managers' gender ideologies constructed a gendered workforce from the beginning, which had significant implications later on for how managers organized work and how women both consented to and resisted this organization.

Chapter 3 explores the rationale behind the transition to *modular production*, the term for lean production in the garment industry, and how management and an international consulting agency translated theory into practice at Moctezuma from 1996 until the year 2000. I examine issues of selection and recruitment of workers, arguing that management selected women for their docility and labor market vulnerability, in spite of the fact that self-managed teams called for assertive workers. For chapter 4, I focus on the practice of modular production in its fifth (and final) year, when I was on the shop floor, demonstrating how both managers and workers were active subjects who shaped and reshaped the contours of self-managed teams. By contesting the rules of teams around issues of leadership, quality, incentives, payment, and supervision, managers and workers affected social relations, and social relations affected production.

In chapter 5, I provide a more in-depth look at the strike of 2001, paying special attention to how workers weighed the decision to act by taking into account the moral economy with the company and the larger economic and political context. With chapter 6, I examine the workers' continued mobilization after the strike as they sought to certify their democratically elected union, and how management and the state used the ambiguities in labor law to subvert worker rights to the interests of capital. Chapter 7 describes management's failed attempt to reestablish control on the shop floor through flexible Taylorism and explains the reasons behind the firm's economic demise. In the conclusion, I provide a follow-up on managers and workers after the closing of the firm while considering the larger implications of the case of Moctezuma for development and women's agency.

# CHAPTER 1

# Contextualizing the Case of Moctezuma

Workers' actions are shaped and constrained by the economic structures and political institutions in which they are embedded. To understand the mobilization of Moctezuma's women workers in 1972 under piecework and in 2001 under teamwork, it is necessary to appreciate how the social, economic, and political contexts—what labor process theorists call the *politics of production*—set the conditions for shop floor relations and working-class struggles.

When Italia, Moctezuma's parent company, opened in 1951, Mexico's developmental state was in the midst of a modernizing campaign, ushering in a hegemonic regime where social and industrial policy mediated worker-capitalist relations. A period of working-class mobility and national industrialization was followed by economic crisis and an abrupt opening of the Mexican economy to global markets in the 1980s. Falling profits lead to intense global competition and an era of hegemonic despotism, the regime predominant in 1996 when modular production was introduced at Moctezuma.

By 2001, Mexican firms operated under conditions of hegemonic despotism as globalization transformed the role of the neoliberal state, now more concerned with setting conditions for capital accumulation than social welfare policy. The state prioritized attracting foreign direct investment (FDI) and promoting exports by keeping wages low, encouraging national industry to enter into production arrangements with transnational corporations and dismantling barriers to foreign investment in production and capital markets. This shift from a developmental to neoliberal state in Mexico affected the trajectory of the apparel industry, the strength of unions, and the organization of households. Significantly, women's participation in paid employment changed drastically, as did their reasons for working and the conditions under which they labored. This chapter sets the context for the case study on Moctezuma, underscoring how state policies shaped the conditions of work.

## From Revolutionary to Developmental State

The contemporary Mexican state has its roots in the 1910 revolution, which resulted in the deaths of over one million people, massive population displacements, and destruction of agricultural and industrial infrastructure. The revolution also shattered the previous state apparatus and class alliances. What emerged from the civil war was a strong interventionist state that sought to control different sectors of society by incorporating them into the ruling party, the National Revolutionary Party (PNR), later known as the Institutional Revolutionary Party (PRI).

The administration of Lázaro Cárdenas (1934–1940) consolidated revolutionary changes by assimilating popular sectors and isolating independent-minded capitalists. He undermined foreign monopolies by nationalizing the petroleum industry, weakened the traditional landowning elites through agrarian reform, and controlled northern Mexican capitalists by establishing competing sectoral organizations and chambers of commerce as consultative government bodies (Saragoza 1988). President Cárdenas also incorporated labor and peasant unions, as well as middle sectors (such as the military and teachers), into the PNR through umbrella confederations. These corporatized sectors, known as *official unions*, served several purposes: to prevent further radicalization of workers and peasants, channel political participation of popular and middle classes, and counterbalance the power of capitalists. The populist Cárdenas policies, however, created a conservative backlash that moved subsequent governments to the right. Although popular sectors remained incorporated, labor and peasant sectors were increasingly weakened as the union leadership traded away rights in exchange for positions in government and patronage for official unions (Collier and Collier 1991; Hamilton 1982).

## Import-Substitution Industrialization and the Developmental State

While worker and peasant demands were negotiated through official unions, the Mexican state increasingly forged alliances with capitalists strengthened by post–World War II anticommunist ideology. International conflicts spurred Mexican industrialization as U.S. demand for industrial and agricultural products grew. Taking advantage of the demand, credits, and FDI from the United States, the Mexican state embarked on import-substitution industrialization, an attempt to foster strong internal markets. This was achieved by increasing protective tariffs on imported goods, preferential taxes, and subsidies for firms producing for the national market; investment in infrastructure; establishment of state-owned enterprises in strategic sectors; fixed overvalued exchange rate; and institution of a 49 percent limit to foreign business ownership (Middlebrook 1995). The goal was to protect national industry geared for domestic consumer markets while state support of strategic sectors helped develop capital-intensive industry.

During the import-substitution industrialization period, between the 1940s and the debt crisis in 1982, the Mexican developmental state sought to control capitalists by favoring some fractions over others. Capitalists willing to stay out of politics and follow state conditions for economic support were privileged and allowed to develop oligopolies, where a small number of industries controlled supply and prices (Garrido and Puga 1990). Not all capitalist fractions were willing to do so. Consolidated under Porfirian rule in the 1880s, the Monterrey industrial elite was composed of densely intertwined family business groups, which strongly opposed state intervention and proworker legislation promoted after the revolution. To fight the progressive labor code, they formed the Mexican Employers' Confederation (COPARMEX) in 1930 and were instrumental in founding the business-oriented National Action Party (PAN) in 1939. As a counterweight, the Mexican state set up a new organization, the National Chamber of Manufacturing Industry (CANACINTRA), which brought together firms dependent on the state for investment. Capitalists were further controlled since business associations were prohibited from participating in political activity (Camp 1989; Saragoza 1988; Schneider Ross 2008).

By 1950, the import-substitution policies garnered support from capitalists, workers, peasants, and the emerging middle class. The establishment of a protected national industry fueled the "Mexican miracle" of rapid economic growth, averaging 7.7 percent annual growth between 1950 and 1970 (Bensusán and Cook 2003). Massive rural-urban migration provided the new workers for the emerging national industry. In 1930, only 33 percent of the population lived in cities; by 1985, 70 percent did (INEGI 2001).

The vast majority of workers were male, with women remaining in their domestic roles as mothers and homemakers. Mexican gender ideologies then, as now, are rooted in a traditional view of the family, with the mother as the spiritual and emotional center, devoted to her children and subordinate to her husband. Employment outside the home was deemed inappropriate for a married woman as it jeopardized her primary role as mother and, thus, the well-being of the family. Notwithstanding the unpaid labor women perform both domestically for their families and for their agricultural lands or businesses, the cultural ideal has been for women to remain within the bounds of the home. And if women were required to work for wages, it would only be until they married (Benería and Roldán 1987; Chant 2007; Tiano 1994).

Until the 1970s, most families followed this normative form. In 1970, 84.1 percent of Mexican households were nuclear families with a male breadwinner. Only 15.9 percent of households were organized around a female head of household, composed (in descending order) of widowed, never married, abandoned, and separated women (Nolasco 1977). While rural extended families reconfigured themselves in urban areas, they tended to do so in separate nuclear households

(Selby, Murphy, and Lorenzen 1990). In 1950, 80 percent of men aged twelve and over were employed, while only 12 percent of women worked for wages. By 1970, women's labor force participation increased to 19 percent, with young, childless women representing the majority. Women's work patterns closely resembled conventional notions of appropriate femininity, with most women leaving paid employment when they married (Healy 2008; Lustig and Rendón 1979; Pedrero Nieto 2003; Tiano 1994).

Industrialization increased urban workers' wages and benefits through the expansion of health services and subsidized government services. The new working class benefited from state subsidies for food, public transportation, and urban services (electricity, water, and city services). Primary education, considered a constitutional right and necessary to obtain a job in the formal sector, was free and more readily available in urban areas than rural ones (Selby, Murphy, and Lorenzen 1990). Through unionized employment, workers in the expanding industrial sector were eligible for additional benefits; these included end-of-year profit sharing (*aguinaldo*), vacation, company share in savings through the SAR (Savings for Retirement System), health services and pensions through the Mexican Social Security System (IMSS), and subsidized housing loans through the National Workers' Housing Fund (INFONAVIT). The hegemonic regime of economic development transformed peasants into workers in a relatively short time, with official unions and government programs playing an important stabilizing factor.

Women and men, however, did not benefit equally from import-substitution industrialization. Women's early withdrawal from employment and concentration in labor-intensive industries led to a sex-segregated labor market across different occupations, where men earned significantly higher wages than women. Average real wages quadrupled from 1952 to 1976, with male industrial workers located in modernizing and capital-intensive industries—automobiles, pharmaceuticals, and chemicals—experiencing the highest wage increases and state-sanctioned provision of benefits. Women workers were overrepresented in the service industries—especially domestic service—and in traditional labor-intensive small industrial establishments like food preparation and apparel; these jobs were sex-typed female, less likely to be unionized, and paid a lower salary with few benefits. As educational levels rose, women entered into nursing and teaching professions. Hence, women and men tended to be concentrated in different industries, and, even when they did perform similar jobs, women earned significantly less (Bensusán and Cook 2003; Lustig and Rendón 1979).

Throughout this period, maquiladoras have been, and continue to be, one of the most important sources of employment in Mexico. As a precursor to export-led industrialization, the 1968 maquiladora program took advantage of U.S. Tariff Code Article 807 to import parts for assembly along a twenty-kilometer strip on the U.S.-Mexico border. Article 807 (later known as 9802) permits firms to import goods manufactured abroad with American components to reenter the United States with duty paid on only the value added to the goods, most often by labor. Mexico's proximity to the United States, lower wages, tax exemptions, and lax enforcement of labor and environmental laws made it attractive to foreign firms. After a slow start, the maquiladora program became a driving engine of the economy, providing employment and foreign exchange.

In 1972, the program was extended to the whole country. At first, maquiladoras consisted predominantly of routinized assembly work and hired mostly women. In 1982, the peso devaluation stretched foreign companies' dollars further; meanwhile, national firms, which earned pesos, struggled to compete as inputs, wages, and overhead costs increased overnight. The resulting economic crisis lowered real wages and made maquiladora employment more attractive to men, which increased their participation in the maquiladora labor force from 20 to 40 percent. In addition, a significant number of the new maquiladoras were capital-intensive automobile and auto-parts firms. These firms, which combined old machinery, new computerized equipment, and selective implementation of flexible production techniques, considered the work skilled and preferred to hire men over women (Carrillo, Hualde, and Quintero Ramírez 2005; de la O 2002).

Official unions played a crucial role in providing the state with political legitimacy; this furthered state-directed industrialization while controlling labor militancy. Although Mexico's 1917 Constitution is considered to be one of the most progressive charters, as it set minimum labor standards—such as minimum wage, an eight-hour workday, overtime pay, and mandated profit sharing—and guaranteed the right to organize in labor unions and strike, it also provided a structure to control workers. Article 123 of the Constitution, which deals with labor issues and protections, established federal and local conciliation and arbitration boards; these form a tripartite body composed of equal numbers of employers and labor union representatives, and a state agent whose mandate is to break any ties. The workers' representative, however, is from an official union, providing little to no voice for dissident worker concerns. Moreover, local boards fall under the jurisdiction of state-appointed labor departments (*secretarías de trabajo*), where labor matters are often subsumed under economic and political concerns. Tasked with ensuring the ambiguous constitutional mandate of "establishing equilibrium between the diverse factors of production, and harmonizing the rights of labor with those of capital," these boards have broad powers to settle work disputes and decide the legality of strikes (Bensusán 1998; translation from Article 123 in La Botz 1992, 49).

Constitutional Article 123 also reproduced the gender division of labor in the family to the labor market. Although the Constitution promised equal pay for equal work and outlawed discrimination based on sex or nationality, it debased women by granting them the same legal standing as children under sixteen. Envisioned as not fully adults—and, therefore, not really citizens—women were only afforded rights through their employed fathers or husbands.[1] In addition, women were believed to need protection, which led to legislation that prohibited them from working overtime, performing unhealthy or dangerous work, or laboring past 10 P.M. or working the night shift.[2] When working women became pregnant, they were exempted from physically demanding work for three months prior to birth, guaranteed their job once they returned from one month of paid maternity leave, and afforded extra breaks for nursing while at work (Healy 2008).

The developmental state was premised on paternalism, interpreting men as heads of families and women as their dependents. The Constitution, in general, and Article 123, specifically, treated workers as members of families, where women played a subordinate role. The 1917 Law of Family Relations (*Ley sobre Relaciones Familiares*) declared women to be legally responsible for managing the household and dictated that men were obligated to provide for their wives (Varley 2000). Moreover, the right to a family wage was explicitly referenced in Article 123, mandating a minimum wage where, "according to the conditions of the region, [minimum wages should] satisfy the normal necessities of life of the worker, his education and honest pleasures, according to his role as head of the family" (quoted in Healy 2008, 12). The family wage underscored that, for women, benefits were obtained through their husbands' and fathers' employment, not theirs (Bensusán 1998). The contradiction of stipulating equal pay for equal work and then treating men and women workers differently stems from the belief that a woman's place is in the home. If women worked at all, they were not expected to work in the same jobs as men. The effect of protectionist policies and the imposition of a family wage was the reproduction of a gendered division of labor, where women were seen as more costly in employers' eyes and men more deserving of higher wages.

The 1931 Federal Labor Law further codified and clarified Article 123, providing additional counterweights to authentic worker organizations and reinforcing the male character of union leadership. One of the new provisions divided unions into federal and local jurisdictions, each with its own bureaucratic organization and under the supervision of federal and local conciliation and arbitration boards, respectively. Another provision allowed for sectoral autonomous national unions in strategic sectors like oil, railroads, telecommunications, textiles, and mining. These laws encouraged competition between unions and deterred the formation of powerful peak labor confederations. The labor code also allowed for all legal powers to be transferred to one person, either the general secretary or business agent (a labor lawyer who advises the union), replicating the male strongman figure on which the revolution (and the PRI party leadership) was established (Middlebrook 1995).

The 1931 labor code also enhanced the powers of the conciliation and arbitration board. While the Constitution gave workers associational rights, unions were legal only if officially recognized by the local and federal boards. The Federal Labor Law also granted recognized unions the right to oust dissident workers from membership. Known as the exclusion clause, if a worker was expelled by the union, the employer was also obliged to fire the worker (Middlebrook 1995). This union disciplinary power, together with the boards' discretionary powers to decide union recognition and strike legality, developed into a powerful mechanism for controlling labor, as we will see in the case of Moctezuma.

The hierarchical system of state-party-union control, as Dan La Botz calls it, provided official unions with state patronage for its leaders and benefits for union workers (1992). The official unions, in turn, supported government policies and delivered votes at election time. In contemporary Mexico, three types of unions have developed in addition to official unions: company unions, independent unions, and protection unions. Historically, company unions, or *white* unions, developed in the conservative northern city of Monterrey. Organized in family groups, big businesses promoted these company unions to fend off the power of official unions. White unions are not connected to any state labor federations (Saragoza 1988).

Independent unions also exist outside of the state's control and take several forms at both the company and confederation level. Most independent unions are the result of workers contesting representation from an official or company union at a particular firm by democratically electing new leadership (Cook 1996; La Botz 1992). A few independent union confederations exist, such as public university unions and the Authentic Labor Front (FAT), which emerged in the 1960s from grassroots progressive Christian groups. In 1997, some of the largest official unions—those representing telephone, social security, and aviation workers—broke away from the official union confederation, and, together with the FAT and university independent unions, formed the National Workers' Union (UNT). The UNT is willing to negotiate with the state and business sectors to increase productivity, but only in exchange for a new social contract, where real union freedom and representation exists (de la Garza Toledo 2003; La Botz 2005).

Both white and official unions often provide *protection contracts* that fulfill legal requirements for union establishment without real worker representation. Some scholars calculate that 80 percent of all union contracts are protection contracts (Xelhuantizi-López in La Botz 2005). However, a more recent phenomenon has developed whereby individuals have taken the concept of protection contracts to a new level by legally establishing confederations that hold title to tens or even hundreds of contracts—resulting in lucrative businesses. Importantly, these *protection unions* exist on paper only (Bensusán 2008; Bouzas Ortiz and Gaitán Riveros 2001; Ramírez Cuevas 2005). According to Preston and Dillon, just one confederation, the National Coordinating Union of Workers (FSCNT), brings together more than 2,000 protection contracts covering over 350,000 workers (2005). Protection unions have grown hand in hand with the maquiladora program.

## EXPORT-LED INDUSTRIALIZATION AND THE NEOLIBERAL STATE

The economic growth and expansion of social provisions under import-substitution development was premised in large part on public spending and financing of the private sector through state development banks, which had increased dramatically in the 1970s with the discovery of large oil reserves. However, when commodity prices collapsed in the 1980s at the same time U.S. interest rates increased, Mexico's debt became especially burdensome. The fall of oil prices ricocheted into high inflation and a foreign debt crisis. Mexico declared bankruptcy. To stem massive capital flight occurring in anticipation of a devalued peso, outgoing president José López Portillo nationalized the banking system (Middlebrook 1995; Schaeffer 2009).

As a condition of debt renegotiations with the International Monetary Fund (IMF) and World Bank in 1982, the Mexican state began the process of instituting neoliberal economic policies, marking the end of the import-substitution model. The payment of debt was prioritized and made possible by privatizing state-owned enterprises (especially the banking system), devaluing the peso to promote foreign investment, cutting wages to internationally competitive levels, opening the national market to international competition, reorienting national production for export, and cutting social spending. By 1988, cheap Asian imports flooded the market, causing many firms to close. Employment in the manufacturing sector fell markedly, and working conditions deteriorated (Garrido 2000; González de la Rocha and Escobar Latapí 2008).

A second crisis occurred in 1994 with the devaluation of the peso just as the North American Free Trade Agreement (NAFTA) came into effect. Neoliberal policies had resulted in a rapid opening of the economy to cheap imports as well as capital (stock and bond) markets, leading to an overvaluation of the peso and inflation. Outgoing president Carlos Salinas de Gotari delayed a correction of the peso to pass NAFTA and avoid political rifts. He also increased government spending by issuing short-term bonds to be paid in U.S. dollars, which drained state coffers (Pastor and Wise 2003).

A key element of globalization is financialization, the explosion and primary use of financial trading and financial instruments to accumulate capital in both domestic and global markets (Epstein 2005; Krippner 2005).[3] The ascendancy of financial imperatives of ever-increasing returns has triggered 24/7 trading in investment portfolios and foreign currencies, introducing increased volatility to national financial systems. Developing countries, like Mexico, are particularly vulnerable to the unpredictability of global capital flows, given the IMF and World Bank conditionality programs that force debtor countries to open trade and financial markets. The inability to regulate financial transactions affects exchange rates, availability of credit, and wages at the national level. Thus, the 1994 Mexican and 1997 East Asian crises were the result, in part, of the local state's inability to regulate financial transactions in their own currency (Dicken 2007; Garrido 2000; Levy Orlick 2006; Motamen-Samadian 2000).

The shift to export-led development through neoliberal policies had a significant impact on Mexican living standards, concentration of wealth, strength of
unions, political democratization, and industrial policy. The effect of the 1982
and 1994 crises on the economy and population were longlasting. Cuts in social
spending, combined with deteriorating employment conditions, severely
affected workers. Subsidies for basic goods like milk and tortillas were cut for all
except the poorest. Services provided by the state—transportation, drinking
water, and trash collection—were slashed, and the quality of health services and
educational facilities declined. While primary schools remained free, requisite
parental contributions kept secondary schools afloat. Food prices rose significantly as inflation surpassed 100 percent, and real wages fell 40–50 percent from
1983 to 1988 (Harvey 2005).

After the 1994 crisis, the Central Bank reported that the economy slowed by
seven points in just one year, bank interest loans tripled, over one million people
were left unemployed, 20,000 businesses filed for bankruptcy, and buying power
decreased by 37 percent. In addition, the crisis revealed how privatized banks
had made scores of bad loans. While making its owners multimillionaires, these
banks now required state rescue (Eckstein 2002; Williams 2001). By 1996, the
state, which had sold off the banks for U.S.$60 billion in 1992, spent U.S.$210
billion to rescue them. Private control remained without the state accruing
any ownership rights (Caplan 1998; Motamen-Samadian 2000).

Macroeconomic policies and rollback of state services, especially social services, also affected women's labor force participation and household dynamics.
Under the developmental state, urbanization and industrialization led to the
possibility of social mobility built around the male head of household. The
expansion of formal employment, accompanied by state and union benefits
(albeit at low wages), provided households with a modicum of stability and
males with authority. The male breadwinner participated in formal employment, supplemented by the formal or informal work of older sons or daughters
when needed. Wives tended to work for pay only during family emergencies
(Chant 2007; Cravey 1998; González de la Rocha 2006).

By the 1980s and 1990s, expanding the number of household members in the
informal economy did not meet families' survival needs. Increasingly precarious
male employment translated into women's augmented labor force participation;
the number of females over twelve years of age working for wages rose from
33 percent in 1980 to 45 percent in 2002, and more married women remained in
the labor market through their childbearing years (Domínguez-Villalobos and
Brown-Grossman 2010; Montaño and Milosavljevic 2010; Tiano 1994). Sons and
daughters quit school at earlier ages, which meant that they were less prepared
for the labor market and had to take the worst jobs. Households expanded, with
young adult couples residing with their parents, as families and individuals
coped with worsening wages and a shortage of formal employment. In addition,
households had to stretch their income to compensate for services previously

provided or subsidized by the state (Chant 2007; Cravey 1998; Escobar Latapí 2003; González de la Rocha and Escobar Latapí 2008). Under these conditions, the poor could no longer count on formal employment, and even piecing together a living in the informal economy became extremely difficult; many turned to scavenging, bartering, and exchanging services (González de la Rocha 2006).

It was not only the working class that suffered under neoliberal reforms; peasant and urban unions, historically pillars of the PRI corporatist government, also lost considerable clout. Peasant unions were devastated by changes made to the Mexican Constitution that allowed privatization of community lands (*ejidos*). Small agricultural producers, already experiencing economic crisis, sold their lands to foreign agribusinesses, which further displaced impoverished rural inhabitants (MacLeod 2004). State-owned enterprises were sold for less than their value to a reduced number of well-connected family business groups, furthering the concentration of wealth (MacLeod 2004; Morera Camacho 1998). By 1994, the sale of state-owned enterprises had also cut employment in the state sector, the stronghold of official unions, by half. In addition, the PRI government pushed for the restructuring of labor contracts to render wages more flexible and increase productivity. Faced with resistance from official union leaders, the state mounted an attack and replaced them with those more compliant. Since 1989, yearly political pacts between official labor unions, peak business associations, and the state have further controlled wages and weakened unions (Bensusán and Cook 2003; La Botz 1992). Hence, neoliberal privatization and deregulation policies weakened official unions, while the shift to export-led development increased the number of protection contracts that favor companies over workers.

The 1982 and 1994 economic crises also had important political implications. The 1982 nationalization of the banking system unified and mobilized capitalist class fractions, especially the northern entrepreneurial class that had long resisted developmentalist policies, against the state through the PAN and peak business associations. Energized business sectors pressed hard for reforms that would deepen the liberalization and deregulation of the economy. They also began to seriously contest PRI control of the government at the same time that the debt crisis debilitated labor and peasant sectors—the political bases of state support. At the same time, a peasant uprising raged in the southern state of Chiapas in 1994 and the scandalous rescue of multimillionaire bank owners mobilized middle and popular sectors affected by waves of bankruptcies. The combination of pressures from business and popular sectors led to the democratization of the 1980s and 1990s. Both business-oriented PAN and left-leaning Democratic Revolution Party (PRD) opposition parties were catapulted to office at the municipal, state, and national levels in the 1990s. The election of President Vicente Fox in 2000 broke the seventy-one-year uninterrupted rule of the PRI (Garrido and Puga 1990; Williams 2001).

Since the ascendancy of the PAN in the 1990s, state and business leaders argue that labor laws harm international competitiveness given its rigid labor protections. COPARMEX, the most important employer association, has advocated for its New Labor Culture to replace the Federal Labor Law. The core of proposed reforms include easing firing restrictions, allowing temporary contracts paid by the hour, increasing work hours, tying salary increases to productivity, and slashing currently large benefit packages—the latter, a historical legacy of corporatism (Bensusán and Cook 2003; de la Garza Toledo 2003). While labor reforms have not passed in Congress, it continues to be debated seriously in government and business sectors.

The shift to export-led development also marked Mexico's entry into GATT (General Agreement on Tariffs and Trade) in 1986, NAFTA in 1994, and a multitude of bilateral free trade agreements. The combination of the 1994 peso devaluation and NAFTA resulted in exponential growth in FDI, totaling U.S.$7.6 billion by 1996 (Motamen-Samadian 2000). Administrative procedures for investing and trading have been streamlined to facilitate such trade agreements. To enhance the attractiveness of proximity to foreign investors, the state provided national firms with training in technological and organizational innovations, promoting Japanese-style quality circles (recruiting workers to improve quality), just-in-time (JIT) inventory (saving capital by increasing communication with suppliers so that inputs arrive as they are needed on shop floor instead of the just-in-case warehousing of the past), statistical process control (SPC; evaluating a percentage of all operations to assure strict adherence to product specifications), and teamwork (composed of multiskilled workers) as well as full-package production (the vertical integration of industries from raw materials to production and distribution; Carrillo, Hualde, and Quintero Ramírez 2005; Frausto Sánchez 2000).

State inducements to adopt organizational innovations, however, have had contradictory results. According to Mexican scholars who have studied the export industry, which is the targeted sector of such state programs, organizational innovations have been only partially adopted, and teamwork and SPC to monitor quality have been implemented without the flattened hierarchies, multiskilled workers, or cutting-edge technology required. This has resulted in what de la Garza Toledo calls precarious Toyotism (2006). Instead, selective adoption of organizational innovations has perfected Taylorist control without the corresponding gains for workers (de la Garza Toledo 1998; Ordoñez 1997). Nevertheless, the Mexican government has emphatically pressured national firms to take on different degrees of flexibility so that they may incorporate into international production chains and, thus, be in a position to benefit from foreign investment. Participating in these production chains is then assumed to foster regional development in the forms of industrial clusters. For this purpose, state agencies have promulgated FDI by advertising abundant cheap labor, tax exemptions, and state-financed infrastructure (Secretaría de Economía 2001b).

Not only has the federal government invested in making Mexico attractive for potential foreign investors, so have the local states. Federal and state resources have been invested in infrastructure such as highways, airports, and fiber optic communication capabilities specifically for trade. The central state where the firm under study is located assisted national and international firms with setting up industrial parks by confiscating community lands and then offering them to companies at nominal prices. This same state also provided electrical networks, potable water, wastewater treatment, access roads to major highways, expansion of local airports, support to train workers, childcare facilities, and exemptions on property and payroll taxes (Grupo Financiero Banamex Accival 1996; Laslavic 1999; Secretaría de Economía 2001a).

The textile and apparel industry has been singled out by federal and state authorities as one of the twelve strategic sectors in the economy given its ability to participate in full-package production arrangements with NAFTA partners and, therefore, to insert Mexico into global production chains. To Mexican federal and state officials, development or upgrading translates into total quality management, lean production, and full-package production (Rabon and West 2000). Moctezuma, the firm under study, attempted all of these.

## The Apparel Industry in Mexico

The history of the Mexican apparel sector demonstrates the crucial effect of state policies on industry performance and work organization. Traditionally, women have sewn most of the family's clothes. In the 1920s, the apparel industry emerged in Mexico City as Lebanese and Jewish immigrants utilized their knowledge in production and trade to manufacture garments in workshops and factories (Arias and Wilson 1997). The nascent industry was strengthened under state import-substitution policies. Given the modest amount of capital necessary to start production and the process of urbanization occurring at the time, the apparel industry became one of the most successful sectors under the state's industrializing incentives. Once wages began rising in the Mexican capital, production moved to its surrounding areas and two other large cities, Guadalajara and Monterrey (Suárez Aguilar and Rivera Rios 1994). From the 1940s to the 1970s, most apparel firms were small or medium sized, with an almost exclusively female workforce, as sewing was perceived to be a "woman's job."

The advent of the maquiladora program increased female employment in the garment industry significantly but limited national industrial development. For the apparel industry, American tariff rules meant that all fabric was imported from the United States and that sewn garments were exported without buttons or labels. The tariff rules also excluded Mexican textile firms from the U.S. apparel production network. The maquiladora program thus promulgated assembly, rather than development (Fernández-Kelly 1983; Sklair 1993).

The shift to export-led industrialization in the 1980s rocked the garment and textile industries. No longer protected by state policies, national firms had to compete with multinational corporations taking advantage of newly opened markets. This proved difficult for the national textile industry since technology was outdated, and, like the garment factories, the textile companies were mostly undercapitalized, medium-sized family-owned businesses (Gereffi 1997). Instead, the garment and textile industries were best positioned to benefit from existing protectionist regulatory institutions like the 1974 Multi-Fibre Arrangement (MFA), a complex set of bilateral trade agreements that regulated textile and apparel trade through tariffs and quotas to protect national economies from Asian imports.

The global apparel industry has been transformed by trade agreements. The MFA fragmented production around the globe (Appelbaum and Gereffi 1994). With the emergence of the World Trade Organization (WTO) in 1995 (replacing GATT), the MFA was set to be phased out in 2005. Under GATT, which Mexico joined in 1986, tariffs on imports fell, increasing competition in the domestic market. The initial effect was stagnation of the apparel industry, with many companies closing. *Twin Plant News* reported that a prominent Mexican manufacturer claimed that 40 percent of the industry had been forced to close (1997). By 1987, a portion of the apparel firms had recovered by retooling as subcontractors for international production. However, with the phasing out of the MFA quotas, many feared apparel production would concentrate in China given low labor costs and efficient supply networks. But safeguard tariffs implemented by the United States and European Union nations have stemmed the flow of apparel production to China. Moreover, rising energy costs and market proximity have kept Mexico and the Caribbean Basin competitive (*just-style* 2005a; *just-style* 2007; Maquila Solidarity Network 2008).

In addition to free trade agreements, the 1980s were a time of big changes in the U.S. apparel industry that had important effects in Mexico. A series of mergers, acquisitions, and bankruptcies resulted in the concentration of power into a fewer number of retailers (such as Wal-Mart and JC Penney) and branded manufacturers (such as Calvin Klein and The Gap). The resulting larger companies were then able to make demands on producers and other contractors for more services at lower prices. Appelbaum and Gereffi note that "[they turned] up the pressure on their contractors to make clothes with more fashion seasons, faster turnaround times [the time it takes from cutting the cloth to distributing a finished product], lower profit margins, greater uncertainty about future orders, and frequently worse conditions for workers" (1994, 60). Retailers and branded manufacturers could now force their unit price on manufacturers, transferring risk down the chain. Thus, with a decreasing return from production, U.S. manufacturers increasingly turned to offshore production, seeking out contractors. Given its proximity and low wages, Mexico became a favorite destination (DesMarteau 1999). Some segments, such as women's fashion, which require quicker turnaround time, continued production in the United States, making use of vulnerable migrant labor and sweatshops (Bonacich and Appelbaum 2000; Sassen 2001).

The liberalization of the Mexican economy in the 1980s has had two main consequences for the apparel industry: polarization and decentralization. Companies have become polarized in size, either becoming large or micro and almost doing away with the small- and medium-sized manufacturers. Large companies tend to be export-oriented, while micro sewing workshops and homework often produce for the domestic market. The majority of workshops operate outside the law, operating in a garage or storefront, while disregarding minimum wage, benefits, and safety requirements. Homework, which pays the least but affords women some flexibility in their schedules, entails workers taking in sewing to be done in their own home. While women often provide the thread and electricity in addition to their labor, they can work around childcare and family responsibilities (Benería and Roldán 1987). Companies have also decentralized to less industrialized regions of the country, establishing themselves away from big cities and the U.S.-Mexico border (Hanson 1994; Suárez Aguilar and Rivera Rios 1994).

In the mid-1990s, another shift occurred as apparel and textile firms in the United States, Canada, and Mexico prepared to take advantage of NAFTA's yarn-forward rule, which states that products with cloth from any of the three signatory countries would have preferential access to all three countries' markets. Lower wages and production costs, together with proximity to the U.S. market, made Mexico attractive to American retailers, textile mills, and brand-name apparel firms. These firms competed to be the organizing agents of full-package production. Many U.S. textile mills either moved south to set up state-of-the-art textile mills and manufacturing plants or made arrangements to work closely with existing national firms. Branded manufacturers and retailers increased contracts with suppliers as well. Moreover, producers from other regions also moved to Mexico to take advantage of the connection with the U.S. apparel market (Jacobs 1998; Kessler 1999; Spener, Gereffi, and Bair 2002).

Exports to the United States skyrocketed as apparel producers took advantage of lower wages and quicker turnaround times. Mexico benefited from increased employment and FDI as U.S. textile plants set up full-package production. Employment steadily increased until 2000, when the market contracted. But rising employment numbers obscure the polarizing effect of apparel industry growth. Although jobs increased, currency devaluations and the state's efforts to keep wages competitive stunted workers' purchasing power. Furthermore, much of the added employment occurred in low-paying sectors like assembly and informal workshops. Government and business associations estimate that 57 percent of total production is carried out in these small workshops, employing 80 percent of the workers in the Mexican garment industry (Román de Santos n.d.; Secretaría de Economía 2001b). According to the XV Industrial Census (the most recent publicly available industrial census), 92 percent of apparel establishments employed from one to fifteen employees (INEGI 1999). Large firms, those employing over 250 workers, constituted only 0.6 percent of the establishments but employed 28 percent of the apparel workforce.

Production in Mexico benefits from shorter turnaround time. On average, turnaround time from Mexico is twenty-five to thirty-five days, while it takes forty to sixty days to source products from Asia (Secretaría de Economía 2001b). However, the advantages Mexico has had in proximity to market has not been enough to overcome the disadvantages caused by wages that are higher than those in Asia and Central America or by underdeveloped communication and transport infrastructures. In addition, the maquiladora program's failure to integrate Mexican supply firms with U.S. producers has made it difficult for supply firms and contractors to achieve the quality and know-how now necessary to export goods (Kopinak 1996; Shaiken 1990). While some areas like Torreón have exhibited successful interfirm networks, the polarization of the national apparel industry has left few national producers able to participate in the more profitable full-package production arrangements encouraged by NAFTA (Gereffi, Martínez, and Bair 2002). Moctezuma was one of these few successful national firms.

## FIRM STRATEGIES IN A GLOBALIZED ECONOMY: THE CASE OF MOCTEZUMA

The central state in which Moctezuma is located transformed from a predominantly agricultural state to an industrial hub in the late 1960s. Import-substitution policies attracted national and international textile firms in the 1950s. In 1966, the state expropriated community lands just outside the capital city to establish an industrial zone. National and international pharmaceutical and automobile companies were enticed with twenty-year land and property tax exemptions, in addition to the provision of water, electrical, communication, and transportation infrastructure. At the same time, peasants were pushed out of the countryside by the modernization of agribusiness and population growth that made subsistence agriculture unsustainable. In his study of the local automobile industry, Roxborough found that 48 percent of the male workforce had been born in rural areas (1984). Another study found that 70 percent of women workers during this period were from the countryside (Mier Merelo 2003). Thus, the new working class was composed of either peasants or children of peasants (Martínez Cruz 2000; Peimbert Frías 2002; Roxborough 1984).

The origins of Moctezuma date back to 1951, when an Italian entrepreneur set up a textile mill in central Mexico. For the purposes of this study, the original mill will be called Italia. Although capital, management, and designs were decidedly Italian, it was legally formed as a Mexican enterprise. Italia's production of cashmere cloth was geared toward the national market to take advantage of subsidies and protections provided by the Mexican state under import-substitution industrialization policies. The great majority of workers were male, tending large machines and moving heavy loads of thread and dyes. A few women were hired in the darning department, where imperfections in the cloth were fixed by hand. This division of labor persisted until the firm closed in 2004. Like most of the workers in the region, Italia's workers were either peasants or children of peasants who were attracted to the city with the hope of better employment.

In 1964, the textile company opened a new division to fashion cashmere suits from its own cloth. The garment division proved successful, and, by 1969, Italia's management expanded the workforce of two hundred and fifty women by hiring a hundred or so temporary workers. In order to maintain flexibility, the majority of these workers were fired and rehired every twenty-eight days. As temporary workers they did not receive legally mandated health care, housing, and savings benefits, to which most workers aspired. From 1969 to 1974, the city in which the firm is located became a hotbed of independent unionism as the growing working classes demanded more rights and union democracy. Given the recent industrialization of the region, official unions were weak, and the need for political legitimacy from the state was high; this contributed to a vibrant social movement unionism. At the time, the women of Italia's new division were an important part of this movement. After temporary workers helped organize a strike to earn full-time status in 1972, the new division became its own company—Moctezuma—and the women workers were represented by an independent union. As I will argue in chapter 2, the successful strike in 1972 is best explained by the strength of the local social movements and character of state-society relations. In the following four years, Italia's management isolated and then fired the independent union leaders, reinstating the corporatist union that increasingly functioned as a company union. It was this union that Moctezuma's women confronted in March 2001.

By the 1980s, when the Mexican economy began to open its doors to foreign investment and promote exports, the Italian management of Italia and Moctezuma took advantage of the new state inducements to import technology and raw materials. High levels of investments poured into the companies, specifically for technology at the textile mill (in 1984) and, later, computers for the design department at the garment factory (in 1990). In 1984, for the first time since Moctezuma's inception, products were exported to the United States and Europe. Given this, it should come as no surprise that the companies had been able to survive the shift from import-substitution to export-oriented industrialization. Both companies had always maintained a direct connection with Italian capital and designers, making a smooth transition, with the liberalization of the economy, to become a leader in production for the national and export markets.

In 1993, Italia and Moctezuma were put up for auction. According to several high-level managers, the Italian owner of the industrial group died and the board of directors decided to sell all overseas investments. A leading northern Mexican entrepreneur, Pérez (a pseudonym), and his family became majority owners of the two firms. Although NAFTA did not become law until the first day of 1994, industrialists in all three participating countries were already positioning themselves to take advantage of the new trading rules (Carrillo, Hualde, and Almaraz 2002). Therefore, it is reasonable to think that an experienced and successful exporting firm taken over in 1994 would have been a prize acquisition. This was confirmed when, in 1995, the Australian International Wool Secretariat named Italia the best textile plant in Latin America and one of the best eight in the world, as often repeated by managers.

The Pérez family set up a new business group, Grupo Mexicano (also a pseudonym), when they purchased Moctezuma, its sister textile plant Italia, and a distribution network. Financed by a Texan global venture firm and a Mexican bank, Grupo Mexicano purchased 90 percent of the Italian conglomerate's shares in 1994 for U.S.$254 million. The Italian clothing conglomerate retained controlling interests in the U.S. distribution center (*Business Wire* 1997). Since its inception, Pérez, his wife, father, and cousins have sat on the board of directors and held important offices in the organizational structure of Grupo Mexicano. Although they did not have any experience in the textile and apparel sector, the majority owner and his family had controlling interests in real estate and in one of the largest (nontextile) petrochemicals in the nation. The latter was purchased in 1992 from the state at below market value during the sell-off of state-owned enterprises.[4]

After the purchase of the apparel and textile plants, the new ownership embarked on an ambitious growth strategy. Expansion was based largely on bank loans, such as the 1998 million-dollar loan taken out to purchase machinery and technology, which doubled cloth production. State support was also secured in the form of development bank loans. Particularly advantageous were tariff-free importation programs, which facilitated wool imports from Australia and large textile machinery as well as computerized sewing technology from Europe. Interested in sponsoring regional development, state government training programs and subsidies were made available for certification and worker training. Between 1996 and 1998, the state, using monies provided by the World Bank to support development projects, paid for three months of training for 900 workers.

Moreover, state development officials envisioned Moctezuma, the largest domestic garment company in the region, as the anchor of an emergent garment and textile industrial district, where national and transnational firms would build links with local supplier firms to increase employment and export production. For this purpose, Grupo Mexicano received further tax exemptions and other favorable fiscal exclusions.

To fully capitalize on the new regulations, the owners realized improvements would be necessary. Among the significant industrial upgrades were modernization of the plant, reorganization to modular production, establishment of full-package production, and diversification of investment portfolios. The Mexican majority owners' stated purpose was to dominate the U.S. and Canadian markets by becoming cutting-edge world-class producers. To that end, one of the first steps taken in 1994 was to move toward ISO (International Organization for Standardization) certification. Both firms—which retained their names, management, and workers—retooled to incorporate quality controls throughout the production process. Obtaining ISO certification provided a stamp of approval that improved the possibility of landing and retaining high-end clients. At the same time, the firm invested capital in the garment factory to computerize key sewing operations. One year after purchasing the textile and garment firms, the new industrial group set up a series of store outlets for their own national brands inside Mexican high-end department stores. The goal was to conquer both the export and domestic markets.

The next step was the reorganization of production around lean techniques. On a state-entrepreneurial tour of innovative foreign firms organized by the Mexican state, one of the majority owners of Moctezuma had visited European firms where he had seen Japanese-style lean production at work. Accounts point to this being the spark that started the reorganization of production at Moctezuma. At the time, lean production was being advocated by management fashion setters—namely, business schools and consultants—as the best way to compete internationally. Management fads translate emergent ideas about progress, rationality, and technical improvements into management packages to be marketed, using overly optimistic rhetoric that posits the practices as the most progressive and efficient organizational forms. Adopting such practices—in this case, lean or modular production—may indeed improve organizational functioning, but, more important, they provide legitimacy and mark the firm as cutting-edge, factors necessary to be competitive (Abrahamson 1991, 1996; Guler, Guillén, and Macpherson 2002).

Adopting organizational innovations became necessary because of client stipulations as well. International buyers, like Calvin Klein and JC Penney, made increasing demands for quality and quick turnaround times with the use of JIT and SPC. In order to avoid penalty fees and retain profitable relationships with buyers, the firm reorganized under modular production. In 1995, the industrial group invested heavily in the services of a high-profile international consulting agency to implement changes.

Reorganization at Moctezuma had four main elements: managed work teams, elimination of midlevel supervisors, increased information-sharing regarding production with workers, and focus on quality. Another crucial element was the presence of a compliant union. Production was reorganized gradually, beginning with one section in 1996, as kinks were worked out by the industrial engineers and the modular production system showed concrete results.

Acquiring full-package production capability was the second strategy for firm upgrading (see table 1.1). In 1997, the industrial group established a small state-of-the-art textile mill to produce acetate lining needed for the suits. With cutting-edge European technology, less than fifty workers at the acetate mill produced enough lining for both Moctezuma and the national market. The textile

TABLE 1.1

GRUPO MEXICANO'S PARTICIPATION IN TEXTILE AND APPAREL COMMODITY CHAIN

| | Cloth Textile Mill | Lining Textile Mill | Apparel Production Company | Distribution Company | Retail Businesses |
|---|---|---|---|---|---|
| Company | Italia | Acetamex | Moctezuma | Distribumex | Several |
| Description | 100 percent cashmere wool | Acetate for lining | High-end men's suits; produced 4 brands under own label; produced for 8 branded clients, all American or Italian | 16 licensing agreements, producing for U.S., Canadian, Mexican, and Latin American high-end markets; U.S., Canadian, and Chilean subsidiaries; exports to 70 clients in 13 countries | High-end retail stores; special arrangement for high-end department stores in Mexican malls to have special display area; specialty international restaurant |
| No. of workers | 537 | 55 | 1,424 | 67 | 84 |
| Female (%) | 4 | 0 | 88 | unknown | unknown |
| Male (%) | 96 | 100 | 12 | unknown | unknown |

Source: Author's own compilation from newspapers, interviews, and company documents. Company names are pseudonyms.

mill functioned efficiently, supplying acetate lining on time and with the quality requirements; however, other suppliers did not fare so well. Just-in-time inventory was adopted to cut in-process inventory and carrying costs by forging closer communications with suppliers, who furnished inputs only when needed. However, not all suppliers could function on tighter time schedules, forcing Moctezuma engineers to assist and train some of the backward-linkage providers, such as subcontractors supplying inputs like buttons, zippers, and foam lining, on the merits and details of JIT.

Control over inputs was crucial if Moctezuma was to fulfill its orders for national and international clients. Contracts with clients included provisions where they could reject an order if the inputs provided by Moctezuma were not up to quality specifications. At one point, no high-quality shoulder pad supplier could be found in Mexico, so they had to be imported from Europe. Meanwhile, technical guidance and loans to purchase European machinery were provided to a local company that in the future would furnish the shoulder pads. Thus, to assure the successful sale of production, managers found themselves developing closer ties with suppliers, which often meant diverting industrial engineers and supervisors to get the suppliers' functioning up to par. If this was not achieved, financing or internalization of suppliers would be required. Both the training and verticalization of domestic suppliers resulted in unexpectedly high costs that drained the firm's reserves.

Forward linkages into distribution and retailing also were secured in order to gain a foothold in higher value-added activities. Moctezuma modernized its design department, plotting out not only the designs given to them by clients like Calvin Klein, Hugo Boss, and Ralph Lauren, but also marketing four of their own labels for the national market. These suits were then geared for high-end Mexican stores like Palacio de Hierro, Suburbia, and Liverpool, where they had special display areas. Furthermore, the industrial group purchased the licensing rights to sixteen high-profile international labels for sale in U.S., Canadian, Mexican, and Latin American markets. That is, they paid for the right to make and market a branded product in order to retain a higher portion of the profit. In order to market products internationally, Moctezuma opened subsidiaries in the United States, Canada, and Chile. Over 60 percent of production was exported to thirteen countries: the United States, Italy, France, Spain, Canada, Australia, China, Hong Kong, Japan, Columbia, Chile, Peru, and Brazil. In another effort to diversify and cement their investments, Grupo Mexicano also moved into another high value-added commodity chain, the international service sector, by investing in a popular global restaurant franchise in 1998.

## CONCLUSION

Italia opened in 1951, during the era of the developmental state. Heavy state intervention in the economy guided investment first to light industry and later to capital-intensive sectors. During this period of hegemonic production regime, capitalists and workers had a stake in the political system. Capitalists profited from subsidies and import tariffs that protected them from international competition, while workers gained in the expansion of social and economic benefits that accompanied industrialization. Many workers were also in the unique position of participating in the government through state-directed labor confederations. Hegemonic control over labor allowed limited spaces for worker mobilization. On the one hand, the incorporation of labor into the state apparatus meant that worker demands resonated with a state that sought legitimacy and whose discourse identified with the revolution and worker interests. On the other hand, union leadership's support had been secured through patronage.

This was the context in which Italia and Moctezuma developed. Italian ownership made use of local and federal subsidies to set up a state-of-the-art plant, adding to the burgeoning industrial growth of the area. At first, the firm sold exclusively in the protected national market, but began exporting in 1984. When the textile plant opened a garment division, however, it tried to limit the benefits it provided the female employees. Women worker's resistance to the informal nature of their employment in 1972 was the impetus for the strike and the eventual establishment of Moctezuma as a separate corporate entity.

When the new Mexican owners took over the firms in 1994, they took energetic steps to sell their products in the global market. However, the political and economic context had changed drastically. State agents and academic circles promoted Japanese organizational innovations and full-package production as necessary to compete in the global economy. Following the 1982 debt crisis, the state implemented neoliberal reforms that cut social spending, deregulated financial markets, lowered barriers to FDI, promoted exports, and advocated the adoption of organizational innovations and technological upgrading through tax exemptions and tariff-free import programs.

Grupo Mexicano began to experience capital shortages in 1998. Heavy investments into upgrading the textile and garment complex, combined with some poor business decisions, would have constrained any company. However, to do so within an institutional atmosphere—where national capital markets were increasingly vulnerable to global financial crises—made borrowing capital expensive and uncertain. In addition, the concentration of power in the global apparel industry in the 1980s meant Moctezuma's clients demanded quicker turnaround times and enhanced quality but at a lower price during a time of intense international competition and low profit margins. Under these conditions of hegemonic despotism, international clients threatened to move their business elsewhere. Workers fared worse since the firm sought to pass the cost on to them by slashing wages and benefits. This was the situation on March 15, 2001, when women workers declared a strike.

CHAPTER 2

# "I Like Piecework More . . . Because I Work for Myself"

This chapter explores the labor process at Moctezuma under piecework, the production system employed since the firm began making men's suits in 1964. Although the factory had transformed to modular production in 1996, the ghost of piecework was always present while I was on the shop floor. Managers continually brought up the disadvantages of piecework in interviews, while workers implicitly and explicitly compared piecework and teamwork in their daily conversations. To better understand how piecework shaped the evaluation of teamwork by both managers and women workers, I describe the 1972 strike, then follow with a discussion of hiring and training as well as the role of supervisors and the union at Moctezuma under piecework.

## STRIKING FOR INCLUSION IN THE WORKING CLASS

At the end of 1971, Italia had more work than it could complete with its permanent workforce of 250 women.[1] The firm hired 110 temporary workers, firing and rehiring them every twenty-eight days in order to not provide them with the legally required benefits for full-time workers. At the beginning of June 1972, the firm made a bureaucratic error and fired them on the thirtieth day. Having already been influenced by the ongoing independent union movement, the fired women sought support. The grassroots school for workers set up by the Authentic Labor Front (FAT), an independent union in which automobile and textile workers learned about the Federal Labor Law next to university students and garment workers, helped stage a citywide protest to demand reinstatement (see figure 2.1). Law students affiliated with the school represented workers in the labor courts and in negotiations with the company. Two weeks later, the fired women workers were reinstated as full-time employees who voted for new union leadership composed of movement supporters.

This marked not the end but the beginning of worker mobilizations at Italia's garment division. The successful campaign galvanized women workers to fight

Figure 2.1. Moctezuma woman worker at protest, August 1972. Poster reads "Greedy hands off workers' interests." Photo by Adrián Carrasco Zanini.

the managerial change in work methods begun earlier that year, which had been rubber-stamped by the official union affiliated with the garment industry's faction of the Confederation of Mexican Workers (CTM). Termed *remethodization* by workers, industrial engineers modified the tasks and times allotted for workers to complete their sewing operations. Productivity and workloads were increased, but wages remained unchanged. Women expressed indignation at not being respected as workers and for being paid 40 percent less than their male coworkers, who were concentrated in nonsewing operations.

The new union took advantage of upcoming biennial contract revisions in August to protest this workload augmentation. By law, unions must notify the local conciliation and arbitration boards (LCABs) two weeks prior to declaring a strike, which is automatically done every time there is a contract revision.

So although the union had declared a strike, the company believed it was only a bureaucratic move. On August 11, much to the surprise of the company and government, workers upheld the strike and refused to go back to work—citing that the remethodization violated the contract. Although workers had voted for a new union executive committee, the CTM still represented all the women workers; the company fired those who supported the strike action.

What followed was a month of frenzied local and national solidarity events as well as negotiations. These actions occurred during the heyday of social movement unionism in Mexico, which united labor and community concerns. The women workers' struggles gained support from cultural figures, intellectuals, and political activists. Even national media followed events closely. Under these conditions, the governor was pressured to resolve the workers' claims quickly in order to avoid tarnishing President Luis Echeverría's reputation as a reformer. In this instance, unlike the strike that would occur in 2001, the state responded quickly to worker concerns. The industrializing project entailed close collaboration between state, business, and labor. Although the women workers had acted without the support of the CTM, the state's political legitimacy was under scrutiny from other unions, which were paying close attention to the official response to workers' concerns.

The governor played a major mediation role between Italia and its striking workers. Of the workers' twenty-three demands, the most important included reinstatement, a halt of remethodization, an end to the practice of hiring large numbers of temporary workers, the right to have a democratically elected union, a nursery and child-care center on factory grounds, and the payment of wages lost during the strike. The company accepted all except the last. The governor was quoted in the newspaper, chastising workers for being unreasonable in demanding all of the lost wages: "It does not matter how much money is spent," he stated, "what matters is that we do not set a precedent, because if you workers get everything you ask for, other workers will also want the same" (*Punto Crítico* in Basurto 1989, 149).

Ten days after the strike began, the LCAB declared the strike inexistent. By law, this reaction must occur within seventy-two hours of a strike's starting.[2] Five days after this ruling, women workers and their supporters responded by taking over the LCAB offices located in the government palace off the main plaza of the city. Tents made of sheets and rope appeared; this demonstration site was guarded by workers and activists for twenty-four hours daily. Through the Institutional Revolutionary Party (PRI) governor, the company sent notice that it was willing to pay 100 percent of lost wages in two installments on the condition that it could fire the union leadership. Workers refused the offer, but cracks in local movements supporting their cause were becoming evident. Importantly, two independent unions wrangled over representation at a nearby Japanese auto plant. Representatives for one of these accused the secretary-general of the new Italia union and the law students advising the union of being too radical.

Recriminations between different factions continued. Interestingly, one of the automobile union leaders involved was the person that, almost thirty years later, would become the legal union representative for striking women workers at Moctezuma.

Italia management used the divisions in the larger social movements that supported workers to their favor. The company proposed another offer, giving in to all worker demands as long as it could fire forty workers of their choosing, including the union executive committee. The workers ended the strike thirty-five days after it begun. In the end, they received 70 percent of lost wages, made temporary positions permanent (with the company retaining the right to keep fourteen temporary positions), stopped remethodization, and obtained a nursery and child-care center. All workers were reinstated, except for the democratically elected union leadership, who were fired. Three days later, women workers voted officially to separate from the CTM and establish their own independent union.

On May 1, 1974, workers from several factories that had won independent unions called for a boycott of the traditional May Day parade, which was meant to show government appreciation. Over 10,000 workers, including the women of Italia, deviated from the parade route and refused to pay homage to the government. A campaign of repression, coordinated by the government and entrepreneurial sectors, swept the region, clamping down on the wave of independent union movements. Women workers continued to produce suits from Italia's cloth, but they were now organized as an independent factory—Moctezuma. According to one high-level manager, the split was directly related to the women's activism; managers did not want women workers' penchant for strikes to spread to the male workforce at Italia. The independent union did not last, as the firm slowly fired movement leaders individually so that they could not claim collective retaliation. The union reverted to old practices of colluding with the company against workers' interests. Most of the strike gains were lost, and remethodization was reinstated.

## ESTABLISHING PIECEWORK AT ITALIA

In the 1960s in Mexico, manufacturing was men's work. Sewing, however, was women's work. When Italia decided to open a garment division in 1964, it needed to ensure that the factory was seen as an honorable place to work, an extension of the family. Unmarried daughters of the growing urban working class were the primary female labor supply available at the time, and they had few formal employment options. Paternalistic policies of firms and the state defined women as supplementary earners, as dependents in need of protection who could justifiably be paid less (Molyneux 2000). Italia portrayed itself as a benevolent employer and father figure through sponsorship of religious festivals. As such, recruiting workers was not difficult, given Italia's image of a moral environment with comparatively high wages and benefits.

The organization of work under piecework, however, resulted in antagonistic rather than benevolent relations between workers and managers. Key to this antagonism was the underlying Taylorist philosophy. In the apparel industry, Taylorist principles guide piecework organization: the production of garments is broken down into many separate and distinct operations, with specific motions to be performed repeatedly by an operator, historically a woman. Industrial engineers, who are almost always male, design operations and methods to provide the most efficient performance movements for production. They then time experienced machinists to calculate the number of completed tasks that can be expected per minute; this establishes a piece rate, or payment, for every operation and is considered the only appropriate method to follow for that operation.

This piece rate is then used to develop daily expected production levels and incentives for workers to surpass that quota. Making one's quota, however, is difficult. New workers often become discouraged and quit, while more experienced ones work as fast as possible without regard for quality, which results in high numbers of repairs and rejects. This, in turn, requires increased supervisory control and pressure on workers (Lamphere 1987; Westwood 1985).

The descriptions of piecework provided by women workers interviewed at Moctezuma closely match those of women at other garment firms (Fernández-Kelly 1983; Lamphere 1987).[3] This chapter demonstrates that a combination of control and autonomy resulted from piecework. Supervisors monitored workers, at times in coercive ways, to extract greater effort. Given the power differentials, sexual harassment was rampant. Women workers used their creativity and ingenuity to outsmart their surveillance by supervisors. Still, the goal at work for most was to earn as much as possible for their families. And, because the women aspired to limited promotions available to them, they ended up consenting to management's imperatives and control.

## Hiring the Right (Female) Worker

The first step in establishing control on the shop floor was to hire the right worker. According to both the human resources (HR) director and Belinda, who was in charge of hiring and training, company policy had long dictated that women be employed for most operations. Age, marital status, and educational attainment were secondary hiring criteria after gender.[4] Interviews with the six women who worked at the firm in the 1960s and 1970s reveal that, during the initial years, young unmarried women were preferred. Two of the women interviewed were sixteen-years-old when they were hired at Italia, another two were seventeen, and one nineteen. Only one woman was married, and she had two small children; she had been twenty years old when hired. This pattern of hiring young, single, childless women repeated itself except during periods of excessive work, when experienced sewers—regardless of their marital or family status—were hired.

Young women's employment was guided by the ideology of familialism, where the family's need stood above individual interests. Sofía, who began working at Italia in 1971 when she was sixteen, turned over 80 percent of her wages to her stay-at-home mother. She had been working since the age of nine as a domestic worker. Her brothers also worked, but they kept their money for their own expenses. Like Sofía, other young women accepted that their labor—but not their brothers'—was subsumed under a family strategy of survival or social mobility.

Married women also subscribed to the idea that their employment was for the good of the family. Gaby, the one young woman who was married, pooled her money with her siblings and mother, with whom she had migrated from northern Mexico. While Gaby worked, her mother took care of her two small children since their father had left. Having previously sold fruit on a corner, she was proud to work at a stable and high-paying factory job that allowed her to provide for her family.

The company was less concerned with the family background of the workers than with their gender. Both male and female managers repeated the managerial trope that women were naturally inclined for detailed work while men were not. Thus the preferred worker under piecework (and modular production) was female. A well-educated, male department manager put it this way:

> I don't know if it's genetic, but statistically it has been proven that women have greater dexterity in their hands [than men]. In this firm, as a garment firm, we require a lot of dexterity. . . . On average women do better than men. Many of the operations require small movements that are needed to give the garment a special effect. Women have shown that they are more patient in learning, in carrying out the operation. They are more social. There are few men that are willing to sit [at a sewing machine] because they say that others might say that he is a fag [sic] or because in his house they taught him that only women sewed. In my case, I sit down at the machines. I have always been interested in machines because of the ability they require.

Managers suggested that women's abilities are natural, couching them in terms of physiology. Gender socialization in the home prepares girls for sewing while only unnatural men or homosexuals, according to the manager, would be inclined to sew. Note, however, how the supervisor asserted his masculinity by describing his interest in sewing machines as an intellectual curiosity. Another male supervisor suggested that men were not ideal workers because of their innate uncontrollable sexual urges. He said: "Men, as Mexicans or any other man, are going to want to have relations outside of marriage." Since often both the wife and girlfriend worked at the factory, he explained, men's presence on the shop floor disrupted work.

In 1996, a pilot program spearheaded by the consulting agency tasked with converting the firm to modular production insisted that men be allowed to operate sewing machines, which had previously only been open to women.

Before 1998, only men worked on vapor irons in final pressing (because managers believed that standing up all day close to heat interrupted a woman's menstrual cycle), and only men were hired for the cutting department.

Despite the new rules eliminating restrictions for men, few were placed in sewing positions. The majority were sent to nonsewing operations in final pressing, cutting, or the stock room. Of those assigned to the pants or jackets departments, they tended to be sent to the preparation or bundling operation, which is considered heavy work, or the stamping and pressing operations with large machines. The HR director explained why, in his opinion, fewer men were hired:

> I think there are [two] reasons why there are not more men here. [First,] the union is afraid. Since the union has been mostly male or at least in terms of its leadership . . . they are afraid that, if men come in to work, they might remove [the leadership], or change them or leave them without work. [Secondly,] I think that, in Mexico, men are still a bit afraid of doing an activity that is supposedly women's work. We have the idea that being a good sewer means [having] feminine tendencies [or being] homosexual, which is totally wrong.

In spite of the more balanced view of this top manager, most managers consistently harped on women workers' natural dexterity. After men were admitted into all positions, they held onto gendered notions of skill while at the same time asserting there was no difference between men and women. For example, a top manager commented: "Men definitely have lower concentration levels [laughter]. . . . Manual work, men are not as capable. . . . Women's labor is more appropriate for this."

At the same time, however, the department manager for final pressing, where women were integrated after 1996, claimed men and women were equally qualified. He said: "I see no difference in the ability between men and women. The men are at times freer, deciding to go out with friends instead of coming to work. But in terms of ability, not a single problem." Questioned on how women were performing in cutting and final pressing, areas previously reserved for men in the garment firm, the female administrator in charge of hiring told me: "We are convinced that women have no problem doing the work."

These quotes are from managers at Moctezuma, but they could have been uttered at garment firms anywhere around the globe (Fernández-Kelly 1983; Lamphere 1987; Ong 1987; Salzinger 2003; Wolf 1992). Whether conscious or unconscious, managerial tropes about gender and skill in the garment industry have served to frame female workers as naturally skilled in sewing and, thus, deserving of lower wages. However, women are also preferred because they are seen as less likely to get involved in worker unrest, in part due to their family responsibilities. When it came to choosing between work and family, several managers said, women always chose family.

By 1990, the firm began experiencing increased levels of turnover. The HR department studied worker profiles, drawing on monthly productivity spreadsheets and exit interviews to find the ideal worker. They determined that family problems and immigration to the United States were among the most important issues that encouraged workers to leave the job. In 1990, turnover levels reached 79 percent annually, which was lowered to 37 percent in 1992, and 25 percent in 1994. According to the director of HR:

> [We hired] people with a bit more of a sense of responsibility. Not just young women as we had previously done, but rather people that maybe had a husband or children—but that the children be a little older so that her parents could take care of them and she could work. . . . We also eliminated some things. We decided to not hire people that had relatives in the U.S.

To lower turnover rates and increase productivity, the company decided that married women with older children were the preferred worker. The age of the children was important since the older ones could to take care of themselves or be left with relatives. In this way, Moctezuma managers were seeking "matron workers" like the Hong Kong managers in Chin Kwan Lee's ethnography (1998).

Another reason for hiring older women emerged in general conversations with two separate high-level managers. One said, "I fought for accepting women over thirty-five years old [into the factory] because they already have kids, they are less love-struck [*enamoradizas*], more responsible, and will be thankful to the company for giving an older woman a job." Fewer employment options for older women meant they would be tied to the firm and less likely to leave in search of another job or as protest over working conditions.

Older women were also believed to be less likely to immigrate to the United States given the dangers of crossing the border without documents. Human resources personnel uncovered a pattern among the U.S. emigrating workers: they often had a male relative who migrated seasonally to the United States. This male relative arranged and paid for intermediaries, or *coyotes*, to take the women on their trek north. Thus individuals who had male relatives in the United States had someone to sponsor their migration north and were considered more likely to quit work voluntarily; they were weeded out in the application process.

Although managers framed the problem of turnover as one of not hiring the right worker, later conversations inevitably brought up another issue: conflict. Piecework required coercive forms of control to keep production moving. As noted by the HR director:

> The turnover rates under [piecework] were higher. And I'm going to tell you why. Under the piece-rate system, workers were directly and excessively pressured by the supervisory staff. Since there was high turnover . . . one had to find a lot of people to substitute for those that left. And to not have to stop production in the plant, people would arrive, receive a very short training program, and go straight up to the shop floor. People were not trained so they did not earn money [reach their quota] and they soon left. And they also left because of the direct pressure from the supervisors.

This top manager believed supervisory pressure caused turnover, which affected the firm's ability to produce high-quality goods because workers did not build up skill and experience. By asserting that sewing and ironing were indeed skilled jobs, he was contradicting management's longtime claim that women deserved to be paid less because they were either unskilled, or the types of skills they had were natural so did not require training (Collins 2002).

Thus Moctezuma's leadership was attracted to modular production not only for its expected increases in production and quality but also, importantly, for the expected improved relations between managers and workers. Management knew that producing high-end men's suits was skilled work. As such, retaining skilled workers (and the investments made to train those workers) was an important component of efficient production.

## CONTESTATION OVER TRAINING

The issue of training proved to be an area of contestation between HR and the production department. Human resources personnel were more concerned with levels of turnover, while production managers focused on filling vacancies on the shop floor as soon as possible. Inevitably, the two departments clashed over how long workers should be trained and under what circumstances they were to be placed on the shop floor. Human resources favored a full month's training, while production saw the training center as a holding place for workers until slots opened up on the shop floor. They considered on-the-job training adequate. In light of this, it is not surprising that power struggles between these two departments ensued both under piecework and modular production: each wanted to control training. Under piecework, the training center fell under the purview of the production department. However, under modular production, the training center became part of the HR department.

Notwithstanding the differences of opinion between the two departments, the connection between training and turnover is not so clear-cut. Undoubtedly, some untrained workers did leave prematurely. However, in interviewing workers in 2001, I found great variation in the amount of time they spent in training regardless of when they began working. In fact, time spent in training did not differ between the two organizational systems. Therefore, the department in charge of training had little impact on workers but did demonstrate upper management's shift in focus: efficiency under piecework and quality under modular production.

## PAYMENT: INCENTIVIZING INDIVIDUAL OUTPUT

In line with scientific management philosophies, each operation was meticulously timed and studied by male industrial engineers. Each operation had a designated value for degree of difficulty, type of cloth, and order specifications.

Ironing a seam open (the operation I performed in the first team) is easier than sewing the waistband onto pant legs, which requires interpolating equidistant belt loops. Sewing jacket back panels is easier when using cloths of one color. Jackets with checkered or striped designs are more complicated because each line must be perfectly matched. Variations such as these were incorporated into the point value of each garment and operation, together with the time— measured in standard allocated minutes (SAMs)—required to perform the task. Complexity was further introduced to the piecework payment system through four different categories for workers, depending on the type of operation performed: (1) sewing; (2) pressing; (3) trimming; or (4) cutting.

Wages were calculated by taking into account the point value for each piece of clothing, each operation (within each category), and the individual workers' level of efficiency. A set amount of work per day was set by industrial engineers in SAMs, taking into account variation in design and cloth. Designs and cloth materials that were more difficult to maneuver received a higher point value and were allotted longer SAMs to perform the operation.

According to workers, an important element of the payment system was the "time-out" feature (called *economía* at the factory). When a worker had insufficient materials to perform her operations, she would use the time-out card to indicate she was "off the clock." Therefore, workers were paid based on their level of efficiency—that is, the number of operations performed divided by the amount of time they were on the clock. This time-out feature was crucial for workers because they were not docked pay on those occasions when the company failed to provide the conditions for them to work. However, timing-out also meant that, on a slow day, a worker may have to stay longer than the eight-hour shift to fulfill 100 percent efficiency.

Under piecework, workers received a base salary with the possibility of attaining four different types of bonuses: for productivity, quality, punctuality, and multiple skills. To earn the productivity bonus, a worker had to reach 105 percent efficiency. The amount of the bonus increased incrementally until it reached the top limit of 130 percent efficiency. The upper limit for utility workers who could perform more than three operations, and were moved daily to where they were most needed, was 160 percent. They earned five percentage points per operation mastered. Therefore, if they performed four operations at 100 percent efficiency, they were paid at 120 percent of the base pay. Working over 100 percent efficiency at an operation could garner even higher bonuses. A bonus for punctuality could be earned if a worker was sitting at her machine at 6:55 A.M. every workday of the month. If a worker had been certified for more than three operations, she became a utility worker and received a multiskill bonus.

Workers biweekly payment was calculated by adding the base salary, overtime, bonuses earned, and amount of time-out used and then deducting for damaged garments, cafeteria, the Mexican Social Security System (IMSS), union dues, savings fund, payroll tax (ISPT; usually 10 percent), and payment for the initial two weeks' worth of wages for the year that was "lent to workers."[5] Paystubs from 1996 to 2001 offered by a utility worker from one of my teams show that she earned $414.98 pesos for the week of November 10, 1996. After deductions, she received $322.41 pesos, which would have been U.S.$42.90 in 1996. Compared to the less well remunerated jobs most women workers held before starting at Italia, this amount was considered high. In addition, women workers received benefits that extended to the entire family, such as housing and health care.

Workers got so caught up in surpassing 100 percent efficiency to earn productivity bonuses that they consented to their own exploitation. Many experienced workers claim to have regularly reached over 100 percent efficiency and thus preferred piece-rate work over teamwork because they controlled their expenditure of labor and returns. If a worker wanted to earn a higher wage, she only had to produce more garment pieces.

Producing above efficiency rates, however, meant that industrial engineers might change the operation's piece rate, which is what happened. Time-and-motion studies were carried out to set a new number of pieces to be produced per SAM. Thus, as workers' skills increased, their workload could as well. Gaby clearly remembers the fastest workers were always selected for the time-and-motion studies. This made fast workers, who self-exploited to earn more money for their families, unpopular.

While sometimes new time-and-motion studies were added as a result of a worker's efficiency, at other times they were a response to changes made to the work method or the organization of the line to increase productivity. These were the remethodizations that angered so many workers in 1972. In Sofía's case, the changes meant adding a device to the sewing machine where she affixed the waistband to the pants, making it possible for her to do more work in less time. However, she did not earn more money.

The changes to Gaby's workstation and method were more serious. Previously, five different operations, performed by several workers, were needed to attach the lapel to the jacket back and front panels. After remethodization, she and another woman were responsible for completing all aspects of this job in one operation. The industrial engineers timed her and the other worker many times to set a new piece rate and to determine which of the two would keep the job. In this way, workers were pit against each other to lower how much money they could earn while increasing the workload.

The problem, however, was that increasing sewing speed also tended to increase mistakes. If those quality defects were caught in time, they would be returned to the worker for repairs, which took time away from producing more garments and lowered the efficiency rate. In interviews, a great many workers, on the one hand, claimed that they could not consistently reach above-efficiency rates and, thus, preferred to make the base salary. The lack of overexertion, in turn, drew greater supervisory monitoring. Managers, on the other hand, recall a significant portion of the workers reaching 120 to 150 percent efficiencies, but with terrible consequences for quality. According to 1991 HR data, 50 percent of workers produced over 105 percent of efficiency.

The piecework system pitted workers against line supervisors. If quality problems were discovered at the end of the line, it was harder to find the worker responsible for shoddy work. As such, workers did their best to sew quickly and hide the mistakes from the line supervisors; the line supervisors, in turn, tried to catch quality defects and return them in time to the person who made the mistake. In addition, it was line supervisors who called in the industrial engineers to retime operations, further exacerbating tensions.

## THE LAYOUT AS SOURCE OF AUTONOMY

According to workers and managers who labored under the piecework system, the layout of the shop floor did not change drastically with the reorganization to modular production. The main difference under piecework was that workstations were arranged closer together so workers need only turn to grab for wheeled carts that carried a large number of garments. Bundles of work were passed, sometimes literally pushed, from one workstation to the next on three-foot-high metal carts that held one bundle consisting of ten to twenty pieces. Each worker performed one operation and then passed it to the next workstation or department. This product-flow process was repeated all day on the shop floor. The cart system, however, had problems. The woman worker who staffed the bundle preparation position in the jackets one (J-1) department vividly remembers the difficulties in finding enough carts to use. Moreover, sometimes there were so many carts in between workers that it was hard to maneuver around them.

To complicate matters of product flow, the piecework system operated on a just-in-case system, which meant having inventory on hand. According to one area supervisor in the J-1 department, it was the supervisors' responsibility to have at least thirty pieces of inventory available *per operation*. Always having garments to work on, it was believed, would ensure the least amount of work downtime for both workers and machines. However, this practice hampered the production process in many ways. Piles of work around each workstation impeded the easy flow of carts while, at the same time, making pockets of privacy around individual workers. Under cover of inventory buffers, it was easier for workers to use their time and energy at their own discretion (Appelbaum et al. 2000).

The congestion on the shop floor caused by inventory and carts was experienced differently by management and workers. According to management, congestion made it hard to follow the flow of production. Some operations had large inventories, and others, according to the speed of the operator, were empty, which caused unbalanced lines. Items were lost along the way. It was difficult to get orders out in a timely manner because the bundles of the same lot number moved at different speeds. Searching for a lost bundle amid the piles of garments was often a Herculean task.

For workers, however, the layout allowed them to have greater control over their labor, enabling them to speed up or slow down as they wished or to carry out operations in ways different from what the industrial engineers required. As one worker noted, "We worked according to the method when the supervisor was nearby. She turned around, and we sped up and did whatever we wanted." One of the 1972 movement leaders, Laura, recalled how she would complete her work then start passing out flyers, taking care to hide behind inventory buffers to avoid supervisory control.

The inventory buffers also encouraged socializing. Hidden by the piles of garment pieces, some workers carried on conversations and planned after-work social events while supervisors were not watching. Doing so, however, probably meant slowing down and not earning a bonus. The young unmarried women were most likely to see the factory as a social arena. According to Laura, there were many parties to attend, especially for birthdays, marriages, and births. Thus workers preferred piecework because it allowed greater individual discretion over the work process—whether to work harder to earn more money for their families, sew according to their own pace, or simply socialize with friends.

## Supervisors and the Gendered Politics of Promotions

Under the piecework system at Moctezuma, the lines were clearly drawn between workers, line supervisors, area supervisors, and department managers. Each department had a department manager who answered to the production manager. The number of sections, area supervisors, and line supervisors depended on the product and length of the line. Both jackets departments consisted of five sections, each supervised by five area supervisors. In turn, these five sections had a line supervisor and a quality inspector, for a total of sixteen supervisors in each jackets department.

Most line supervisors and area supervisors began as workers and rose through the ranks, though mobility differed by gender, as it does in most workplaces. For example, one area supervisor, a midlevel manager who had been at the factory since 1965, described herself in the interview in this way: "I was there [at Moctezuma] for thirty-five years as a worker, utility worker, area supervisor, adviser [under teamwork], trainer [under hybrid system]." Her story was not unique. Another midlevel manager told of her mobility in the company:

> I began as a worker [obrera] when I was nineteen years old in 1969. I came from [a neighboring state] to visit family who convinced me to stay. I came in as a machinist in the first sections [of the pants department]. I arrived with knowledge about sewing. If they saw that you knew what you were doing, they would give you opportunities. After five months, I became a utility worker.

I learned about pants starting from the first operations. After that, noticing my capacity and attitude, they proposed me for line supervisor. I must have been around twenty-two years old. And I rejected it. Later, I accepted and became line supervisor for the first sections in pants. From that you learn what is needed and I kept jumping [up the ranks]. From there I became a trainer and then assistant area supervisor and, now, [area] supervisor. That is how I began at [Moctezuma]. This is a company that has given us opportunities. There are many *compañeras* who have been machinists, and now they are the bulk of the supervisors. We have had opportunities.

This supervisor's experience was not uncommon. Indeed, one of the main characteristics of Moctezuma under the piecework system was the mobility of workers through the internal labor market. Almost all supervisors had started as workers, although women reached a glass ceiling at the department level, rising only as high as area supervisor. Both aforementioned female midlevel managers began and remained in one section of a department. By the time each was supervisor of an area they knew every operation and had probably trained most of the workers.

Department and upper-management positions, however, were only attainable for the few men that worked at the company. During my time as a worker at the factory, which was after the changeover to teamwork, all five department managers were male, including two who had risen through the ranks. The other three had entered into the position with a technical degree. The head of final pressing described his rise within the factory as follows:

I have been here . . . fourteen years. I came in as a worker, doing sewing operations. From there, [I moved] to the stock room, later as supervisor of quality control. After that coordinator for production flow, then head of the sixth section [in jackets]. In pressing, after a year I was trained by [the production manager] in traditional pressing. Now I am the head of final pressing.

The head of finished products—also a man—had a very similar trajectory. Both the production manager and the quality director, at the highest levels of management, also began at the company as machinists. It was a matter of pride among management that two top managers had entered the factory doors as workers. Under piecework, the director of corporate manufacturing was always an Italian manager, representing the foreign ownership. Hence, with the exception of the position held by the Italian, all top management positions were theoretically open to male workers.

The internal labor market under piecework was clearly segmented by gender.[6] Women workers followed a more linear and shorter trajectory from worker to area supervisor. They were very knowledgeable about a subproduct. Male workers, on the other hand, which represented approximately 15 percent of the workforce, were overrepresented among higher management. Their on-the-job training followed a different path. Male workers rising through the internal labor market were taken out of their initial work sections to learn how the product evolved from the stock rooms all the way to finished products. Their knowledge of production was more extensive, though probably not as in-depth as that of their female counterparts at lower managerial levels. Men were groomed to be high-level managers while women could only rise to midlevel positions.

The highly visible internal labor market helped ensure worker consent. Although a glass ceiling obstructed women workers' rise in the company beyond area supervisor, their example proved to other women that if you were loyal and worked hard, you could be promoted. Greater promotional ladders for male workers, however, demonstrated to the men—whom management labeled as more likely to rebel and lose interest in work—that the payoff for consent was considerable. The presence of career ladders is an important source of workplace consent (Doeringer and Piore 1971).

## SUPERVISORS: SOURCES OF COERCION AND CONSENT

Women workers were also controlled by supervisors through coercion and dissemination of favors. Under piecework production at Moctezuma, every machine operator's wage was based on characteristics of the operation, the cloth, the worker's category, and his or her productivity levels. This information was collected on a daily basis by the line supervisor. Therefore, the supervisors were continually checking and looking over the shoulder of workers. In describing the supervisory system under piecework, one worker commented: "It was very different before [under piecework]. A supervisor was your immediate supervisor. And if they said, 'Stop doing that and do this' . . . you had to do it." The central role played by the supervisor in distributing work provided him or her with opportunities to play favorites, demand sexual favors, and carry out reprisals such as writing workers up for infractions and controlling bonuses.

Workers complained of feeling pressured while being pushed in both direct and subtle ways. When a machine operator ran out of thread, required the acetate lining for the pockets, or needed a replacement cloth from the cutting department, she asked the line supervisor to fetch it. At first glance, this seems to give the worker power over the line supervisor. However, if the supervisor did not retrieve the necessary work materials quickly, the worker's efficiency level could fall. Lower productivity directly translated into lower wages for that worker. Moreover, it was the supervisors' prerogative to assign workers for the easy jobs when they opened up or, on a slow day, to be paid extra for fixing defective pieces. In this way, compliant behavior toward supervisors was rewarded with easy work, extra work, and a steady supply of work materials. In fact, the line between coercion and consent appeared blurred to workers who suffered negative consequences if they did not assent to do what the supervisor asked.

Although many workers tended to describe all managers as the same, line supervisors, who were more likely to have been women who rose in the ranks, claimed to be caught in the middle. While area supervisors checked quality at the end of the section, returned defective pieces, and monitored the lines, line supervisors took care of materials and tabulating efficiencies. One line supervisor described her responsibilities as overwhelming and said that she was at the mercy of workers, higher management, and the union. Although lengthy, the following description of her work clearly shows the amount of labor that line supervisors did. She described her duties as follows:

> We [women line supervisors] had to request raw materials from the stock room—from threads, buttons, collars, to adhesive we used to glue the pockets, for example. From the repair room [we requested] needles, and from the cutting department the interior components like the pockets, the backing for the lapel, and exchanges [of defective or torn pieces] whether they be lining or cashmere. From the design department the task sheets, the changes in identifying tags, machine parts, the position of the pockets as well as the lapels. Ahhh! We could also request a physical prototype of the model we were going to produce. Also, when the machines broke down, we had to report them and run around after the mechanic for it to be fixed. This is regarding production. In terms of personnel, we had to report those who missed work, those who had permission to miss work due to illness, as well as the daily production of every worker under our charge. We had to note the number of operations that each one did because that is how we calculated their wage. Every operation had a price per piece of clothing, so some operations were paid better than others, but it balanced out when they knew how to do more than one operation. We were responsible that their pay arrived and that it arrive on time, including overtime. Together with the department manager, we also planned the theoretical framework for the line according to the specific characteristics of the models to be produced, the personnel required by operation, the machinery required by operation. [W]e were responsible for almost everything. And, well, we had to run to fetch everything because we had to go to the stock rooms, the cutting department, design department. . . . And, as you know, [those places] are pretty far apart. [W]e ended up so tired!

Immediate supervisors shouldered a great amount of responsibility for keeping the assembly line moving and in balance. In fact, these responsibilities clashed with their ability to monitor workers' progress, allowing for greater worker discretion. Not only did they respond to worker requests for parts but also to higher-management requests for detailed information on individual workers. Caught in the middle, between the workers and top management, line supervisors were known to be the most "despotic," as one worker called it, pressuring for increased and improved production.

Workers also complained of sexual harassment. Women who worked under both piecework and modular production asserted that more male supervisors pressed workers for dates in the earlier period, but they denied pervasive harassment. However, workers interviewed from the 1960s and 1970s described an atmosphere rife with despotic control and sexual intimidation. According to Sofia, who began working at sixteen years of age, "There was extreme vigilance by the department head. [H]e used intimidation. He counted how many times you went to the bathroom, if you talked. . . . And there was sexual harassment. We hated him." Gaby, the only married woman interviewed from this earlier period, discussed how managerial treatment affected her:

> There were such heavy workloads under piecework. There was no rest. And bosses [jefes] would pass by and touch your hand. They were always asking you out on a date. The general manager, he was a horrible man. He would throw garment pieces to be fixed at my face. . . . I got sick [with] nervous ulcers. I felt so much pressure.

It is not surprising that both women who participated in the 1972 strike described ruthless managerial control. What is not clear, however, is if this portrayal is due to their adversarial relations with managers or if managerial despotism and sexual harassment were curtailed by worker mobilizations in 1972. After all, the HR director had criticized piecework for the way it pit supervisors and workers against each other, resulting in worker dissatisfaction.

## PRODUCTION VERSUS QUALITY UNDER PIECEWORK

Under piecework, workers were concerned with their individual efficiencies. Earning productivity bonuses was the best way to increase one's take-home pay. Much like Burawoy's description of "making out" in a machine parts factory in Chicago, garment workers used their ingenuity to produce at high levels while controlling their speed and using their time-out cards wisely during slow times (1979). The net result, however, benefited the company. One woman at Moctezuma described her day in the following way: "I arrived [at the factory] and started to work. . . . If one hurried up and said, 'Yes, this week I want to get a bonus,' you hurried up and got it. The productivity bonuses were really good."

Although earning as much as possible was highly desirable, most workers mentioned the ability to control their own work, more than the bonuses, as the best part of piecework. One woman said, "I like piecework more because I pressure myself. I work for myself. I did not earn more but I did fine. . . . I have been one of those people who preferred that what I work is what I earn, as long as it's enough to live on." In another interview, one young woman commented she liked piecework for the following reason: "It's personalized. Your work is something personal, it arrives and you are responsible for it. And you can do something better with it." For these women, piecework was fulfilling, not the robot like experience that managers claimed was one of the reasons for changing to teamwork.

Under piecework, women worked according to the established method and times when the supervisor was near. When the supervisor left, a worker could either slow down or speed up (often resulting in poor-quality work). By managing their time, speed, and use of the time-out card, workers felt they controlled their work. One worker commented, "One would hurry up for one's own benefit. If you got more than 100 [percent efficiency], then you could relax and take it easy." In fact, most workers did not relax but rather worked harder to surpass quotas to reach productivity incentives.

In management's view, the piecework system systematically neglected quality in favor of quantity. One male supervisor recalled, "I think that the piecework system is the worst system in terms of quality because all that people have in their little heads is to get as many pieces out to make good money." Managers often described workers in patronizing ways. This attitude was prevalent with management who berated workers for watching out for their own economic interests. However, as will soon be evident, management could also be shortsighted, setting aside a commitment to quality when expediency demanded it.

According to managers (and some workers), levels of rework and rejects were unacceptably high. Both managers and workers agreed that, technically, every worker was supposed to repair their own work. Every bundle had a task sheet that noted which workers did which operation. However, as bundles passed from section to section, task sheets were lost. If shoddy work was not registered by the area supervisor, there was no information about who performed an operation. In that case, finished garments were returned from the end of the line to utility workers who then repaired the jackets or pants. However, utility workers checked their time-out card and were paid extra for repairs. Rework or repair levels were astronomical, at times reaching over 90 percent of production according to managers. The seconds rate—that is, the number of suits that were beyond repair or not up to par after repair and thus had to be discarded—reached 42 percent according to several line and section managers. This represented enormous levels of lost capital for the company.

Paradoxically, even with such high rates of rework and discards, workers did at times earn bonuses for quality. When I asked a supervisor how this could be, she recognized that quality bonus calculations were only measured in the final products department, thus not taking rework and some discard statistics into account. Moreover, from her own experience in quality control at the end of the line, she knew that if orders were urgent, higher-level managers directed poor quality products to pass inspection. She told me:

> When I worked in final quality control, I did not like it. For example, I would say to the quality director, "This does not pass." He would say, "Pass it." "But it does not pass; it does not fulfill the requirements, the specifications,

the concept of what we ask for. . . ." [The quality director] then would say,
"You'll pass it because I say you pass it."

The point clearly made is that priorities for quantity over quality were set at the
highest levels of management. Although workers admitted to working too fast to
perform operations with high quality, it was management who set up the incentives to produce more and then rewarded poor quality by forcing it through
quality control and doling out quality bonuses. Both line and area supervisors,
as well as workers, understood this. Blaming workers for poor quality is only
looking at half of the picture.

Incentive structures at each level of management encouraged supervisors to
ignore poor quality work. Production goals encouraged managers to be concerned only with their portion of the production process, making decisions to
increase their output although it contravened larger organizational goals. To
point out defective work was to take responsibility for repairs and lower production numbers. The fragmentation of managerial decision making had the unintended consequence of structuring production in ways that made sense for
departmental goals but were irrational for the functioning of the firm (Prechel
1994). Thus management also had a hand in perpetuating a system that prioritized volume over quality.

## THE ROLE OF THE UNION

When women workers replaced the union leadership after the 110 temporary
workers were fired in 1972, they discovered that the documents being filed with
the labor authorities by the CTM union for contract revision were the same documents first provided in 1964. Details like names and wage levels had not been
adjusted at all. The role of the union was to make workers believe they were
represented while company interests were protected.

At the beginning, workers did have some expectations that the union would
stand up for them against management. Given the rapid urbanization occurring
in Mexico, most women workers were the children of peasants or of the first
generation urban working class, yearning to benefit from industrialization. And,
comparatively, they did. Jobs in large factories provided higher wages and access
to state housing programs, social security, and pensions. But local struggles by
male textile and auto plant workers pointed to interests shifting toward issues of
workplace democracy. When the company fired the 110 temporary workers and
the union did nothing, such a shift made sense to many women workers at Italia.

The bitter thirty-five-day strike turned many women workers into experienced activists. The women were proud of having stood up to management,
but the condition set by the company for reinstating all 350 workers meant the
dismissal of their independent union. Once inside, women workers thought
they could elect another independent union and continue their struggle. However,

according to the few women from that period that I interviewed, management soon bought out the new union, and scrupulous union members were fired one by one and placed on a blacklist, unable to find work at any other factory in town. Most women followed the only recourse they had: to place a suit with the labor authorities against the company for unjustified dismissal, which normally took years and rarely ended positively.

Back at the factory, however, the pay and working conditions improved. Gaby, who was not fired until 1974, recalls how supervisors were more respectful. Women were afforded more freedom of movement, without as many recriminations for going to the bathroom or breaking to drink water. The nursery and child-care center opened for a brief period, with nursing mothers allowed two half hours per day to feed their babies. After a while, remethodizations commenced again.

As union control reverted to leaders working closely with the company, union leaders focused on solving individual worker problems without delving into workplace issues. Thus, if a woman worker complained of excessive yelling by a manager, union leaders would speak to the particular manager and smooth over the problems as a matter of misunderstanding. If a worker was docked pay for staying home with a sick child, union representatives talked to payroll to explain the difficulty. The union became adept as resolving individual problems, building a role for itself in the factory without challenging workplace concerns like low piece rates and remethodization. It was a so-called white union, fulfilling legal requirements of representation for workers but responding to the needs of the company. The occasional disciplining of management was more a move to retain some degree of legitimacy than real protection of workers' rights.

## CONCLUSION

How should we assess the piecework system at Moctezuma? Some in management pointed to increasing market shares and output levels to defend piecework. However, this was a highly inefficient system. Piecework resulted in the need for high levels of rework, together with escalating antagonism between workers and managers. High levels of production were achieved through multiple levels of line and area supervisors who exerted strict control over workers—determining who did what job, who did how much, who got paid extra for repairs.

For women workers, piecework was a combination of autonomy and control. Workers discovered ways of improving their individual production and take-home pay. Making use of the piles of inventory to hide from supervisory surveillance and using the time-out card to increase downtime resulted in greater discretionary power for workers. Many felt they had outsmarted management, controlling their own time and labor. Yet to earn the productivity bonuses, workers had to consistently work at 105 percent of efficiency levels and put up with heavy-handed supervisors. Self-exploitation was part and parcel of piecework.

The way workers and managers later remembered piecework during my interviews with them provides some hints to their respective reactions to team-work. By a great majority, workers preferred piecework over teamwork; they felt like they controlled the extent of their work and related earnings, which provided them an opportunity to help out their families. In contrast, management was partial to modular production. But, as we will see, there was resistance to change among managers as well.

Piecework, an antagonistic yet stable model, would have probably continued indefinitely had it not been for the changes going on in the global apparel commodity chain. In 1994, when the company was bought by Mexican entrepreneurs, the garment industry was being shaken by the increased power of brands and retailers as well as the popularity of new forms of production organization. Increasingly, buyers pushed manufacturers like Moctezuma to adopt organizational innovations that increased turnaround time and improved quality for lower unit costs. The expense of converting to the organizational forms that buyers required, however, was shouldered by the producing firm. Central to the conversion at Moctezuma was the hiring of consultants to direct the process of becoming a lean factory and to hire and train workers in the new philosophy—the subject of the next chapter.

# CHAPTER 3

# From Piecework
# to Teamwork

## TRANSLATING THEORY INTO PRACTICE

The concentration of power in the global apparel industry changed the conditions under which Moctezuma functioned. The firm's clients demanded quicker turnaround time, higher quality, and lower costs. Several high-profile buyers stipulated the use of just-in-time (JIT) and statistical process control (SPC), where work is measured at preset intervals to chart and assess whether production is within quality parameters.[1] To retain high-value clients, in large part, Moctezuma reorganized production from piecework to teamwork.

### THE THEORY OF MODULAR PRODUCTION

In 1995, the industrial group invested heavily in the services of a high-profile international consulting agency, which proposed Japanese-style lean production, termed "modular production" in the apparel industry, to respond more quickly to client demands through smaller batches of more varied models. Lean production is a combination of social relations and techniques (Kaplinsky with Posthuma 1994). Theoretically, production is organized under three core principles: *quality consciousness, teamwork,* and *flexibility.*[2] Together, they strive for the ultimate goal of *kaizen,* or continuous improvement. Quality consciousness refers to quality from the source, taking place at each step, not at the end of the line, so that mistakes are corrected immediately. Assembly lines are reorganized around product families and workers into teams, where rotation and further training aim for a multiskilled workforce. Skilled workers can then use their ingenuity to solve problems and improve functioning on the shop floor. Managerial tasks of translating experience into scientific method can then be returned to the workers through teams. In these ways, management relinquishes significant control over the labor process as quality and production are dealt with by team leaders and team members in coordination with management.

Flexibility is built into the system by reducing inventory on the shop floor by pressuring suppliers to deliver parts JIT. Such a tight system demands quality and coordination to reduce waste and production time, freeing up capital for reinvestment. Client demands create a pull on a product stream that is followed as closely as possible. Smaller-batch production, ability to reorganize the line and machinery, and multiskilled workers respond to this goal. The use of *kanban*, or visual marker cards, performs a dual function. First, the markers direct JIT production by specifying what supplies are required for immediate orders on the shop floor. Only those inputs are supplied to each worker's station. Second, kanban pull products through the line. The cards move upstream on the shop floor designating what operations are to be done and who does them. In this way, inventory, quality, and flow can be constantly monitored so that workers with bad quality are signaled out; this ensures continuous improvement at work.

In the garment industry, modular production theories are seen to lower production costs by decreasing work in process, inventory, through-put time (the time it takes the garment to go from the first to last operation), and rework (repair of pieces flagged for bad quality). As a result, productivity and quality improve, providing augmented responsiveness to clients in terms of turnaround time and model changes (Abernathy et al. 1999; Abernathy, Volpe, and Weil 2006; Appelbaum et al. 2000; Bailey 1993; Dunlop and Weil 1996). Workers are empowered to take control of the work process, having the challenge of producing a larger segment of the garment and focusing on issues of quality (Berg et al. 1996). Increased worker satisfaction arising from the trust and responsibility given to them, in turn, should translate into greater productivity. Furthermore, since teams are self-managed, middle management disappears, lowering payroll costs and providing direct and constructive communication between workers and management (Arthur 1994; Tello and Greene 1996).

Japanese-style lean production has become so popular that many academics, policymakers, and practitioners have overlooked the particular ways in which lean production emerged in Japan. In order for workers to consent to working smarter (and many say harder as well), industrial relations in Japan developed in ways that connected interests between management, unions, workers, and the state (Chalmers 1989; Cole 1979). Japanese employment relations secured consent of workers through life-time employment, seniority-linked wages, and company unions (Elger and Smith 1994). Yet life-time employment applied only to men in the big automobile companies while women made up a large portion of the part-time, contract, and temporary workers in supplier firms (Carney and O'Kelley 1990; Kucera 1997). Women's family responsibilities were used to move them out of work during economic downturns, further denoting skill as a male characteristic. Therefore, a segmented and gendered labor market regime emerged as men were considered the breadwinners and women (occasional) supplemental earners (Besser 1996; Cole 1979).

Although lean production established a less antagonistic regime than Taylorism, work practices that secured employment were not sufficient to manufacture consent in Japan. Life-time employment for men and weak organizational representation were buttressed with corporate welfare policies. Cole argues that, for an internalization of organization goals to take place, Japanese firms had to provide incentives and benefits that responded to workers' main concerns, such as housing (1979). Workers traded increased effort for increased security, participating in what he called a *community of fate*, where workers and managers cooperated for a common goal.

The notion of shared vested interests in the company implies that both managers and workers should be willing to sacrifice for the good of the company. However, the community of fate is a normative ideological construct used to elicit consent from workers in Japan. Although rarely fully internalized, it was a convenient way to bundle workers' interests with those of management in everyday practice. Similar ideological constructions have been found in the U.S. auto industry organized around teamwork (Besser 1996; Graham 1995).

## The Practice of Modular Production at Moctezuma

When Mexican entrepreneurs purchased Moctezuma in 1994, they faced a highly competitive and rapidly changing economic environment. As one top manager put it, "We had to become cutting-edge to compete [globally]." To best compete internationally and retain their global clientele and reputation, the owners decided to upgrade by reorganizing as a modular producer. Implementation of lean production occurred slowly and under careful direction of an international consultancy firm and top management.

Reorganization around lean techniques had four main elements: self-managed work teams, elimination of midlevel supervisors, increased information sharing regarding production with workers, and focus on quality. I have reconstructed the outlines of the implementation process of lean production at Moctezuma from company documents, internal communications and planning manuals that document the transition to lean production, and interviews.[3]

The process began in 1996 when new ownership hired an international consulting firm, American Consultants (a pseudonym). This firm was based in the United States, with offices all around the globe providing services in a wide range of areas, from accounting to labor process. With a satellite office stationed in Mexico City, consultants began by conducting in-depth training with top production, quality, and human resources (HR) managers on the benefits and methods of modular production. Training included a trip to an auto parts firm on the U.S.-Mexico border that had been successfully operating under lean production for three years. An industrial engineer from this Ciudad Juárez firm signed on as a consultant at Moctezuma, working together with American Consultants.

The next step was the training of middle management. The production manager joined the consultants to impart courses for department and section managers. These sessions took place after the workday, often going until 10 P.M. or midnight, with only one break. Top management and American Consultants detailed a plan of action, with deadlines and people responsible for each activity. The consultants and top managers participated in *every* meeting and *every* part of the implementation.

The reorganization to modular production at Moctezuma was a two-pronged process spearheaded by two main departments, HR and production. Human resource personnel meticulously planned the training necessary to produce in workers, in their own words, "a cultural change." Not only did they need to convince workers to think of production in different terms, but they also needed workers to feel personally invested in the process. As one of the handwritten notes found among the reports provided to me read: "[Need to] make people emotionally involved!" Meanwhile, industrial engineers deciphered how to reconfigure the assembly line into self-sufficient teams and how to pull production instead of pushing it down the line. Human resources followed a normative logic, while the production department followed a competitive one. Both departments shared the task of training workers in the skills and attitudes needed to make modular production function.

## HUMAN RESOURCES: CONSTRUCTING THE SOCIAL RELATIONS OF MODULAR PRODUCTION

In September 1996, courses to explain the new philosophy to workers commenced. Workers learned that they would be directly in charge of managing production, assuring quality, and securing the working condition of the machinery. In effect, under the new production system, workers were to take on the responsibilities of line supervisors, industrial engineers, and mechanics on top of their own duty of producing 1,900 pieces of clothing a day.

Since Moctezuma decided to convert to modular production with its existing highly skilled workforce, they had to convince workers to participate in the new organizational innovations. Constructing a community of fate would maintain and reinforce the behavior of ideal workers and prevent resistance from workers who did not want to change the way they worked. To do this, HR managers were tasked with devising a profile of the preferred worker, enhancing corporate welfare programs, forging closer connections between management and workers, and reinforcing the new philosophy.[4]

### *Constructing the Profile of the Ideal Worker*

Under teamwork, constructing the profile of the ideal worker was important not only because it would continue to lower turnover but also because the firm expected resistance to change.[5] As the reorganization began, over 200 workers were in the process of being selected to fill vacancies that opened up if workers quit or were fired by the firm. Close scrutiny of both applicants and current workers and their attitudes ensued to weed out poor candidates for teamwork. Selecting workers on attitude is not uncommon if management believes that attitude is an essential component of getting the job done (Callaghan and Thompson 2002).

For the most part, workers at Moctezuma who were unhappy with the proposed changes or who proved obstacles to team functioning were pressured to leave voluntarily. If a worker was very disruptive and did not leave of her own accord, she was fired.[6] Women remember many people quitting during this period, pointing to the fact that management was able to disguise the weeding out process so that it did not cause further resentment (see Appendix C).

While in the past Italia, and later Moctezuma, had preferred unmarried, young women with at least primary education, American Consultants insisted on hiring the most qualified applicant, whether male or female. As noted in chapter 2, however, managers' deeply ingrained gendered assumptions that women were naturally more skilled at sewing and more willing to put up with monotonous work still guided their hiring practices.

The worker profile, constructed and updated assiduously every year since 1996 by the HR staff, consisted of the following characteristics: age, sex, educational attainment, experience, compound measures of life-cycle stage, medical requirements, and personality. Belinda, who was responsible for hiring, described it this way:

> There are two profiles. We have to watch for characteristics that affect production and medical requirements. [T]hey must . . . [be] the ideal age (over twenty-five years old), and preferably that they be female. We have seen that women have greater dexterity when it comes to sewing; however, we do accept men. [They must] have junior high school [education]. The civil status does not matter, as long as they are stable, whether they are single or married. [What matters is] that you have a steady place to live, live no more than an hour away, that you have someone to take care of your children, . . . and that you not plan to have a child in the next year and a half—so that you can be integrated into productive [work] life . . . and experience. If they have [sewing] experience, it's very easy for them to get in.

According to this description, productive imperatives required mature young women who knew how to sew and did not have life circumstances that would interfere with work. Managers assumed most women would eventually become mothers. However, the greatest problem with hiring women was not motherhood but lack of stable childcare.

According to the HR office, medical requirements called for specific heights so workers could fit comfortably at the workstations; thus, requirements meant shorter height (women) for sewing machines and taller height (men) for cutting tables. Upon a visual inspection of the shop floor, however, there were women and men of all heights in all departments. Another medical requirement prohibited any kind of tattoo. When I asked about the proscription, I was told that people who had tattoos were likely to belong to a gang or, at the very least, were antisocial and had poor judgment. Since men were more likely to have tattoos, they were more often excluded from the pool of employable workers. The effect of the height and tattoo requirements thus justified an ideological preference for women in teams.

The last medical requirement, while not found anywhere in writing, was certainly official. Every female applicant who made it through the first phase of tests and returned for the medical exam underwent a pregnancy test. While this practice is illegal under Mexican law, it is common practice in the export assembly and manufacturing industry and has been in place for years (Fernández-Kelly 1984; Jefferson 1996). When I first arrived at the factory, I asked an HR manager about this common business practice. She denied it, underscoring the illegality of the practice. Eight months later, after having reviewed hundreds of worker files with old pregnancy test results attached, I asked her again. By this time, not only did I have evidence to rebuke her denial, but we also had established a friendly working relationship. She told me that the pregnancy exams were still performed but were no longer reported in the worker files after a complaint to the labor authorities was made against the firm for this practice.

Although managers predicted that women would inevitably experience motherhood, hiring pregnant women was frowned upon.[7] While women were the preferred workers, surveillance to determine where they were in their reproductive cycle was used to discriminate against certain women. Management knew that women were likely to become pregnant, but their preference was to have the women working at peak productivity before they took time off to have children.

Another characteristic sought by recruitment officers was the all-important team attitude. At the beginning of the reorganization to modular production, workers' interactional attitudes were assessed to limit worker resistance. It was later institutionalized as part of the desired worker profile. Company memos from the reorganization period show how managers made lists of workers who were natural leaders and those who did not approve of changes. One memo read:

> This team is very motivated . . . with the exception of two people, [names], who are easily signaled out by their attitudes. They resist changes proposed and seek ways to be the leaders of the group. However, the other workers don't pay much attention to them. . . . [W]henever we broke up into teams, they called others to them instead of them seeking out their teammates as the [group] dynamic intended. . . . Regarding the feedback sessions and group

dynamics to detect leadership qualities or apathy, the following people were
found to be lacking in interest or apathetic: [two names]. Another worker,
[name], is insecure. I think she has problems adapting to teamwork.

The managers' main concern was to find just the right (female) workers
who could get along with others. The change from individual piecework to
teamwork required not only technical training but also an openness and commitment to teamwork. It required workers to put the interests of the team and
the firm above their own—that is, it required a cultural change in attitudes
towards work.[8]

Information culled from training sessions and initial teams served to filter
out potential troublemakers and construct a profile for future team workers.
Workers with certain characteristics were avoided: those with leadership qualities, assertive personalities, or lacking in self-motivation. Team attitude, in
contrast, meant being confident (but not too confident, which would be seen as
assertive), following directions, and getting along with others. Such characteristics favored certain more submissive femininities over self-assured ones. The
past-work experience of applicants also was closely scrutinized for possible troublemakers. If an applicant had worked at a place known to have had problems
with strikes or work stoppages, they were automatically rejected. This was common practice among large employers in the city; Moctezuma was no different.

To be employed, applicants had to pass four exams, entailing several visits to
the factory. Although applicants took psychometric exams to measure intelli-
gence, aptitude, manual dexterity, and ability to follow directions, the personality evaluation with written comments by the HR interviewer carried the most
weight, reflecting subjective assessments of the person's ability to interact with
others. Reports from many interviews in worker files that I examined clearly
indicate that the company sought accommodating, pleasant, and quiet workers.
Some comments even warned when applicants appeared to be too forceful or
outgoing.

Thus, the ideal worker profile—a social, submissive woman with junior high
education and networks for childcare—was then used to screen applicants.
Situated in central Mexico, where there were more workers than jobs available,
the firm saw a steady stream of applicants show up at the factory gates. When
there were vacancies, workers were encouraged to recommend family members.
I was told family members felt more pressured to perform at work and were thus
preferred.

According to the manager who oversaw the recruitment and examination of
applicants, approximately one hundred people applied monthly in 2000 and
2001. Of those, only thirty-five to forty matched the desired worker profile.
Of these, a large number were denied when they did not pass the medical,
psychological, eyesight, or dexterity exams. In the end, approximately ten out of
the hundred applicants began training every month at the training center.

## Enhancing Corporate Welfare Practices

Previously, Moctezuma provided only the medical staff required by law: one doctor and one nurse. In the effort to tie workers to the firm and elicit loyalty, the firm established a family clinic. It covered two shifts for the garment and textile factories and was composed of four doctors (two specializing in industrial medicine, one nutritionist, and one psychiatrist) as well as a dentist, two nurses, a hygiene and safety specialist, a paramedic, and a laboratory technician. The clinic offered services to workers and their families, including women's health (birth control, yearly pap smears, uterine and breast cancer detection, pregnancy checkups, and breast-feeding classes), deworming, and dental campaigns (fluoridation and education). Moreover, the medical clinic provided free annual vaccinations for the family and high doses of vitamin C during winter.

The expanded medical services served two purposes. First, as the clinic doctor stated, healthy workers work more:

> We can see the positive changes in workers' health in the lower levels of absenteeism; fewer and fewer cases of missing work due to diarrhea, due to infections in the upper respiratory tract, for situations that could have been foreseen. And these are measures that we quantify. . . . Everyone benefits. The workers receive treatment without having to travel [to the government health services], wasting both time and money. And our firm avoids a worker having to leave the worksite to receive medical service, leaving their machine abandoned [for extended periods]. Production will not be affected. The quality of the production is better [with] a healthy worker than one with ongoing health problems.

It was in the interest of the firm for workers to be in good physical health. However, the medical services were expensive. Expanded medical services had a second goal: to convince women workers that Moctezuma valued its employees above all else. Given that one of the workers' greatest concerns was their family's health, these services were a powerful incentive for workers to remain at the firm.

The firm also enhanced its educational, cultural, and sport programs. Junior high school and high school equivalency programs operated in the afternoon. Outings to musical concerts and parks were organized by the HR office. Soccer and volleyball teams played on company fields. The firm's objective was to demonstrate their commitment to workers and their well-being.

In addition to federally mandated benefits, Moctezuma provided thirteen gifts and opportunities that were included in the contract as "additional benefits." They included (1) the equivalent of 650 days of wages to the family of a worker if she or he died; (2) additional wages (on top or regular wages) for the union executive committee members and delegates, in addition to assistance for social and cultural union events; (3) eyeglasses for workers who needed them to perform their job; (4) subventions for one meal per day from Monday to Friday; (5) promotion of sports events through the union, including uniforms;

(6) $125 pesos (U.S.$13.89) in recognition of a child's birth; (7) scholarships for ten workers to complete high school, university, or a technical degree; (8) a one-time marriage gift in the form of a two-piece suit or three meters of cashmere cloth; (9) three days off (five if out of state) with pay if a family member died; (10) $1,000 pesos (U.S.$111.11) if parents, spouse, concubine, or children were to die;[9] (11) 20 percent of their wages after the sixth day and up to the seventieth day of disability provided by the Mexican Social Security System (IMSS); (12) retirement with a special compensation package for workers with twenty years of service; and (13) food coupons prorated by seniority.

The last benefit deserves further explanation because it became a point of contention before the strike in 2001. Food coupons were given twice monthly according to seniority, a gift to help women fill their kitchen pantries. Workers with zero to two years on the job received coupons equivalent to 10 percent of their wages; for workers with three to fourteen years, it increased to 15 percent; and for those with over fifteen years of seniority, food coupons represented 20 percent of their wage.

These additional benefits embraced workers as family members, offering gifts for births, marriages, and deaths in the family. The image and discourse of the firm as a family was reinforced by the rules for pregnant women. Moctezuma allowed women to work at 70 percent efficiency after the sixth month of pregnancy and to leave work an hour early while nursing. Although women workers had to fight in 1972 for the right to nursing breaks to feed their children, it was now offered as a present from the firm. Together, the enhanced corporate welfare programs depicted the firm as a generous patriarch who cared for his workers. However, the problem with this strategy (which was evident when the firm experienced an economic crisis in 2000) is that it is expensive, especially when a firm operates in a highly competitive economic environment.

### Forging Closer Relationships between Management and Workers

The company also fostered a feeling of family by removing status markers that differentiated workers from managers. The cafeteria served everyone alike, with no special areas reserved for management. Special cultural and sports events were held where managers and workers participated equally without regard to rank. Supervisors danced and joked with the workers at religious festivals and end-of-year parties where workers' children received Christmas presents. At these celebrations, managers brought their families and sat at the same table as the workers, breaking down barriers. One of the department managers put it this way: "I very much believe that [a person's] permanence at a job is provided by a sense of belonging, a sense of being a part of something. It is this sense of being part of something that gives you the desire to work harder." Moctezuma invested heavily in constructing this feeling of community.

Another mechanism to forge closer connections between managers and workers was the presence of one of the top managers in the firm—whom I call

Mr. López—on the shop floor during the implementation of teamwork. He spent much of his day in the midst of the three teams, working out issues as they arose. His main task was to help teams coalesce and to convey the firm's commitment to the new system of production. Mr. López had been a machine operator who rose from the shop floor to the highest levels of management. His daily, jovial presence among these first teams was meant to demonstrate the new philosophy of worker-management relations: horizontal instead of vertical communication.

Managerial hierarchies were also flattened in accordance with lean production theory. During this initial period, psychological evaluations of line supervisors were conducted to ascertain their intellectual capacity, commitment to the firm, and ability to relate in a nonauthoritarian way with workers, which informed later supervisor profiles. Based on analysis of these evaluations, supervisors were dismissed or moved. In the first section of the jackets one (J-1) production line, three line supervisors were reduced to one during the pilot program.

New rules for supervisory management highlighted their changed role. Instead of supervisor, they were called "advisers," and they could enter into self-managed teams only when invited by the team leaders (as discussed in chapter 4). Their role was to assist workers in reaching their productive and quality goals, not to direct them. Instead, advisers focused on gathering information to carry out SPC by measuring seams to calculate minute deviations from method specifications and graphing data on progress reports. Just-in-time production also required that they carefully orchestrate the operations, supplies, and workers required for upcoming client orders.

By the time I arrived on the shop floor in 2000, the numbers of middle management had been heavily pruned. Under piecework in J-1, there had been a department manager, five area supervisors, five line supervisors, plus five quality inspectors. Quality inspectors under piecework could check garments but had to speak to the line supervisor to request any changes. Under teamwork, there was a department manager, two advisers, and a quality auditor. Team leaders, technically workers, were positioned between the managers and the team members. Thus the middle layer of supervisors was heavily cut, changing from sixteen supervisors to two advisers and a quality auditor/adviser; the latter now had the power to require changes directly from workers, demonstrating the elevated concern for quality.

The changed role of middle management was also gendered in nature. Under piecework, women workers could aspire to line or area supervisor. But modular production required technical skill rather than workers' tacit knowledge. Thus new advisers were required to have a university degree in industrial engineering, a predominantly male profession. This educational requirement removed internal promotion ladders for both male and female workers; however, it transformed this middle-level of management from one that was predominantly female to one predominantly male.[10] Mr. López's story of promotional opportunity was no longer possible.

### Reinforcing the New Philosophy

A series of posters were designed to inculcate the new work philosophy. The posters read: "Multiskilled means being better"; "Recipe for a good service: Make good suits; Make the exact number requested by the client; Deliver on time"; and "With teams we will be the best firm and will beat the competition." The promotional campaign, making use of colorful cartoonish characters with male superheroes and childish-looking female workers, highlighted the new-found central role played by workers and the appreciation of them by the firm.

Management also used posters to respond to specific issues that arose during the implementation. In one case, the top manager, an Italian, had the following placard made in reaction to worker resistance:

> Work under teamwork is not easy or relaxing. It requires additional effort from every worker since one has to be concerned not only with one's operation, but also with coordination, communication, reaching team goals, balancing flow, controlling inventory, etc. Teamwork is for more qualified workers and, for this reason, qualified workers are better paid.

This message was directed both to the workers already organized in teams and to the rest of the shop floor, which was intently watching them.

A monthly bulletin prepared by HR personnel also responded directly to workers' concerns. Using a comic strip format known to working-class sectors in Mexico, the bulletin informed workers on the progress of the pilot program. Women workers in the first three teams were interviewed, their comments and suggestions printed. Here are a few of the comments from the first bulletin:

> Aurelia from Team One tells us: the work in teams is good. Even though I still have some doubts about how to deal with the bundles, I feel that work is better in teams because we can be more interconnected. Lourdes from Team Two comments: the change is good because [by] improving the quality of our work, we will have more clients. Besides, we need more companies [in Mexico] who are open and willing to change in order to have more clients and create more jobs. . . . Working like this is more family-like, we get along better and we help each other.

Whether Aurelia or Lourdes really said these things, the message was clear: teams were good for workers and the firm. The comments projected a picture of workers who had internalized the interests of the company as their own. Teams improved production, which improved the economic viability of the firm, which, in turn, secured employment for all. Human resources and American Consulting devised feedback mechanisms to evaluate the degree to which workers were internalizing these messages.

The subtext of the posters and bulletin not only equated the firm's interests with those of workers but also helped construct a gendered understanding of work. They highlighted the idea that teamwork is family-like, coming *naturally* to women workers. Posters written in the format of a recipe and bulletin articles on cooking and childcare reminded workers that, above all else, they were mothers. Just as in the home, women's work at the factory was an integral survival strategy during hard times. Moctezuma framed work as an extension of the home and equated women's central yet subordinate role in the home with their role in the firm.

A welcome packet provided to every new worker also highlighted the fragility of international competition and, by extension, the importance of women's work. It read:

> Our country is going through a stage of great changes that affect us all. In response to these changes, firms have also had to change, giving ourselves the opportunity to improve. Moctezuma, and the industrial group to which it belongs, have been following a process of improvements and changes because we are aware that every day our clients are more demanding. We have national and international clients. They can choose to [leave and] go to our competition.

Company documents referred to larger processes of globalization and the need to remain competitive through organizational innovations and full-package production.

A video shown on the first day of employment further explained that teamwork, JIT production, and quality at the source were necessary to satisfy clients, produce a better product, and reduce internal costs. Posters even had Japanese words on them: "Rules for Order and Cleanliness: *Seire*-Selection; *Seiton*-Order; *Seiso*-Cleanliness; *Seiketsu*-Progress; *Shitsuke*-Discipline." The posters could have come straight out of a how-to book on Japanese-style lean production, furthering management fads that equated development and progress with a specific organizational form. During this time in Mexico, lean production was touted as *the* way to upgrade. Through these posters, the company was implicitly urging workers at Moctezuma to act more like Japanese workers who had traded job security and expanded benefits for peaceful worker-management relations. Fearing a reprise of 1970s mobilization, management worked hard to construct the feeling of a community of fate to manufacture consent.

## PRODUCTION DEPARTMENT: IMPLEMENTING THE TECHNIQUES OF MODULAR PRODUCTION

While HR personnel were manufacturing a cultural change in workers' attitudes, the industrial engineers crafted the technical aspects of the reorganization of production. The pilot program encompassed thirty-eight workers in the first section of the J-1 line. The plan was to successfully execute modular production in one section and then begin a rolling transformation of the shop floor until all of sewing, pressing, and cutting activities were organized around the goals of teamwork, continuous improvement, and JIT production. The idea was to accomplish this over a period of thirty two-months, but change was slower than expected.

The pilot program was released from managerial tutelage in February 1997, five months after the training of workers commenced. In the middle of that same year, all of the jackets two (J-2) production line switched to teamwork. A whole year later, in August 1998, the rest of J-1 began to function in teams. In October 1999, the pants department followed suit, and, seven months later, half of final pressing converted to teams—all working side by side with the other half that remained under individual piece rate. Although plans were made to likewise transform the cutting department, it never happened. When I began working on the shop floor, one thousand workers labored under teamwork, while more than two hundred still worked under piecework. Four years had passed, and the process was still incomplete.

Much was riding on the pilot program in 1996. Effectively implementing modular production in the first three teams was crucial, for they were to be a showcase for the rest of the shop floor. The pilot program had to convince other workers of the benefits of teamwork not only for the factory but, more important, for the workers themselves. It was also an opportunity to work out the kinks in the system before committing the whole factory to such drastic change. For this reason, implementation of the new work system followed a haphazard schedule, with changes along the way.

To set the conditions for this change, industrial engineers reorganized how garments were pulled through the shop floor by the kanban system; they also improved the quality of supplies as well as the capacity of suppliers. Two specifics tasks had direct impact on how workers responded to the organizational transformation: the payment structure and layout of the shop floor.

### Aligning Payment with Effort

Management's change to teamwork promised to reward extra effort with greater take-home pay. A system of bonuses was instituted for producing above 100 percent of productivity with quality quotas, having multiple skills, being a group leader, training coworkers, and working on difficult operations. The productivity-quality bonus was calculated according to the weekly totals in the finished products warehouse, individually prorated for days missed. The generous bonus ranges, starting from $175 pesos (U.S.$19) for 2,300 daily garment pieces produced to $420 pesos (U.S.$47) for 3,000 daily pieces produced, were posted in large posters in prominent places. The goal was to incentivize workers to increase their productivity while maintaining quality requirements.

Purposefully named to underscore the need for 100 percent volume of work with 100 percent of quality, the productivity-quality bonus was originally calculated at the team level to encourage adoption of modular production and deter resistance. If the team produced more than their weekly quota, they were eligible for a range of bonuses. However, the fact that some teams were able to produce more than others unbalanced the lines. By April 2000, the rules were changed for totals to be calculated by departments at the same time that the daily production quota was increased from 1,900 garments to 2,299. While not an uncommon practice under piecework at Moctezuma (and the industry in general), it undermined the firm's message of shared management. In August 2000, management decided to change the calculation of the productivity-quality bonus again, basing bonuses upon the production of the entire shop floor as counted in the finished products area. Changes in the incentive structure demoralized workers as their bonus depended increasingly on more people working above their peak capacity.

The bonus for multiple skills incentivized learning and certifying new operations. Acquiring multiple skills was an important way to augment take-home pay, adding $80 pesos per week for two operations and $110 pesos for three. The more operations a worker could perform, the more flexibly and quickly teams could respond to production glitches. Workers who were certified for more than five operations were labeled *utility workers.* Each department had a team of utility workers who were sent out to cover daily work needs. Utility workers were the best-paid workers as they proved invaluable in making it possible for teams to reach their production and quality goals. The bonuses for utility workers were also paid weekly and according to days worked. The weekly bonus ranged from $230 pesos (U.S.$25.56) for five to six operations certified, up to $380 pesos (U.S.$42.22) for eleven or more operations.

The highest-paid utility workers earned over 82 percent of the base wage. Through messages on posters and the incentive structure, the firm constantly reminded workers that becoming multiskilled was in a worker's and company's interest. What was not so clear, however, was how people were selected to be trained in further operations to become multiskilled.

Team leaders received a bonus of $120 pesos (U.S.$13.90) per week for the duration of their rotation. While the role of team leader had not changed much since the inception of teams in 1996, the specific time and work requirements had. At the beginning, teams suggested candidates for team leaders, who were then chosen by management. The position lasted for two months, which, at a later date, was changed to six months. By the time I arrived at the factory in 2000, team leaders were automatically chosen by seniority and rotated every four months. Also at the beginning, team leaders were expected to take on added responsibilities while completing 100 percent of their work. In 2000, that was changed to 75 percent of production, which workers still deemed unjust.

The last bonus recompensed workers who performed especially difficult operations. The twenty-seven operations were outlined in the collective-bargaining contract and amounted to $75 pesos (U.S.$8.33) per week. Since it took longer to master and be certified for complicated operations, they deserved an extra bonus. Each operation had been calibrated by industrial engineers so that easy operations were repeated more times per hour than difficult ones. In the end, the labor expended by each worker theoretically balanced out.

The training bonus rewarded team members for training coworkers, but it caused a great deal of tension. First, eligibility for any bonus was contingent on being certified for an operation. Industrial engineers certified operations by conducting time-and-motion studies, where workers had to produce 100 percent volume and quality in the standard allotted minutes. Second, not all workers had the same opportunity to be certified for multiple operations. Women workers in bottlenecked operations did not have the free time to learn new operations. Third, at times production needs required workers to move to a new operation before they could complete training, lowering their take-home pay.

Last, workers who were certified for an operation had the right to name those who helped train her, which provided the trainer with a onetime bonus of $297 pesos (U.S.$33). The problem was that many felt training by team members had been deficient or nonexistent. But if other team members were not named as instructors, repercussions could follow. Workers spoke of resentment, illtreatment, and even physical retribution in the form of *caballito* (the attack of the worker by several people, bringing her to the floor to be hit and kicked). The doling out of training bonuses thus became a political issue among teams, extracting an emotional cost on workers as they navigated conflictual relations in teams.

In the end, bonuses could add up to a significant amount of one's paycheck. A March 2000 paystub for the same utility worker discussed under piecework shows that, of the $1,385.73 pesos (U.S.$110.43) in payment, over $500 pesos were bonuses. She received the same benefit deductions as under piecework—IMSS medical coverage, National Workers HousingFund (INFONAVIT) subsidy,[11] and payroll taxes (ISPT), as well as firm deductions for union dues, initial advance, savings fund, and meal subsidy—but with two new additions: workers could borrow money from the firm, paying it back through payroll deductions, and they could purchase imperfect suits at lower prices. The savings fund entailed deducting 15 percent of weekly wages to be put in a fund; this was supplemented by an additional 13 percent provided by the company and could be withdrawn either at the end of the year or upon termination of employment. Additional benefits provided by law but not noted on the paystub were meal and transportation subsidies as well as vacations and profit sharing. After deductions, this utility worker took home $737.42 pesos (U.S.$58.77).

Working at Moctezuma was highly desirable. One of my coworkers had waited a long time to be hired by the firm. She lived an hour away, in an area overrun with informal workshops and an industrial park with several large modern multinational garment firms. When she worked at one of the workshops, she earned $230 pesos (about U.S.$26) per week without any benefits, and during peak season she was forced to work extra hours and holidays without the legally stipulated time-and-half wage increase. "Workshops are not secure employment," she told me.

When I asked why she did not work at the industrial park, she said, "They pay too little." Her aunt worked at a U.S. garment firm earning $360 pesos, the same as a trainee earned at Moctezuma. She told me, "At least here, once you get to the shop floor and are certified for an operation, you can earn up to a $1,000 pesos (U.S.$111) per week plus great benefits, at least that's the rumor."

Wages at Moctezuma were higher than those at most other garment factories in the area, but they were not subsistence wages. The base weekly wage at Moctezuma began at $462 pesos (U.S.$55) and could easily rise to $700 pesos (U.S.$78) with incentives. Minimum wage for a garment sewer in the central region in 2000 was quite a bit less, $214 pesos (INEGI 2002). The Mexican government defined the cost of a basic food basket, known as *canasta básica*, as $3,300 pesos per month for the average Mexican family for that year. Thus, although considered one of the best garment jobs in the area, and even though take-home pay had improved under teamwork, a job at Moctezuma did not provide wages that covered the basic financial needs of most individuals, let alone those of their families.

Under piecework, this utility worker's overtime and individual productivity bonus constituted 37 percent of her paycheck. Under modular production, productivity, quality, and multiskill bonuses added up to 58 percent of her take-home pay. The incentive structure under teamwork provided a powerful inducement for workers to increase discretionary effort, in exchange for augmented physical, mental, and emotional labor.

### Improving Control through Shop Floor Layout

The second major task tackled by industrial engineers, who made up the backbone of the production department, was the shop floor layout. When modular production is set up in new factories, termed *greenfield sites*, teams are often set up in semicircles (Juárez Nuñez 2003). However, in brownfield sites, which are already established, as Moctezuma was, only incremental changes that make better use of space and realign operations are possible.

Physical and social impediments to change existed at Moctezuma. Structurally, sewing and pressing operations were intertwined, with vapor ducts, electrical connections, light fixtures, and even walls already in place. Some of these could be changed, while others could not. Moreover, making big changes in the layout from piecework to teamwork would signal big changes in social relations. Some workers had worked side by side for years and resented drastic alterations. Thus organizational change was planned as a gradual process, the layout modifications piecemeal. According to company documents, the goal was to optimize floor space and team building by doing away with "vertical and horizontal barriers" to work and communication.

The streamlining of the shop floor layout followed the tenets of JIT production. Each workstation contained only materials needed for scheduled orders. Tables or carts with extra bundles were taken away as inventory buffers were no

Figure 3.1. *Poka-yoke* lights, control panels, local supply shelves, and altar to Virgin of Guadalupe, pants department, 2001. Photo by author, February 2001. Photograph taken with permission from top management at Moctezuma.

longer necessary. Each workstation was to be completely visible to everyone else (workers and managers) as information regarding efficiencies, quality, and flow was now of public interest. Team members were responsible for each other's work and, thus, needed to know what each was doing. Using Foucault's conception of power as pervasive, Barker (1993), Oliver and Wilkinson (1989), and Salzinger (2003) describe this type of layout as surveillance through the panopticon.

Besides workstations being moved closer together, white boards (used as control panels) and local supply stations (for reduced inventory) were set up in every team area. Production and quality information was updated by team leaders every two hours on the control panels so that managers and workers could gauge the day's progress. In effect, everyone could see which teams reached their goals and which had not, providing a tool for peer pressure and all-encompassing control (see figure 3.1).

The local supply stations used the kanban system to supply workers on a JIT basis. There was no longer the need for workers to leave their post in search of materials or have large inventories stacked up on the shop floor. Small amounts of only the necessary materials (such as threads, buttons, and pocket lining for specific operations) were placed within the team perimeter, which was clearly marked with blue paint. Young men from the stock room would then be responsible for monitoring the material levels. Visual aids, part of the kanban system, signaled which and how many supplies were needed for the week's work. Stockers also cleared clutter so workstations were visible to all.

The new layout also included tall poles with lights at the top (*poka-yoke* lights). These lights were a signaling system: yellow meant out of work; red, the machine needed repair. Women workers were instructed in basic machine-repair methods, but if that proved insufficient, they put the red light on. Mechanics, group leaders, and advisers responded to the signals. These light signals were analogous to cords used in automobile assembly lines organized around lean production. Auto workers could pull a *poka-yoke* (Japanese term) or *andon* cord to stop the assembly line when there was a defective piece or errors. The colored signals on the Moctezuma shop floor were used instead since there was no assembly line to stop. Together, the open layout, production panels, and kanban system increased the ability of managers and coworkers to surveil and control workers' efforts.

## HUMAN RESOURCES, PRODUCTION DEPARTMENT, AND WORKER TRAINING

All workers participated in six months of daily training in 1996, consisting of two hours of small and large group sessions on the meaning of teamwork and JIT production. After the reorganization of the shop floor, training took place mainly on two occasions. The production department headed a two-week refresher course on the theory of modular production for workers hired in the last calendar year. They stressed how workers' deviation from the theory weakened the firm's economic viability. Human Resources led *la escuelita*, or training school, teaching new workers rudimentary sewing and pressing and modular production fundamentals, and weeded out possible troublemakers as well.

### The Refresher Course: Managers and the Union Holding Workers Accountable for the Firm Crisis

In December 2000, before I began to work on the shop floor and after having spent four weeks at *la escuelita*, I joined workers in the refresher course. Some women workers had already been on the shop floor for almost a year, and others, like my fellow trainees and myself, had yet to start. The refresher course took place from three to five o'clock in the afternoon. Workers from the first shift stayed late and those from the second shift arrived early to attend. The classes took place in a big hall, surrounded by soccer and basketball fields on one side and the family clinic on the other, making it a perfect location to bring workers for talks on the merits of teamwork and the importance of working interdependently as a community of fate.

The first day, we were greeted by the top production manager, a sharply dressed man in his fifties who had risen through the ranks. With a serious but affable style, he began by pointing out the destructive nature of piecework.

People had been working like machines since the 1900s. The result, he said, was poor quality, increased costs, and losses for companies. Moctezuma changed to teamwork as a response to world competition, to cut waste (a point every presenter would harp on consistently), and to provide workers the possibility of self-fulfillment. The logic, he said, was that if workers labored without oppressive supervision, a congenial work environment would lead to employees taking pride in their work, enhancing quality, and improving the firm's bottom line. He painted a nice picture; next he detailed the operational nuts and bolts of production and how workers were falling short.

The production manager discussed the basic building blocks of modular production, or *teams* (the shorthand used at Moctezuma), explaining the importance of clients, teamwork, and quality. Every team had to continuously supply their internal client, the next team, to keep production moving without wasted capital and inventory in order to satisfy the ultimate client, the buyer.

Teamwork was essential in this process of continual work flow. Teams were responsible for a semiproduct, moving people around to deal with bottlenecks, cover absenteeism, or solve technical issues.[12] Teamwork, he emphasized, improved the work environment, sharing of knowledge, leadership, responsibility, and take-home pay. Under piecework, he continued, it took workers eight to ten weeks to reach 100 percent efficiency and be eligible for productivity bonuses. A worker could do that in two to three weeks under teams, he claimed.

In response to this extremely rosy picture of teamwork, women workers started to complain. One said, "I started October 3 [2000] and barely have one operation certified." Several yelled out, "It depends on the difficulty of the operation." He replied, "You have to want it." His words silenced the room. Despite claims to close manager-worker relations, this exchange shows the lingering importance of hierarchy in the firm and frustration over the truncated character of training.

The next day, the top production manager explained how quality was the linchpin of the team system. Performing quality work from the very start, he said, led to a more satisfactory work experience and a more profitable product. A commotion from women workers signaled discontent. Relationships in teams could be difficult, he acknowledged, but if individuals made an effort, thought about how their actions affected others, and took care to have shorter morning meetings and not waste time, teams could function superbly. He used the blackboard to show how the inefficient use of time by workers caused production lags, not teamwork. He stated that the workday was 9.1 hours long for the first shift.[13] Then he listed how women workers "cheated" the clock:

| | |
|---|---|
| 5 minutes | arriving late |
| 30 minutes | in a team meeting |
| 5 minutes | leaving early to the cafeteria |
| 5 minutes | leaving the cafeteria late |
| 10 minutes | leaving shift early |

| 10 minutes | meeting in the middle of the afternoon |
|---|---|
| 5 minutes | talking with a friend |

1 hour 10 minutes of lost time
+36 minutes   teams had changed schedule to leave at 4 P.M. instead of
                  4:36 P.M.[14]
1 hour and 46 minutes of lost time per workday

Evidently frustrated, he announced that, in the end, there was a 17 percent loss of productivity during the workday. He continued:

> If each person in a team of twenty loses 1.5 hours, thirty hours of labor are lost. Thirty hours in a 9.1 hour workday means 3.29 hours are lost to wasted time daily. For the 1,400 workers, that would be like 230 people not showing up to work per week. Then the price of our product goes up. So don't tell me that the daily production can't be done; it's you who are wasting time.

The hall was silent. He ended the discussion by saying, "Teamwork can be a very beautiful system or it can be a very destructive one." In other words, it was women workers who were slacking off.

The production manager then returned to the overhead projections on quality. Properly handling work materials secured high quality. Mishandling cloth or inputs could ruin a product or cause shortages. In a more somber tone, he added that the firm was experiencing material shortages at the moment. "During the day off last week, we [managers] picked up in just one of the jackets departments over 800 cones of half-used threads. Over 100,000 buttons were picked off the floor. We have to use materials efficiently!" he asserted.

After defining production terms, explaining ISO 9001 (the most recent quality guidelines from the International Organization for Standardization), and the kanban system, the top manager concluded by asking, "I know there are distortions, but these are the principles. What do those of you who have already been up on the shop floor think about it?" A litany of complaints followed: team leaders did not know how to lead, so the team fell apart; others said the opposite, that team leaders did not get any support from the team; most complained that everyone did not put in the same effort. The production manager listened. To specific problems, he proposed solutions: "Have you told the team leader or the adviser about this? They are there to assist you, use them as resources." Other times, he wrote down the number of a particularly problematic operation and promised to investigate.

His responsiveness to women workers' grievances, especially compared to his previous defensiveness, boosted the morale in the room. The difference in attitude toward management was remarkable. As Elton Mayo (founder of the human relations movement) discovered, positive interaction with management and within work groups increases productivity (Mayo 1933).

Interestingly, a union delegate imparted the next training module. She asked women workers if they knew the respective responsibilities of team leaders, members, utility workers, and advisers. A boisterous discussion echoing complaints of the previous day ensued. After listening to grievances, she agreed that some problems, such as not allowing workers to train fully on an operation before having them learn another one, had to be studied by the union. However, she chastised workers for cutting corners and undermining the system. She noted how self-managed teams misused their ability to give members permission to miss a day's work (called permits) by granting too many and requesting utility workers to cover their place. This, the union delegate said, was an abuse of the trust given to workers by the company.

Another problem the union delegate highlighted was the drop in efficiency. She asserted that the firm performed at 100 percent efficiency under piecework, compared to 70 percent under teamwork. However, the number of suits required, standard allotted minutes allocated, and training were the same.[15] "What gives?" she asked. Then she warned that the company had the right to decertify operations if workers did not perform consistently and that sanctions could be applied. "So be careful about demanding and demanding without giving anything. Not everything the company does is bad. But, if they wanted to, they could demand 100 percent efficiency." While she listened to worker complaints, she also cautioned them to hold up their end of the social bargain. Her words mirrored those of management uttered days before.

At the end of the class, the union delegate and I were walking to the union office when a worker approached her, concerned with rumors that the firm was going to fire workers. The union delegate told her not to worry. While it was true the firm was in dire condition, they were not going to start firing workers. A careful evaluation of workers' efficiencies, quality, and attitudes would take place first. The woman left relieved. I was struck at how she had just told the filled hall that the company was benevolent in not sanctioning people for low efficiencies, and now she said workers would be fired based, in part, on their inefficiencies. More striking still was the assertion that workers could be fired for their attitude. The Federal Labor Law does not sanction this as a justification for expulsion; however, it seemed the union did.

Last, during the refresher course, Mr. López, the worker who had become the top quality manager, discussed quality issues. He began by explaining Maslow's pyramid of needs and how work satisfied the fundamental human need of self-fulfillment. The goal of teams, he asserted, was to allow individuals to live up to their potential; only quality people can make quality products.

He then explained why workers should care about producing quality suits. He asked, "Did you know that JC Penney quality auditors come to inspect orders? For an order of 2,800 suits," he said, "they take twenty off the racks. If they find two defects, they take another twenty suits. If they find three defects in these, they reject the order. Last year's first shipment was rejected. Managers and workers spent five days inspecting every single suit for the second audit. JC Penney rejected the order a second and then a third time." Mr. López then asserted,

"If we begin to satisfy our internal clients, our final client will also be satisfied. That's why we must do quality work from the start." In the end, JC Penney decided to take its business elsewhere, while the firm lost a great amount of money paying for extra hours and penalties for delays. Although the firm believed that the client had exaggerated the "quality problems" to lower the unit cost, there was no way for the firm to contest this—the buyer had the final word.

At the end of the refresher course's two weeks, presenters consistently underscored that the workers and company's fate were intertwined. After providing detailed information on the ins and outs of teamwork, managers beseeched women workers to participate and cooperate. But, in case these pleas did not work, woman workers were also constantly reminded that the firm was in economic trouble, which meant that workers had to consent to the team system of production.

### La Escuelita: *Training as Constructing a Compliant Workforce*

Training at *la escuelita* served the manifest purpose of teaching necessary skills and the latent function of providing cheap labor and screening out any possible troublemakers who might have made it through the hiring process. Theoretically, training lasted four weeks, at the end of which the instructor made recommendations to the production department as to whether and where trainees should be placed on the shop floor. Trainees, considered temporary workers, received zero remuneration the first week, $150 pesos (approximately U.S.$17) the second week, and their full trainee base pay of $362 pesos (close to U.S.$40) the last two weeks. According to the 2000–2002 union contract, trainees only had a right to subsidized transportation and meals.

*Learning Skills.* I began the participant observation portion of this study on November 6, 2001, with fellow trainees (seven women and three men). The ability to go through the training center allowed me to better understand the firm while, at the same time, providing workers an opportunity to learn about me. I explained that I was doing research for a dissertation, which many likened to "a work internship for a degree [*práctica*]." Very often, they asked, "Why don't you punch a timecard?" I explained that I was not employed by Moctezuma, nor was I being paid. In the end, my coworkers either left bewildered ("Why in the world would she work without pay?") or thought it was a great idea ("Oh, she's improving herself").

On that first day, we all gathered in the training center at 7 A.M., just as the first shift began. The classroom had two rows of tables arranged lengthwise in the middle, lined with old industrial sewing machines on all four sides. Metal and wood chairs that looked at least twenty years old were in front of each sewing machine. Against one side wall were two steam irons; and, across the room, there was one drawing table and another for cutting. Cubbies for odd-sized practice cloths were in the corner by the electric scissors. As in any other classroom, at the front of the room was a desk in front of a blackboard.

The instructor—a forty-something woman who had worked on the shop floor for seven years—began by emphatically stressing the importance of quality at the source: if we produced shoddy work, the company would lose clients. She made it sound as though there were a direct correlation between individual performance and client behavior. The instructor introduced us to a series of fourteen exercises that every trainee had to complete, passing a rigorous timed exam for each to measure accuracy (quality) and efficiency (volume).

She walked us through the operation of steam irons, sewing machines, pattern making, and cloth cutting. Then we were all given an eight-inch square piece of cloth and told how to sew. The goal was to "dominate the machine." Our first exercise consisted of filling the cloth with straight lines, each half an inch apart, then repeating the same motion with perpendicular lines. We did this exercise repeatedly for seven hours, until it was time to leave.

The next day began just as the previous one had ended, at our machines sewing straight lines; this time, we rotated between cashmere and acetate lining, learning how to control for cloth differences. If we made a mistake or the thread ran out, we had to remove the stitching and begin anew. The instructor walked around the room checking our work. After four hours of continuous sewing, she checked the quality of our work and counted the number of squares we had sewn, calculating our efficiencies.

To my surprise, I reached 65 percent, which I thought was very good for someone who did just a little bit of quilting for a hobby. Two of my coworkers who had never sewn before reached 45 and 50 percent. Naively, we congratulated ourselves on this achievement. The instructor, however, loudly scolded the class for poor performance. Had we not been listening to her for the last two days? If we did not do the work correctly, it was not worth doing it at all. Our efficiencies, she announced, were extremely low. If we wanted to move up to the shop floor we had better change our attitude.

By that time it was 1 P.M., our turn for lunch at the cafeteria. Lunch was harried. We had thirty minutes to form a line; pick up our trays, silverware, food, and drink; scan our worker IDs at the cashier; bus our dishes; and be back sitting at our machines. The workers on the shop floor had to add two further steps for their break: form a line to clock out, and then another one to clock back in. If they took more than thirty minutes, the team leader was advised to hurry them along.

Hurried as it was, we were always happy when lunch break came around. We were hungry and our bodies ached from being in the same position for six hours before the break. Not only were the metal and wooden chairs not ergonomically designed, many did not even function properly. When we arrived in the morning there was always a mad dash for the better chairs. Some were too high for the machines, others too low. The backing on some was broken so you could not lean back. To make matters worse, the poorly ventilated room quickly became stuffy and uncomfortably hot with all the machines running.

*Providing Underpaid Labor.* At the end of the first week, the trainees were told there would be no exercises that day. Instead we were going to the microproduction department to "help out." Micro, as it was called, was a large room filled with all types of machinery in a small building between the textile and garment factories. Six employees (*empleados*), under a supervisor, prepared samples, special-order suits, made changes to orders, fabricated vests, and sewed new models. In Mexico, there is a marked difference between employees and workers. Employees at Moctezuma were not governed by a contract or represented by a union, nor did they have a set schedule. They earned a little more but had to be at the beck and call of the firm. While the wage differential was not great, their status was much higher. For the most part, employees had been line and section supervisors who were displaced by the team system. It was a demotion, but it was preferable to being fired.

For the next four days we—the two morning-shift trainee groups—were divided into groups to help change labels on a large order of jackets. There were around twenty of us who lined up in groups to do a series of tasks: to carefully remove labels from the inside right breast pocket and nape of the jacket and left sleeve, clean stray threads, gently iron the lining back into shape, pin new labels in place, sew the labels onto the inside pocket and nape, attach a small rectangular label on the left sleeve, press suits in a large steam iron, and then place them on a rack with a plastic cover. I mostly removed the lapel label and ironed the lining back into shape; both tasks were done standing up. If before we complained about sitting all day, now our feet throbbed from standing all day. However, in micro, we could talk to each other when the instructor was not in the room. The employees did not care; they enjoyed the company.

We were changing labels because the company had an urgent order but no production, so it modified suits with similar characteristics. While I did not know why these particular suits were hanging around the factory, there are several common practices that could account for them. More and more, retailers and branded manufacturers stipulate in the purchasing contracts that the producer (or contractor) must accept unsold merchandise (Bonacich and Appelbaum 2000; Collins 2003). Furthermore, buyers can refuse orders that are incomplete or considered deficient in quality. The net result is to transfer risk down the commodity chain to the contractor or subcontractor. In this case, Moctezuma could have been forced to take back unsold merchandise or could have had an order rejected, so these suits needed to be modified to be sold, even if at a lower cost.

Although trainees expected to move to the shop floor after four weeks, this did not happen. They "helped out" instead of completing training exercises. During the second week of training, Moctezuma workers were furloughed at half pay for one day due to supply shortages. The morning and afternoon trainee shifts, however, continued. Since the forty of us did not fit in the microdepartment, half of us were sent to work on the shop floor. I was working there when someone from HR saw me and complained to the instructor. From their point of view, I was closer to a manager than a worker and, thus, should not be put to work.

After this incident, I spent the rest of the second week and all of the third doing exercises while the rest of the trainees labored in the microdepartment. Every so often, when there was not much work, we would all do exercises. However, my fellow trainees were starting to complain about the low pay and indefinite stay in *la escuelita*. I was the only one to complete training from my cohort. I later discovered the prolongation of training for the others continued for several months. In the end, most of the trainees quit. Low wages and the increased financial uncertainty of the firm made a secure job unlikely. A few trainees continued to help out in the microdepartment. This practice of extending the training period, in effect, was a subsidy for the firm as workers labored for less than market wages in the hopes of later earning more.

*Weeding Out Independent Women Workers.* At the end of the third week, the instructor informed us that workers were needed in the second shift. If we wanted to secure our position in the firm, she said, we should jump at this opportunity. However, the company was in economic crisis; so no one knew what would happen. She coaxed and prodded but only three workers were willing to move to the night shift from 5 P.M. to 1:30 A.M. One woman said her husband would not let her; another said that her neighborhood was too dangerous to get home at that hour—even taxis would not enter after dark.

Two single women in our cohort accepted the next day. One lived at home. This schedule would allow her to help her mother with her baby sister during the day. The other was a single mother who liked the possibility of being with her baby daughter during the day to feed and care for her and then leave her sleeping in the care of her mother. Significantly, the only male in our group quickly accepted the night job. With no one to answer to at home, he decided his own schedule. The women, in contrast, made decisions based on their family circumstances and in negotiation with their families. They had to balance the double shift of work both at home and Moctezuma.

The workers who were able to be flexible graduated to the shop floor with permanent employment. Those that were unable or unwilling to work the night shift, however, remained trainees and were seen as uncooperative by the firm. The instructor mentioned to me that, if workers really wanted the job, they would accept the offer. Not doing so proved they were not committed to the firm and, thus, more likely to quit voluntarily, a huge concern for HR. In the end, the women workers did quit, but it was out of frustration in being trainees for much longer than the four weeks promised and at very low pay to boot.

Another way the firm weeded out potential problematic workers during training was by evaluating attitudes. While I was in *la escuelita*, at least four trainees were fired, three of them because they were "hard to get along with" and had "an attitude." Having worked with these three young single women for three weeks, I was struck by the fact that all three could be described as confident and free spirited. Two of them were excellent seamstresses, and all three were progressing well in the training module. They did not exhibit difficulties relating with coworkers or following the instructor's directions. However, they were self-assured young women. "Hard to get along with" seemed to be code for "independent."

Another coworker, a single mother with older children, was not progressing well at all. Yet she remained, although she consistently got the lowest efficiencies with the worst quality. Management was constructing a workforce made up of "vulnerable women" who would feel economically tied to the firm. Thus decisions about skill, aptitude, and attitude were very subjective, suggesting that management was more interested in a compliant rather than skilled workforce.

## THE CONTESTED NATURE OF ORGANIZATIONAL CHANGE
### *Managerial Resistance*

The reorganization of the shop floor, led by American Consultants and top management, demonstrates how distinct levels of management held different interests.[16] The implementation of modular production was contested as top management wrestled with the practical implications of the new flexible work system. Disagreements arose around what to do with midlevel managers, how to deal with managerial turnover, and how tensions grew between the HR and production departments. Resistance to change, however, is not surprising.

Organizations undergoing structural change often face managerial resistance. Smith's study of restructuring at American Bank demonstrated how top and midlevel managers interpreted and defined their interests differently (1990). Thus adoption of organizational innovations by midlevel managers occurred in ways contrary to top management's intention. Instead of cutting employees by *managing out* (getting rid of employees), middle managers found ways to calculate and report productivity to save jobs.

In addition, studies of organizational change often find that unintended consequences lead to contradictory results. Vallas's study of participative arrangements in the paper and pulp industry shows that teamwork paradoxically increased boundaries between hourly and salaried workers as technical knowledge was privileged to provide productivity data to clients (2003a). Similarly, Prechel argues that, in the process of decentralizing decisionmaking at a large steel company, top management centralized control and reduced midmanagement's span of authority (1994, 2000).

Organizational change can also occur in multiple ways. Work theorists have debated the necessity of high performance or participatory teamwork for organizational effectiveness (Smith 1997). Post-Fordists argue that high-road options built on well-paid skilled labor empower workers to use their discretionary effort to improve production. Enhanced responsibility must accompany greater authority to overcome worker resistance prevalent in Taylorism. The key to success is to implement clusters of organizational innovations and HR practices; this includes production teams, selective hiring practices, and incentive pay based on objective performance (Appelbaum et al. 2000; MacDuffie 1995).

Neo-Fordist and neo-Taylorists, however, show that low-road options, based on routinized, low-skill work with low wages and increased control, have been used together with flexible organizational forms to increase productivity (Dohse, Jürgens, and Malsch 1985; Knauss 1998; Taplin 1996; Vidal 2007).[17] McKay's study of high-tech firms in the Philippines demonstrates that there are multiple ways to organize production, combining different elements of high- and low-road options, while still being internationally competitive (2006).

### Debating How to Achieve Flexibility

Organizational change at Moctezuma was strictly controlled by top management and American Consultants. Every change had to be approved by them before implementation, whether for quality-control panels, guidelines for teams, layout improvements, or worker profiles. However, these two guiding forces differed significantly on how to deal with middle management. In accordance with lean production philosophies of flatter hierarchies, American Consultants insisted on cutting the number of midlevel supervisors. For them, flexibility meant closer communication between management and workers by cutting intermediary levels while at the same time freeing up capital to be reinvested in the firm.

Top management, however, preferred to retain midlevel supervisors as additional labor. They knew that suit orders oscillated throughout the year, requiring highly skilled additional workers at peak times. Most of the midlevel supervisors were women who had risen through the ranks. They had substantial skill and seniority, making them indispensable; at the same time, they were expensive to fire due to legally stipulated compensation. Retaining midlevel supervisors provided flexibility to deal with problem orders or during busy times and was essential to retaining increasingly demanding clients.

The compromise between the consultants and top management was to relocate the majority of supervisors to the newly set up microproduction department. While irrational in terms of the implementation of lean philosophies (since expenses were not cut but shifted), this move was rational given the local industrial relations context and industry. According to Weber, this is the irrationality of the rational, a characteristic of organizational change (Prechel 2000).

*Dealing with Managerial Turnover.* In January 1996, twelve newly graduated industrial engineers—all but one male—were hired with the express purpose of working with teams. American Consultants had been adamant that team supervisors be technically trained. Following the long-established firm practice of learning by doing, the industrial engineers were trained by learning the job from the bottom up.

These mostly male industrial engineers believed they were not accorded the authority and status they deserved. They objected to being trained alongside women workers. According to the female industrial engineer Cecilia, as university-educated professionals they expected to be making decisions about production behind a desk. Furthermore, they objected to the rude and dictatorial leadership of the firm's top manager, an Italian. Cecilia recounted the stress and ill treatment experienced during the initial reorganization period:

> We handled changes to be made on 2,000 repairs, that is, 2,000 finished jackets that would have to be reprocessed. . . . It was terrible. . . . On one occasion, we [supervisors] were all called into the [director of corporate manufacturing's] office . . . and he started to yell at us—screaming and with vulgar expressions. I remember that I left the room almost crying because he said to us, "Take your finger out of your asshole!" Frankly, you are prepared for pressure, but not this type of thing.

In response to the harsh treatment and perceived lack of status, all eleven of the male industrial engineers quit within one year. Supervisors did not have much recourse other than quit or take the pressure. Only Cecilia remained. While she also disliked the insults, she did not believe it would be easy to find another job as a woman in a male-dominated field. Her best option was to learn as much as possible before moving on. Cecilia was subsequently moved to most departments, learning the entire process.

In response to losing the male industrial engineers, the firm followed two strategies. First, some of the women supervisors who had been transferred to microproduction returned as teams advisers. Second, care was taken when hiring more (male) industrial engineers to explain the hands-on approach to training supervisors at the firm. Following these changes, midlevel managerial turnover was no longer a problem. A further factor, however, was that Moctezuma's jobs were considered among the most stable in the area. In 2000, several transnational and national garment firms in the nearby industrial park closed their doors, making the cost of leaving higher.[18]

*Competing Logics between the Human Resources and Production Departments.* Tensions between the HR and production departments were evident from the beginning. Under piecework, communication with workers was under the purview of HR. With the move to modular production, the Italian top manager instructed all communication to be channeled directly through Mr. López—the production manager who was acting as team supervisor for the pilot program—to enhance his authority. Paradoxically, the purpose of his presence among the new teams was to breakdown manager-worker barriers and hierarchies.

Tensions continued throughout the pilot program. Three months in, HR complained to the board of directors that the production department was not sharing information on completed certifications. The production department objected to HR's direct communications with workers. The change in work organization shifted the sphere of influence of each department, disturbing the power balance within the firm.

The conflict also pointed to competing logics. While HR's main concern was to find the right kind of worker that would both remain at the factory and consent to management directives, production was more concerned with getting workers onto the shop floor as quickly as possible to churn out production. Human resources looked at the long-term effects of worker-management relations; production, at short-term efficiency.

The clash between HR's "planning change by changing industrial relations" and production's "doing change by calibrating operations and workers" resulted in a disorganized and uneven implementation of modular production. Different goals were also rooted in the makeup of the departments. While the HR personnel, who sided more often with American Consultants, were mostly young women with college degrees in business administration, the production managers were either workers who had climbed the ranks or industrial engineers beginning their careers.

## CONCLUSION

The transformation from piecework to modular production combined a change in social relations and work organization. Top managers and an international consultancy agency decided how the theory of lean techniques would be implemented at Moctezuma. Then both workers and managers participated in extensive training in the philosophy and mechanics of the new system.

The implementation of the new work system was not seamless. Organizational change is often piecemeal and contradictory. Change at Moctezuma was no different. The HR department spearheaded the task of convincing workers that the change was in their best interests and would provide a more humane form of work organization. Preventing worker resistance and manufacturing consent was essential. To this end, the department devised a new profile of the ideal worker (a woman over twenty-five with stable family networks), set up new employee benefits (such as the expanded clinic and health campaigns), fostered closer relations between workers and managers through social events, and reinforced the ideals and techniques of modular production through posters and bulletins.

The production department was in charge of executing the technical changes. Planning a more efficient way to pull, rather than push, work through the shop floor necessitated a new system of providing supplies, setting up teams, and sequencing operations. It also required greater control over women workers' discretionary effort. To achieve this, the department developed a payment system to reward greater effort expected of workers and redesigned team layout on the shop floor to allow for augmented visibility.

The work of both the HR and production departments contributed to instilling a community-of-fate belief at the firm. Moctezuma needed skilled workers to efficiently produce high-quality suits. The enhanced corporate benefits and closer manager-worker relations, together with a payment structure that increased take-home pay, had the express goal of tying workers to the firm and convincing them that the company had their best interests at heart.

The HR and production departments both participated in the training of workers through a yearly refresher course on the theory and practice of modular production and through the training center. The refresher course unveiled significant worker resistance and discontent with the changes. Management responded to women workers' complaints by reproaching them for their sloppy work and wastefulness, pointing out how they worsened the firm's economic difficulties.

The implementation of teamwork also demonstrated how the HR and production departments operated under different logics. Human resources' efforts were geared toward persuading workers of the personal and firm-level gains to be had from teamwork. An important component of this was weeding out assertive women through *la escuelita*. The production department focused on increasing efficiency and quality in the shortest amount of time possible, pressing workers to begin work before they were fully trained.

The practices of both departments reflects management's "flexible" adoption of teamwork as it responded to real production constraints such as short turnaround on garment orders. While management acknowledged the need for skilled workers, its practices demonstrated the preference for a compliant labor force. Management was more concerned that workers believed in the *ideas* rather than understand the *techniques* of modular production. This contradiction was most evident and problematic in the functioning of self-managed teams, the topic of the next chapter.

# CHAPTER 4

# Becoming a Worker

## DISCOVERING THE SHOP FLOOR AND THE
## CONTESTED NATURE OF SELF-MANAGED TEAMS

When the training modules ended at the end of November 2000, I requested permission to work on the shop floor. However, with company holiday events and work slowdowns caused by lack of material, the human resources (HR) director suggested I wait until the new year to begin working on the shop floor. December in Mexico is saturated with religious festivals to honor the Virgin of Guadalupe and *posadas* (the reenactment of Joseph and Mary seeking shelter in an inn) as well as company and school festivals. December at Moctezuma was no different.

On December 12, the day of the Virgin of Guadalupe, all workers from the three Grupo Mexicano firms (Moctezuma and the two textile factories) and their families were invited to the annual celebration. A competition took place with every department boasting an altar to the Virgin, decorated by a volunteer group with great pride and effort. My family and I began the day, together with approximately three hundred people of all ages, with a procession through the company grounds to sing *las mañanitas* (happy birthday) at each of the many altars. Undoubtedly, my six-foot-tall partner and light-haired, blue-eyed child stuck out like a set of sore thumbs. As a short Latina, I fit into the crowd more inconspicuously. Most workers who had not heard of me probably thought we were family members of a manager or factory owner.

The festivities continued with a mass, speeches by the bishop and majority owner, and raffles (everyone received a number when they entered the factory gates). We were all continually reminded how thankful we should be to work for such a giving company. The majority owner even publicly noted that, although this had been a terrible year for the firm, the annual raffle and special honors could not be cancelled because the company put its workers above monetary considerations. Dozens of home appliances, small and large, were raffled off throughout the morning as people sat in the chair-filled parking lot, children played games on the manicured grass, and babies were fed under the shade of trees.

By early afternoon, it was time for the big event. I gathered with some of my fellow trainees; we giggled in anticipation of the draw. Much to our surprise, the grand prize was a brand new car! A man from the main textile plant with ten years seniority won. The majority owner and he got into the car and took it for a quick spin around the company. At the end of the celebration, all children lined up so the majority owner and top managers could distribute Christmas gifts to each. What a symbol of community and generosity: the firm as one big family under the protective embrace of a patriarch.

## BECOMING A WORKER

I returned to Moctezuma after the holidays on January 2 along with the other workers. One of the HR managers, Belinda, set up a meeting for me with the pants department manager for the second week of January. At that time, I described my project, now linking turnover and teamwork, and asked for permission to work in the department. The department head asked me many questions, fascinated with the idea of doing research by participating in the process. Much later, I discovered that he had had the opportunity to earn a master's degree in industrial engineering in the United States but had not been able to leave his job to do so.

The pants department manager called in two advisers so I could explain my project to them. The advisers were both women who had started as workers. One had been at the factory for thirty years, and the other six. Before I had a chance to discuss my project, they were already planning how the research was to be done. Right away the advisers suggested that I work with every team for a little bit to get a solid sense of the work. I explained my preference of working only within one team, to get to know the workers better while learning the processes in depth. Then they debated which team would best suit my needs. I expressed interest in working in one they considered to function best or worst. "Oh," they said in unison, "then she has to go to team four." They continued, "They have lots of problems, and lots of work. May be you can tell us how to make it work better."

The advisers also suggested that I work the afternoon shift since it had three times the turnover rates of the morning shift. I defensively responded that since I had a small child I could not do that. In response, the younger adviser exclaimed, "But that's why we have such a problem with the women too; it would be perfect." She encouraged me several times during the next month to study the afternoon shift. By the time I was ready to accept this scenario, the second shift was cancelled.

While I debated the merits of an expanded study with the advisers, the team leaders were called into the office over the loudspeaker. Soon the office, which had a big glass window that looked onto the shop floor just a few feet away, was overflowing with women of all ages. Some stood and others sat as we all crammed into the room. I was pushed into the corner behind the department manager who remained seated at his desk. He introduced me as a researcher and asked me to explain the reason for my presence at Moctezuma.

Essentially, I repeated what I had told the managers, being careful to highlight that the study was for my degree, that all conversations were confidential, and that I would only provide a general summary of my results to the company. The department manager interrupted me, underscoring that the study had already been approved by the company and the union but that I was *not* employed by the company. As he said this, the union president happened to pass by and was invited in. He reassured workers that I had permission to be there. Trying to appear as nonthreatening as possible, I shared that I had a one-year-old son. Then I asked if it was okay if I worked with them as part of my study. There was a general hum of approval but definitely not a resounding endorsement. In reality, it would have been difficult for them to deny the request given that the department manager and union president were present. I started working with team four immediately.[1]

### Getting to Know the Physical and Social Layouts of the Shop Floor

The team four leader, Luisa, looked like a teenager, light-skinned and dressed in a red strapless tank top, tight jeans, manicured nails, and tasteful makeup. In fact, she was twenty-seven years old and had worked at the factory for six years. Although she was the team leader, she told me go to see Betty for instructions, which I did. Betty was matronly, although only a few years older than Luisa. She always wore loose flowered T-shirts with her hair down and no makeup. In a soft voice she said: "Why don't you start where the product starts? José, show her how to put bundles together." With this, the only male in the team motioned me over.

José was tall and lanky, had hair spiked up with gel, and wore his baggy pants fashionably low with an oversized soccer T-shirt. He was treated more like everyone's younger brother than a rogue teenage worker. At twenty, José had worked in a supermarket and as a mechanic's assistant before coming to the factory a year ago. He patiently showed me how to put bundles together, going to one team to pick up the waistbands, then another for the front and back pants panels. Lot, size, and model numbers had to be checked to pair them correctly. Then, gathering same-colored bundles so machine threads would not have to be changed, he would put two or three bundles of ten each on a cart. He would tell me where to put the carts, since different models required different operations. I did this all day, quickly learning the system (figure 4.1).

When I arrived the next morning, Betty sent me to the next operation (Op-3) in the queue, sewing front and back panels together. As I nervously watched one worker do the difficult operation, the team leader came over. "You know," she said, "we could really use you to help move bundles through." I had told them in

Figure 4.1. Picture of bundle preparation (Op-1) and first sewing operation (Op-2), José and Luisa in the foreground. Photo by author, February 2001. Photograph taken with permission from top management at Moctezuma.

the department office that I wanted to help the team as much as possible, so I was glad they were putting me where they most needed me. For the next few days, I moved bundles from one set of operations to the next so the women did not have to leave their work posts to fetch them.

Although the distance to pick up new bundles was not great, it broke up the rhythm and pace of work. This job was perfect for me because I got to move around and meet all the workers as well as discover some of the repercussions of working in teams. Team four was located directly off the departmental offices, where advisers and top management walked in and out of meetings. It was a strange feeling to be watched by both workers and managers as they tried to figure out who I really was.

In team four, José prepared bundles (Op-1) and then passed them in carts to either Luisa, who was on the computerized linear sewing machine that was used for open-seam pockets (Op-2), or two other women, who were on sewing machines required for double-seam pockets (Op-3). Operations 2 and 3 coupled the front and back leg panels, preparing the garment for the waistband to be attached (Op-4). The latter was the most difficult and time-consuming operation because the waistband had to be sewn onto two separate leg panels, while belt loops were affixed equidistantly. Each pant model had a different distance and loop size. Since this was the bottleneck operation in our team, José had to keep moving carts from operations 2 and 3 to operation 4. For operation 4, the carts were used to hold the bundle being worked on as workers sewed the

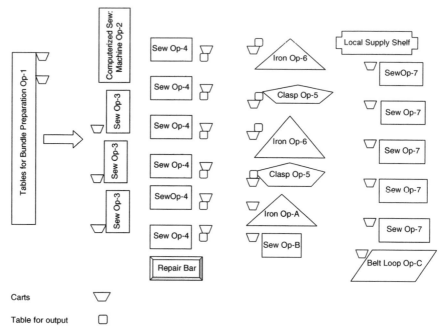

Figure 4.2. Production flow and work posts in the pants department, team four. Diagram by author.

waistband; the finished product was then placed on the table. Once a whole bundle was completed, the worker retied the bundle. The woman who affixed clasps (Op-5) had to get up and get the bundle from the table and put it in the cart by her post. When she finished, she left it at the table next to her for the person ironing the waistband seam open (Op-6) to pick up. (See figure 4.2.)

This was the area I worked in the most, moving bundles from operation 4 to 5 and then 6, giving women the opportunity to work without having to stop to get more work. However, when there were JoS A. Bank or Calvin Klein models, several other operations had to be performed. I pressed the pant pocket open (Iron Op-A) and then passed it on to sewing operation B, which made a special pocket stitching. Calvin Klein models further required a belt-looping fastener done by a special, dedicated machine (Belt Loop Op-C). It should be noted that producing for Calvin Klein and JoS. A. Bank entailed buying specialized machines that stood unused most of the time. Such additional expenses, including the training of the workers for these operations, were covered by the firm, not the client. And, as workers for operations A, B, and C did not have regular work, multiskilled workers jumped to this operation when needed.

All other models followed the path from the steam iron (Op-6) to the last sewing operation (Op-7), which completed the important aesthetic step of the right front pants panel. From here, the pants went on to team five for the zipper, buttons, and inseam. It was at this final operation, Op-7, that production was counted by the team leader every two hours and added to the daily production totals. This information, posted on a whiteboard above the last team operation, let workers in the team, other teams, and managers know whether production was on schedule. It was a form of public accountability and pressure.

Team four was one of the largest teams, though typical in its age and gender composition. There were eighteen members in team four, with ages ranging from nineteen to forty. Five of them, including the only male, José, were single, young, and childless. They all lived with their families, with whom they shared 20–30 percent of their income. Three of the single women were taking classes of some sort in the evening or weekend, two of them for technical degrees, and one to complete high school. José had a junior high school education.

Another five women were single, with children ranging in age from one to twenty years of age, with an average age of eleven. Of these, four had second jobs as waitresses or store clerks, sold crafts made at home, or prepared food to sell in the neighborhood in the evenings. Four of the single mothers lived with their immediate family who helped with childcare, while one lived independently. The only single mother who did not have a second job was also the one who owned her home, purchased with remittances from her husband who worked in the United States.[2] While two of the single women with children had a grade school education, the rest had attended junior high school.

One of the women, Elena, was in the process of purchasing a small piece of land and building a house on it. Every paycheck went to pay for the land. I visited her home, a ten-foot square, corrugated cardboard and metal shack with no running water, sewer connection, or electricity. She lived there with her six children and ailing mother who provided childcare. Her eldest son was the only one who worked, packing bags at the supermarket for tips. She was the poorest among my teammates. Elena, who had dark skin and indigenous features, also traveled to Mexico City every weekend, where she waitressed at a friend's stand in a big open-air market.

The rest of the team consisted of eight women, ranging in age from twenty-nine to forty; all were partnered, with children.[3] In general, partnered women had more stable and economically secure home lives. The partnered women had twenty-seven children among them, with only six children under the age of five; the average age of the remainder was fourteen. Thus, childcare was not a crucial issue for most partnered women, as the older children watched out for themselves and relatives or husbands cared for the youngest children.

In all but one case (because of illness), the spouses contributed to home expenses (five husbands provided 100 percent of their wages to the home, one provided 80 percent, another 50 percent, and the disabled husband had no income). The husbands were employed as factory workers (two out of the three worked at Italia, the textile mill belonging to the industrial group), a villa caretaker, a waiter, a security guard, and one working in the United States for three years. All but two of the women said they turned over their entire paycheck for household expenses. The two women who provided less set aside the same proportion as their husbands, 80 and 50 percent, respectively. One partnered woman had a grade school education, and the rest had completed studies to the ninth or twelfth grade.

Unlike the single workers, none of the partnered women had second jobs. Six of these eight women owned their own homes, with the other two renting. The partnered workers also lived independently from their extended families, though they still relied on grandmothers and sisters for childcare.

Thus, in general, single workers without children lived at home but used the great majority of their wages for their own expenses and education. Partnered workers with children contributed almost the entirety of their wages to household expenses but, with the addition of the husband's income, were able to live frugally but comfortably.

Single mothers had the greatest difficulty making ends meet. In that sense, they were as the company estimated them—more vulnerable. However, four out of the five single mothers lived with their parents, where they received child-care assistance and pooled their income with the male head of household, their father. Single mothers were not the poverty-stricken women management portrayed. Moreover, these women did not think of themselves as victims; rather, they thought of themselves as mothers performing their duties. They did not ask for special consideration as single mothers.

There existed an unspoken belief that motherhood was, or should be, everybody's priority. Some of the young childless women voiced frustration that their needs were trumped by coworkers who were mothers and felt targeted for increased work by the mothers in the team. The working mothers often commented that these single childless women were irresponsible with their money, but, while these young women were more fashion conscious than the other team members, this was not necessarily so. Lety, a single childless woman who lived in an indigenous town an hour away, studied computer programming in the evenings and Saturdays, using 80 percent of her wages to pay for classes and the requisite computer. Working at the factory was a way to save money and be able to move to a better job. As pressure increased at work, she spoke of quitting. However, her mother convinced her to stay; she still had many payments left on the computer, and other jobs were hard to find.

That first week in team four, many workers asked me who I was and what I was doing there. Betty asked me why I was interested in this topic. I explained that most studies on teamwork only surveyed management; I wanted to ask workers what they thought and study work from their perspective. "Yeah, maybe they will hear us then," she said, smiling. Another day that week, when I was taking bundles to the back of the factory, a group of women stopped me. "You are not from around here, are you?" they observed. "No," I replied, "I am Chilean and American." "What are you doing here?" they queried.

So, I explained. They were utility workers who had been at the factory for many years and had experienced the conversion to teams; they offered to meet with me some day. I was getting to know the physical and social layout, and the workers were getting to know me.

This acquaintance period was abruptly interrupted by a three-week-long bout with bronchitis. It was the first time I had ever had bronchitis—and a serious case at that—but my main worry was that the workers would think that I had abandoned the project. When I returned, people asked me where I had been; they thought I had gotten tired of the work and left. I explained repeatedly that I had been sick, to which they replied with some insistence, "Oh, it's the lint." Even the department manager and one of the advisers nonchalantly asserted that the lint had made me ill. A reaction to lint the first weeks of working on the shop floor was a common occurrence, they said. By the end of my stay at the factory, I had bronchitis three times, each time becoming more asthmatic.

The longer I was there, the more I found out about other people's upper respiratory problems, including asthma, sinusitis, nasal bleeding, and sinus headaches. Workers could request masks, but they were not always available. Besides, it was so hot on the shop floor that wearing a mask was suffocating. I tried it but did not even last a day. When I asked the doctor on call about it, he said they regularly test the lint particles in the air: they are completely safe, well below the allowed parts per million. I was not very convinced.

I quickly reincorporated into team life. Besides moving bundles around, I began to help out in other areas such as repairs, following the flow, and ironing. After moving bundles all day for several days, I was happy when I was put to the task of carefully ripping apart seams of defective pieces for others to resew correctly. Then I was told to follow production, making sure urgent orders were given priority, and to find bundles that had been misplaced along the way. While this allowed me to get to know workers outside my team, and even in other departments, it placed me in the awkward position of being under the sometimes conflicting direct orders of both management and teams. Lastly, the need arose for someone to perform an ironing operation not often required, for which I was trained.

## CONTESTING THE EFFORT AND AUTONOMY IN SELF-MANAGED TEAMS

### The Theory of Self-Managed Teams

Self-managed teams were central to modular production at Moctezuma. In theory, self-managed teams embraced experienced workers as independent thinkers and agents who used their ingenuity to improve the production process: *kaizen* at work. Workers, no matter their gender, were to be chosen for their skill, and team leaders were replacing middle management.

The shape and rules of self-management were established by the production department, which arranged workers into teams according to the order of required operations. According to management, a precondition for self-managed teams included sharing detailed production information (what they called the company's theoretical framework) so that workers and management knew which orders were on the shop floor and what problems arose; this allowed both parties to find joint solutions. Armed with such information, teams were to decide which operations each member would do to fulfill a preset quota of a semiproduct. In an effort to do away with free-rider problems, teams could even expel members for unruly behavior or poor performance, enhancing the efficiency of teams.

Team leaders rotated according to seniority. It was their job to be channels of communication between department managers and workers, translating company requirements to the workers, and workers' opinions and ideas to management. Team leaders had the responsibility for moving workers around to cover absenteeism, shoring up bottleneck operations, and dealing with other problems.

In return for increased mental and physical labor, workers gained the right to provide their own members with permission slips to miss hours of work. Only one permit (*permiso*) could be granted per day, with missed work to be made up after regular hours. Such decisions occurred in morning meetings or quick assemblies, called by the team at any time. In this way, team members were directly accountable to each other and, through the team leader, to the department manager.

Another prerogative of self-managed teams was to limit contact with advisers. Instead of the previous system of supervisors roaming the shop floor, only a few advisers per department remained. They could participate in teams only when invited or if there was a serious problem in a team.

Instead of micromanaging the shop floor, advisers were responsible for following client orders through the production line; calculating quality statistics; and coordinating with suppliers, as well as supervising them, for upcoming client orders. If they observed a problem, it was their job to make the team leaders aware of it. Only after repeatedly unanswered requests could the advisers speak directly to workers responsible for shoddy work. This rule of nonintervention in the team's business, often repeated by workers, was outlined in the collective-bargaining contract.

Participant observation on the shop floor and through interviews, however, revealed the contested nature of self-managed teams. The effort bargain—increased effort in exchange for expanded autonomy and wages—was continually negotiated. As discussed previously, managers increased the likelihood of retaining control over workers by hiring women for their docility, then weeding out assertive women in training. The division of work along gender lines further reinforced appropriate femininity and masculinity on the shop floor.

Self-managed teams produced contradictory outcomes.[4] The everyday demands on leaders required the involvement of advisers even though that infringed on the rights of teams. Issues around training and certification sparked conflict in teams. Pressure to reach and exceed production as well as quality quotas resulted in the coercive control of some teams over others.

Workers, however, used the rules and rhetoric of self-managed teams to different degrees of success, broadening the boundaries of autonomy. Moreover, traditional expectations of motherhood furthered the interests of workers as women. A motherist work culture developed. Team solidarity, constructed around a shared identity as mothers and potential mothers, governed the allotment of permits and work hours. In addition, self-managed teams diminished the power of managers and thus the opportunities for sexual harassment.

The contested nature of self-managed teams had three important unintended consequences. First, trust in management eroded, as did their ideal of the community of fate. Second, women's contradictory location—hired for docility but placed in positions of authority over the work process and their fellow workers—resulted in their reproducing and resisting gender subordination. Third, learned leadership skills were used to both increase output and resist managerial control. The motherist work culture—initially used in defense of motherhood while reappropriating its language—increasingly took on more workerist tones. All of this slowly became more evident as I worked on the shop floor.

### Placement on the Shop Floor: Women's Work and Men's Work

Given the differential treatment men and women received at the training center, it is no surprise that they performed different jobs on the shop floor. Men were generally assigned to be bundle boys and cutters, with a few operating pressers. Women invariably became either sewers or pressers. These jobs carried distinct responsibilities and privileges.

Cutting occurred exclusively in a dedicated department, where workers, aided by machines, laid down the cloth on long tables. Electric scissors, connected to an overhead system of wires and tubing, were used to cut the carefully stacked cloth. At the end of the long tables stood the ticket and labeling operation, where each piece of cloth—cashmere and acetate lining—was given a ticket that indicated the client order, to which piece of clothing it belonged, size, color, and input details. After the cut cloth was bundled, it was taken to pants or jackets.

The first operation in every assembling department consisted of organizing the cut pieces into a series of bundles that would be distributed to particular teams for them to complete a subproduct. Most teams contained mainly sewing operations with pressing intermixed to facilitate further sewing. At the end of the department were the teams that conducted finishing operations—buttons, brand labels, finishing stitches—as well as cleaning of loose threads and the final pressing of products.

While production imperatives did not require a particular gender for each operation, jobs were indeed gendered. In the cutting department, women laid out the cloth, but predominantly men cut the fabric with electric scissors. The few women cutters had entered the shop floor with previous cutting experience.

When asked why men were chosen explicitly for this operation, I was told that the cutting tables required a particular height of worker usually found only in men. Upon closer inspection, cutters were of varied heights but were mostly male. Another manager claimed that cutting cloth was dangerous work; so it was given to male workers. In fact, the work of cutters was highly skilled: one minute deviation from the model could ruin large quantities of cloth. However, managers did not frame the work as skilled; instead, they framed it as dangerous and necessitating a particular height. Had it been framed as skilled work, cutting would have been more difficult to keep as a male enclave; after all, at Moctezuma, women were said to be "naturally" skilled and best suited for detailed work.

While men did the cutting, women operated the ticket and labeling machines located at the end of the same tables. This work was not considered difficult or dangerous; rather, it was monotonous. The gendered division of labor in the cutting department was thus propelled by management ideologies, not productive or physical imperatives.

There was an added layer of gender inequality in cutting; it was the last full department that operated under piecework and received a higher base wage. As pieceworkers, those in cutting could control their own pace of work (within reason) without being pushed by a team. This meant they could either self-exploit (working over 100 percent to earn individual bonuses) or work at a leisurely pace. Most cutters worked over 100 percent, earning higher wages as individuals than the rest of the shop floor's organized teams.

A similar gendered division of labor occurred in jackets and pants. Theoretically, men and women were able to work at any operation. In practice, however, women were concentrated in sewing operations and men in bundling. Both performed ironing operations, although there were fewer men on pressing machines than women. The bundling operations were described by a manager as "heavy work, where a man's strength is needed to move bundles."

Curiously, the first job I did on the shop floor was that of bundling. Indeed, it *was* physically demanding work, but no more than the pressing operations I later performed. The only "heavy" part of the work I encountered came when one of the three previous teams delayed the collating of materials, resulting in stacks that later had to be moved. Bundles of ten pant panels quickly add up to a significant weight, but this was never unmanageable. Indeed, the bundling operation was considered the easiest—and partly the reason they had me doing it! Moreover, in the jackets one (J-1) team where I later worked, the bundling operation was normally done by a man but had been recently given to a woman returning from disability for back problems. Thus, the rationale that bundling was a man's job because of the physical demands of the work does not stand up to scrutiny.

The other operation I observed men doing was pressing. This work consisted of standing up on either side of large pressers, which are pulled down over a humped board (to make curved creases) or using small overhead steam irons with thin boards to open seams for further sewing. While both men and women operated both types of pressing, men were more likely to operate the large presses and women the small steam irons. During my nine months on the shop floor, I operated both types of presses, finding specific challenges with each but not noticing different physical or skill requirements for either. Placement on pressing machines was decided by the instructor and the department head during training. Recall that the (female) instructor did not allow male workers to train on the sewing machines, with the exception of male workers coming in as tailors. Thus, when a presser was needed, men would be more likely to be ready for work. In this way, the gender ideology of managers shaped the gendered division of labor at the pressing machines.

Sewing, in contrast, was clearly marked as woman's work. In the pants and two jackets departments, a minuscule number of men sat at the sewing machines. I recall no more than ten men, out of approximately seven hundred day-shift workers in these two departments, who sat at sewing machines.[5] However, of the ten, two worked on new computerized state-of-the-art machines. In pants, there were two of these computerized sewing machines, one operated by a recent male hire with no sewing experience, the other by Luisa with eight years of seniority. While these computerized machines were considered to require skill, unskilled males could aspire to use them. Thus, even within the sewing operations, the result of worker placement often led to the exclusion of women from the more technically advanced machinery.

Importantly, it was not only management's but also workers' gender ideologies that buttressed this marked division of labor. During interviews, I asked coworkers why so few men operated sewing machines. One woman who had worked at the factory for five years responded: "Sewing has always been women's work." Other women echoed this belief, explaining: "Women are more patient." And, "Our hands are softer and gentler. Men are brutes with their hands. They cannot do the work."

The men interviewed, however, had a different perspective. Juan, one of four men that I worked with in J-1 (of whom two sewed) responded: "Well, supposedly women have more skill, but it's not true." José, who taught me the bundling operation, said, "We men are rougher with our hands, but, with practice, we can become more skilled." Thus, it was the men—denying the feminization of their work—who claimed equal skill between the sexes.

Only one woman interviewed seemed less certain of the natural superior dexterity of females. María, a highly skilled worker, said, "[Men] are ashamed to be seen at the machines; they say it's for women. But if there is a job, just be thankful there is a job. It does not matter if a man or woman does it." Women workers rarely questioned the gendered division of labor on the shop floor. Their beliefs mirrored the larger patriarchal gendered ideology of Mexican society, taking for granted that sewing was women's work. While not surprising, it is important to note how workers participated in their own gender subordination. It is, in fact, both managers and workers who produce gendered divisions on the shop floor.

### Team Leaders: Overworked and Isolated

With the shift from piecework in 1996, the system replaced a substantial number of middle managers with team leaders who were transformed into *worker-managers*. Most team leaders felt the company inadequately utilized the position for which they earned a bonus of $120 pesos (U.S.$13.33) per week. Team leaders were responsible for 100 percent of their production quota (later reduced to 75 percent in 1999); at the same time, they attended requisite daily departmental meetings to discuss production matters and weekly union–team leader meetings to check for problems. They also kept daily absenteeism and permit records, reported and followed up on repairs, counted inventory per operation in the morning, recorded units produced by the team every two hours and end-of-day totals, facilitated daily team meetings, made sure the team ran smoothly, and answered questions about company regulations, product specifications, and quality problems. On top of this, team leaders mediated often conflictive interpersonal relations between team members. Not one team leader claimed to be able to juggle the leadership responsibilities along with his or her own work. Instead, they found themselves stressed and in the middle of antagonistic relationships.

One of the most important duties for team leaders was maintaining amicable working relationships between members. Performing this emotional labor— where the leader's own demeanor set the tone for team interactions—required patience and negotiating skills. Women and men performed this task differently, with management's tacit and sometimes explicit approval, which was evident in the two teams where I worked.

An affable and seemingly shy young woman, Luisa carried out her team-leadership duties in an understated manner. She smiled often, greeted everyone cordially, and went to great lengths to make peace between teammates who did not get along, gently coaxing and cajoling people to follow the rules of team-work. She carried out her duties with confidence, although she often stopped by the workstation of the older female workers to ask for advice, deferring to their opinion on most issues. In meetings, training and production-related decisions were made after she described the issue at hand, requested opinions, facilitated a quick discussion, and put the issue up for a vote. Rarely did Luisa put forth her own opinion or dominate discussion. She carried out her leadership duties with feminine sociability.

Juan, in contrast, had a flare for the dramatic. Although it was common knowledge that he was recently married and had a newborn son, Juan took

advantage of his location at the pressing machine next to the aisle to yell out cat-
calls as young women passed by. More often than not, he started meetings with
his opinion of what should be done, cut off discussions, and called for a quick vote.

Negotiating interpersonal conflicts was not his strength, as he loudly
reminded other team members when they asked him to solve a conflict. I witnessed several shouting matches filled with obscenities between him and two
older women in the team. The fact that the older women demanded respect
based on their seniority and expertise, and called attention to the ways in which
he did not perform his duties as team leader, irritated him to no end. Since I was
his assistant at the ironing press for several weeks, he confided that he refused to
be held accountable to those "old hags" (*viejas*). Juan was unwilling to perform
the emotional labor that came along with being team leader. Even though his
position called for equality, he stuck to gender norms and performed his role
with a highly aggressive and dominating form of masculinity.

Management and other team mates excused Juan's hostile behavior, claiming
that, as a man, he could not help himself. The subtext was that men are brutes;
they cannot control their aggression. Luisa, however, was expected to conform
to the role of peacemaker, acting as a caretaker of team relationships, putting
the team's interests above her own. The fact that management allowed Juan's
belligerence and encouraged Luisa's caretaking evidenced a continuation of
traditional gender norms on the part of both management and workers. When
I questioned coworkers about whether Luisa's or Juan's actions as leaders were
typical, they responded affirmatively. My own observations and interviews with
others who had been team leaders confirm this convention of gendered behavior. However, even with Luisa's willingness to exert substantial emotional labor
at work as peacemaker, the requirements of team leadership put workers in
impossible situations. Management pressed team leaders to push teams harder
for more production, while team members often accused leaders of being pawns
of management at the expense of worker's rights.

Toward the beginning of my stay in pants, Luisa called a meeting. She quietly
announced that she had been told by management to tell the workers to hurry
up, to get more production out. Immediately, several of the women began complaining. "But the models they are sending through now are different; the waistband is thicker and it does not come out in the time they give us. Have you told
them that?" Luisa responded, repeatedly, "Yes, I already told them." "Well, tell
them again!" exclaimed one angry woman. All Luisa could do was shrug her
shoulders in frustration and go back to the office. Later that day, an industrial
engineer, department manager, and adviser all stood close to watch over Betty,
one of the most senior workers, as she was timed doing the problematic operation. Although managers reevaluated the operation as requested, they did so
using the fastest and most capable worker, and with three managers watching
her every move so that she could not slow down the pace. In the end, that model
was allotted a few more seconds per piece.

Another downside to team leadership was the tension it created with team members. All workers interviewed who had been or were presently team leaders claimed friendships with fellow team members had been severely fractured, sometimes irreparably. One of the single mothers in team four, Vicki, almost always sat alone at lunch. One day, I joined her and asked why she did not sit with the others. "I lost all my friends when I was team leader," she said. Most workers would have gladly returned the team-leader bonus instead of performing the job. As Vicki put it, "Now we do all the work supervisors used to do but we don't get paid for it."

In order to accomplish all the tasks required of team leaders, some relied on advisers, which caused more tensions. My team members in pants complained in meetings that the adviser Frida "butted in too much" and should be told to keep out. However, the team leader felt overwhelmed with her duties and thus depended on Frida to take an active part in pushing coworkers to reach production quotas and respond to quality concerns. Besides, Frida and other advisers had extensive knowledge and often were very helpful.

However, another team further down the line, which was one of the best-functioning and well-organized teams in pants, complained to the union and top management of Frida's overreaching presence. She was no longer allowed to enter their area without invitation. Thus, constraints on management could be enforced if workers decided to force the issue. That said, workers could only demand the enforcement of rules when they fulfilled their end of the production bargain.

### Training: Power and Politics in Teams

Issues around training also caused tensions in teams. The contract stipulated that workers who knew the operation in question were to train new workers and receive bonuses for this task. If no one in the team knew the operation, the adviser would train the new worker. One of the problems was that training another person was time-consuming: you had to show them how to do the operation, watch over them, correct them by demonstrating the work again, and inspect their work. Depending on the operation, a new worker could be in training for as little as three weeks or, at most, one year. During this time, the trainee could not pass any work to the next operation without having it inspected by the trainer. Thus, it was very difficult for persons doing the training to reach their individual production goals with such interruptions. Therefore no one wanted to train new workers.

Even when workers acceded to acting as trainers, the trainer-trainee relations had the potential to become tense for other reasons. First, since training was so time-consuming, several people would provide advice to new workers; they then expected the training bonus no matter how small their part was in the training of a operation for certification. Second, having several instructors sometimes proved to be counterproductive when instructions were different or conflicting, leading to confusion and delays. In the meantime, the prolonged submissive role of the trainee could end in open conflict with the one(s) who did the training, leading to a refusal on the part of the newly certified worker to recognize the trainer so that she or he would be given the training bonus.

When I was learning the ironing operation, two workers and an adviser directed me—each in their own distinct way. I was confused and I did not know whom to follow. One day, the woman next to me, who had been the first to offer instruction, asked why I was not following her directions. In truth, another worker, with whom she did not get along, had demonstrated an easier method, but I did not want my presence as a participant observer to cause tensions. So, I reverted to this first woman's direction. It quickly became apparent to me that negotiating competing directions was the norm. Fellow team workers had experienced similarly conflicting training methods for their tasks, resulting in finger-pointing disputes. (Since I was spared the pressure of matching their daily production quotas, I escaped blame.)

### Certifying Operations: Individual Interests versus Team Benefits

Another issue with training was that pressures to provide multiskilled capabilities to team members, no matter how contentious a process, had the added effect of truncating the internal labor market. Under piecework, workers who exhibited skill or were especially close to the supervisor were allowed to train in new operations. That is how machine operators became utility workers.

Under teams, however, it was the team that decided who was to train on a new operation, not the supervisor. It was extremely unusual that the team would allow one member to learn the many operations needed to become a utility worker. Moreover, the number of workers and operations required to fulfill production were so carefully calibrated that team members did not usually have time to learn new operations. It was only when material shortages slowed the line that workers could take advantage of the lull to become multiskilled. Thus, even though the company encouraged a multiskilled workforce, it did not provide sufficient opportunity for workers to acquire this status.

Still, according to the rules, every new worker was to be given a fair chance for certification on one operation before training in another. Yet sometimes advisers overreached their authority and moved people around before they were certified on an operation. Without actual certification for a skilled operation, the worker earned only the base wage and was ineligible for any bonuses.

Another area of contestation had to do with determining who would train for a second operation. The answer depended in part on whether the operation was a bottlenecked procedure. If a worker was positioned in a bottleneck operation, she or he would not have time to train for second operation. Also of importance was the worker's status in the team. In both teams that I worked, power struggles between members were exacerbated around this issue of deciding who would have the opportunity to be trained in another operation.

Such tensions also worsened when the line was unbalanced. Theoretically, there would be a smooth and organized procession of several models of suits passing through the workstations. Hence, everyone would receive combinations of difficult and easy models, evening out to an average price paid to the worker per suit completed. In practice, however, most often a series of urgent orders, each for a specific model, followed in succession on the assembly line. These required exact operations, thus causing bottlenecks. For example, there were two ways to sew front- and back-pant leg panels together, depending on the type of pant pocket. If the pocket had a "V" opening, a computerized machine could perform the second operation fairly quickly (Sew Op-2). However, if the pocket openings attached top and bottom to the seam, this called for more time with careful manual sewing at the next station in the line (see Sew Op-3 in figure 4.2).

The industrial engineers' plan called for a combination of models so one Op-2 worker (on a computerized machine) and two Op-3 machinists (on regular sewing machines) were always working at 100 percent. Most of the time, however, single-model rush orders were pushed through—all of which required either one or the other operation. Thus, a utility worker was placed where needed, while the two other singly-skilled operators had little or no work.

Such bottlenecked situations further complicated matters for subsequent operations, where similar situations occurred. Not only did bottlenecks stunt training opportunities, but workers also ended up producing the more complicated models for the price of an average suit. More often than not, the rush (and larger) orders were higher-cost suits, which did not even out for the workers. And they were very aware of this.

### Production Efficiencies and Quality Control as Increased Labor and Coercive Control

Self-managed teams can increase lateral conflict, deflecting tensions with management (Barker 1993; Hodson 2001; Vallas 2003a). Teams can police their own members, enforcing production and quality rules without much assistance from managers.

This was very much the case at Moctezuma. For many, self-managed teams were code for *control*. Now it was not only management pressing workers to work harder but also their teammates. Interviews revealed that pressure from team members was perceived to be the worst problem on the shop floor by far since the change to lean production. In fact, most workers had considered, at one point or another, voluntarily leaving their jobs because of the unpleasant atmosphere caused by continuous pressure from coworkers.

Most conflicts in teams rose from someone not fulfilling 100 percent of their production-quality quota, or the perception that they did not do so. I witnessed several discussions in team meetings where complaints were made about others spending too much time in the bathroom or drinking water. Slower workers experienced constant pressure—even harassment—from team members since bonus payments were based not on individual merit but on shop floor perform-ance. In one case, one of my coworkers preferred to resign rather than be expelled from the team for poor performance, forfeiting the substantial com-pensation that would come from dismissal. Peer pressure could be the strongest form of control and surveillance.

Almost everyone on my team had problems with one particular worker, Elena. An informal rule governing teamwork was that everyone worked on a combination of easy and hard models to even out the workload. José, the bundle boy, distributed work to the first operations this way. Workers further down the line had to get up from their seat to retrieve work. Elena picked which jobs she would do, selecting the easiest work. This angered most workers, but she did not change her practices. She seemed impervious to the team's complaints and derision. Elena's dark skin and high cheekbones, combined with the metallic crowns on her front teeth, marked her as poor and indigenous, an outsider even among working-class women. Her lack of status in the group freed her from following group norms.

Another issue that caused rifts was the increased individual responsibilities under teams. Under piecework, line supervisors fetched supplies. When a machine broke down, it was the supervisor who reported the machine and fol-lowed up on repairs; likewise, if a defective or incorrectly sewn piece appeared, he or she sent the defective piece of the garment back to cutting for replacement or returned it to the person responsible for the poor quality and waited for it to be resewn. In the meantime, workers continued to accrue units worked per hour. If for some reason they had to stop sewing to concentrate on rework, or if there was no work to be done, they punched their time-out card so the down time would not be counted against them.

Under teams, it was the responsibility of the worker to stand up and go to local supply stations for inputs. When a machine broke down, the worker first checked for basic problems, then informed the team leader, who reported the problem with the departmental office. The red *poka-yoke* light was lit to remind mechanics and managers of the breakdown. If it was not repaired immediately, the worker had to keep pressuring the team leader to have it fixed.

In the meantime, if the worker was multiskilled and there was another machine available, she simply relocated and continued to work. If she was singlyskilled, she had to sit idle; when production, and thus efficiencies, were recorded at the end of the day, this wasted time went against the worker since the time-out card no longer existed. Moreover, under teamwork, when a defective piece appeared, it was the worker who was required to go to the cutting depart-ment for an exchange. Perhaps the most controversial change was that, instead of the team leader intervening, one had to return poor-quality work directly to fellow workers.

Somewhat ironically, improvements in quality control were one of the main goals of the conversion to lean production at Moctezuma. But under teamwork, which was premised on workers controlling and disciplining each other, quality control was often compromised.

For instance, consider the situation in which a worker received a piece that was done incorrectly. She had to stop her work, check who was responsible for the defective work (since every person wrote their worker identification number in the operation slot of each bundle's task sheet), return the piece, and then either wait for it to be repaired or pick it up later. This stalled her work and that of the team's, generating ample reason for discontent. If a particular worker always performed poorly, tensions escalated. Often, defective work was thrown at the person responsible, who in retaliation did not repair the garment until later. Thus, conflicts between workers made teamwork more difficult, often affecting the quality of the work.[6]

## THE CONTRADICTORY NATURE OF SELF-MANAGED TEAMS

Buttressed with enhanced benefits and high wages, workers often internalized the firm's dictates in self-managed teams, transforming them into mechanisms of hegemonic control. Describing quality circles in Japan, Tsutsui writes that teams were "'controlled participation' . . . which offered a voice, but one which could only speak in a language provided by management" (2001, 234). Workers interviewed at Moctezuma displayed similar engagement. When I asked if self-managed teams empowered workers, one young woman in J-1 responded as follows:

> Yes, it is to our advantage because [the worker] can solve problems. You are responsible for your own work. You become one with the company. You have to do that and I have to do this, and you become more responsible with your own work and toward your *compañeras.*

Another noted:

> [Under self-managed teams . . . ] one administers oneself. Like, "Oh good, now that I have finished my work, I can go and help you with that." You know, move around so that more production gets out.

However, quite tellingly, she also added a critical note of skepticism regarding this internalization of the firm's goals of self-management: "At one point we had power and independence, but it's not like that anymore." Most workers expressed contradictory opinions about teams.

### Challenging Managerial Boundaries through a Motherist Work Culture

While the work environment became more stressful because workers had to negotiate relations between team members and themselves in the team environment, there were also clear advantages to self-managed teams. The most important one, according to workers, was the fact that they decided what occurred within their team.

By 1999, self-managed teams had gathered momentum. According to the firm's dictates of self-managed teams, they were autonomous. Team members exercised this autonomy by deciding that they should be able to end their shifts at 4 P.M. instead of 4:36 P.M. if their production quota was complete. Their argument was presented to management based not only on fulfillment of production imperatives but also on the need of working mothers to get back to their domestic responsibilities. After all, their workday did not end with the regular shift at Moctezuma; there were children to be picked up from school, homes to clean, laundry to wash, meals to cook, children to bathe.

Given the company's work culture, it was difficult for management to refute workers' self-identification as mothers first and foremost. Especially since Moctezuma furthered its supportive company image through the community of fate construct, with the firm as a family and the majority owner as the benevolent patriarch. Religious festivals, sports venues, children's summer camps, and health campaigns pressed this message interminably. In addition, training and visual markers around the firm highlighted how managers and teams, pitted against unfair international buyers, found their strength as a family. Struggling to survive in a hypercompetitive global market, managers and workers would sink or swim together.

While such gendered logic may not have swayed managers to acquiesce to the earlier departure time, women (with the support of their male coworkers, who benefited) utilized the discourse of autonomy and motherhood to frame their demand. Given that the teams were fulfilling their end of the production bargain, management was forced to agree. They could not contest usage of self-management rules without causing great discontent among workers and, thus, putting the reorganization of production in danger. Moreover, while allowing workers to depart early when they completed their work might seem irrational, it ultimately benefited the larger goals of the firm by securing high levels of production.[7]

By the time I arrived in the pants department in January 2001, daily production quotas were not being met. On February 17, the department manager sent word through Luisa that we had to stay the full workday, until 4:36 P.M. "No way," chimed young and old, single and partnered. A teammate exclaimed, "No! They are not paying us enough money. They are cutting our benefits. We are not going to stay late!" I looked over at Vicki, next to me, and asked, "What's going to happen at four o'clock?" Her response: "What the majority decides." On the hour, Vicki came up to me and said "C'mon let's go home." "Let me just finish this one," I said, having inadvertently internalized company goals myself. "No, now! Let's go." I dropped everything and left. So did the others around me. The team was battling management's attempts to regain control over team decisionmaking.

While team unity served to contest managerial dictates, solidarity in teams did not need to be antagonistic to management. Workers used self-managed teams to further their interests as mothers by providing permits for absence. Under modular production, workers regulated tardiness and absenteeism in their teams. No longer did workers have to ask the supervisors for permission slips, or permits, to miss work. Under teamwork, workers asked the team leader to call a meeting where the worker related the special circumstances she believed required time off. If an absence was unforeseen, permits could be requested after the fact.

In the pants team, which did not function well, teammates questioned the person requesting a permit, taking into account how many times permissions had been granted previously and her record of tardiness. The merits of the case, the person, and if she would be required to repay the hours were debated, with a show of hands at the end of the meeting. Central to these discussions were the importance of motherhood and motherly duty.

Teams could give only one permit per day to workers requesting permission to be absent or arrive tardy. Single, childless women were both sympathetic and frustrated by the fact that, if they had a medical justification and a mother had a sick child or appointment at school, teams repeatedly voted to give the mother the sought-after permit. This meant that the worker who missed work hours without a permit would not be paid for hours lost.

When I was present in team meetings where such issues were discussed, conversation invariably turned to the demands of motherhood. For example, one time the team was deciding to whom to grant a permit: to Berna, whose child had been sick and in the hospital, or to Lety, a young woman who had been to the doctor's for an appointment. Lety had a note from the doctor excusing her from work; Berna had no proof that her child had been to the hospital or had even been sick. Ana, a partnered woman with three kids, did not get along at all with Berna; still, she spoke in favor of the mother, reasoning: "Our kids can't tell us when they are going to get sick. When they get sick we have to put everything down to care for them." In her defense of Berna, Ana tapped into norms of female solidarity based on their identities as mothers. Lety put the doctor's note into her apron pocket and sighed with resignation; as she did so, she looked at me and said, "It's always like this."

Managers expressed great displeasure and frustration at how workers were—in their view—abusing the power of self-managed teams to give excessive permits. Moreover, depending on the team, their sense of internal solidarity, and the reason for the absence, workers were granted permits without having to repay the hours they missed. If a woman's absence or tardiness was caused by familial responsibilities, especially having to tend to a sick child, teams were more likely to pardon the missed work. Workers used the discretionary power given to them by the team system to recompense mothers for their dutiful familial labor. In doing so, women justified and used the language of motherhood to favor their interests instead of the firm's.

In J-1, the team I participated in that functioned well, most permits were granted without discussion; however, in cases where several permits were requested, mothers did receive priority. In contrast to the pants team, which discussed whether hours would be replaced, the workers in J-1 repaid the hours missed on the honor system. In pants, where team conflict was rife, workers used the occasion of permits to decide if hours were to be repaid according to the merits of the person in question. This opened up terrain for continued internal conflict and competition between cliques.

The ability to grant permits could also be used to build team unity. One day Lupe, whom I assisted at a huge vapor pressing machine in the J-1 team, asked if I wanted to go with her to buy lunch for the team. They had given her a permit to attend to "personal business" before lunch. In fact, the team had conspired for her permit; she had taken orders and collected money to go a mile away to a favorite taco stand. Since I could go in and out as I pleased, I was actually being groomed to do this task for the team in the future. We took a bus to the taco stand, ordered large quantities of food that we hid in our purses, and returned to the factory.

Using permits for things other than emergencies was not allowed. To avoid being caught, Lupe and I slightly staggered our return to the factory. Once inside and exactly on cue for lunch break, we went behind the factory, where the team was waiting for us to eat. This area was hidden from managers, providing a good space to hang out.

The previous year, this J-1 team shared a meal every Friday. However, under Juan's conflictive leadership, the ritual was more sporadic. On this occasion, the older women, with whom Juan had ongoing issues, organized the shared lunch. For this reason, as leader, he did not support this informal teambuilding exercise. Nonetheless, Juan had also placed an order.

This example of the J-1 team lunch demonstrates that, depending on the team's wherewithal to take advantage of the autonomy afforded by the team system, permits could be used to benefit members personally and to build a group identity vis-à-vis management. And when company and team allegiances are intertwined, actions to enhance the team inevitably support firm goals.

However, self-managed teams cut both ways. Team autonomy could translate into empowerment, not only to produce more but also to enhance the working environment and experience of work since supervisors had less say over the individual lives of workers. That said, the fact that teams provided permissions did not automatically empower them. In fact, this provision of permits could be misused, as was the case with the pants team, as a contentious tool to dole out punishment or reward in an arena of shifting alliances and interests. Besides, even though teams were self-managed, department managers had been known to veto team-approved permits or provide them discretionarily to individuals who had been refused permits by their team. Such cases served to reinforce some workers' skepticism about self-management.

Notwithstanding the contract, advisers in both departments where I worked attempted to rule over workers and team leaders in much the way they did when they were supervisors. Whether or not advisers were able to succeed depended on the unity of teams and their ability to get production out. If teams were unified, it was easier to use the rules of self-managed teams to contest the power of both advisers and managers.

An important example of how teams could be used to workers' benefit is the case of the pants department manager who overstepped his authority and faced empowered workers. The women loved to tell how they used their newfound power under self-managed teams to have him fired. Over 150 workers in the pants department protested what they described as inappropriate behavior, accusing him of speaking to workers in vulgar and aggressive terms. The complaint to company leaders and the union was framed as an affront to workers' feminine sensibilities as well as their rights as workers. This resulted in HR telling him to "take a vacation." Six months later, when he was rehired at Moctezuma, he changed his attitude toward workers, treating them with greater respect. Interestingly, most high-level managers were light skinned. The pants manager was the exception. While women complained of him being crude and "low class," it is possible that this was in part due to the ideology of colorism present in Mexico, where class and race are intertwined, so light skin is perceived to denote higher-class status and worth, and darker skin the opposite (Bonilla-Silva 2002).[8]

This was one of the few times that workers went to the union with a labor relations complaint. Women workers invoked the discourse of traditional femininity, together with workerist discourse, to protect themselves from an overly aggressive manager. Women told and retold this story often on the shop floor as a morality tale of sorts, an example of empowered women.

### Decreased Sexual Harassment under Self-Managed Teams

The abuse of power that mostly male management had exerted over individual workers under piecework decreased significantly with self-managed teams, affecting women workers directly. Most notably, recalibrating the manager-worker power differential on the shop floor translated into fewer cases of sexual harassment. And, while women certainly appreciated this improved work environment, they had differing views regarding the advantages. Some underscored the importance of feeling safe and free of sexual pressures on the shop floor; others eschewed the inherent sexism of the workplace, welcoming this leveling of the manager's power differential as an opportunity for independence and autonomy of teams.

For instance, when interviewed, a shy and quiet female single coworker described why she liked self-managed teams: "You feel independent because no one is harassing you [acosando] to do your work. One knows how much production to give at the end of the day. There is no need for them [managers] to be all over the worker." While my coworker might have only been referring to managers' demands for work, she did use the verb *to accost* (*acosar*), utilized in Spanish to define sexual harassment (*acoso sexual*). Most other women used a less-loaded term, *pressure* (*presionar*), when describing the ways managers under piecework related with workers. As noted by another young woman: "[The best thing] is that the supervisors are not over us, pressuring us. We don't let them come [into the team]; the team is the only one that decides [who can engage with us on the shop floor]."

In contrast with piecework, with the previously ever-present supervisor on the shop floor, now under teamwork there were far fewer occasions for managers to be alone with a team member. Furthermore, advisers no longer directly controlled payment or dismissal powers over workers; formerly, this power had been used to exert pressure on young women for sexual favors.

As in most workplaces, there were romantic relationships at play in the factory. I encountered several examples of managers dating female workers; however, it is not clear if these were cases of coercive power. Interestingly, the cases were interpreted by most workers—especially the older, partnered women—as managers doling out special favors to pretty, light-skinned single women. The young women were seen as flaunting their sexuality in hopes of social mobility in the form of worker status, gifts, or marriage. In other words, they were considered to be loose women, and their behavior inappropriate. Rarely did workers interpret these situations as abuses of managerial power. However, this probably says more about how women perceived themselves in relation to others than about abuse of power in the workplace.

My own experiences at Moctezuma evidence the persistence of sexual harassment, even if diminished under teamwork. I had many opportunities to be in contact with male managers and workers while on the shop floor. Most interactions were very professional. However, there were two male coworkers—one an adviser, the other a team member—whose behaviors were improper for the workplace. The adviser would come to my workstation to talk or provide instruction, and, on several occasions, he put his hand on my arm or shoulder while obviously letting some of his fingers linger to stroke my skin. The other case involved Juan, my male team leader in J-1, who assigned me as his assistant on a large steam presser. I spent the whole day by his side placing the garments on the press while he recounted his sexual exploits and predilections. With the benefit of critical analysis, as a participant-observer, I interpreted his sexual banter as a way to reaffirm his masculinity and distance his work identity from the feminized work tasks (Collinson 2003). Still, in the 2001 workplace, his behavior should not have been tolerated.

I mention these personal examples of sexual harassment that persisted from piecework to point out that, if they happened to a North American researcher, they likely occurred with the other women workers.

### Eroding Trust in the Community of Fate

The contradiction between the theory and practice of self-managed teams gnawed away at workers' expectations of self-rule. Issues around training, certification, and team policing of individual's efficiencies and quality increased conflict within teams. The unintended consequence of this was to erode trust in management.

The community of fate belief began to slowly fracture as management was not able to provide workers with the means to fulfill their work and, therefore, earn a bonus. Supply shortages slowed and even stopped work, as happened when I was in training. (This problem had existed since 1999 but worsened as the firm's liquidity problems deepened.) Moreover, management's changes in payment structure undermined their message of shared vested interests. At first, bonuses were calculated at the team level. This unbalanced the lines when some teams consistently outpaced others. By April 2000, bonuses were instead being tallied by departmental production. Four months later, they changed again—this time, they were determined by the output numbers for the entire shop floor.

Workers complained that, no matter how hard they worked, their individual levels of remuneration were not in their own hands but in those of their coworkers. Solving what was considered a free-rider problem became all consuming, with individual workers aggressively making sure that others were working as hard as they were. However, each change made controlling others' labor more difficult. Between the material shortages and the changes in calculating the bonus, it was increasingly challenging to earn bonuses that were intended to incentivize increased production, quality, and loyalty.

Based on the payment slips provided to me by a pants utility worker by the name of Raquel, production-quality bonuses had all but disappeared by 2001. From October 1998 until April 2000, when the first change occurred, Raquel earned a bonus 91 percent of the time. Given that utility workers were organized into a team in each department and were more skilled, they may have earned bonuses more often than other teams. Yet since utility workers moved around to different operations, they did not necessarily work at 100 percent efficiency all the time. It is not clear if Raquel's team's situation was anomalous.

During the period when bonuses were assessed at the departmental level, Raquel earned a bonus 80 percent of the time. However, within four months, from September to February 2001, that percentage decreased to 40 percent, when the bonus was calculated based on shop floor production instead. In the first two months of 2001, Raquel earned a bonus only two times. By this time, workers had come to expect a bonus as a reward for increased effort, even if they did not reach the production goals. They blamed management for not providing them with the conditions (supplies) they needed to earn a bonus, not their lack of effort.

Workers claimed to be initially excited about self-managed teams until they saw how management rolled back the rights given to teams. Irene, who had been at the company for twelve years, described her experiences this way:

> [At the beginning,] self-managed teams meant that [workers] could make decisions within the team, decisions regarding work, how to organize themselves in order to get the production out. . . . They made decisions about permits and then got the production out. That's what it was supposed to be. But later, a permit had to be given by the department head. And that is not what the rules say. The team was supposed to give the permits. The boss was only supposed to sign it. But lately this is not respected anymore.

The more women workers demanded to make use of the rights accorded to autonomous teams, the more managers resisted losing control over the labor process. A struggle ensued between workers and managers over the right to operate as self-managed teams and the role of workers on the shop floor.

Most workers interviewed (before and after the strike) ultimately concluded that teams were not truly self-managed nor were they in the interest of the worker. They involved, in the words of one woman, "greater responsibility [for the worker] and a big savings for the company."

### Learning to Be Leaders

Another unintended consequence of self-managed teams was workers learning how to be leaders. Situated in a seemingly contradictory location, women hired for their docility were placed in leadership roles, where they were forced to coordinate with both management and workers. In the process they gained valuable interpersonal and communications skills. Other studies of self-managed teams have produced similar findings (Barker 1993; Smith 1990; Vallas 2006).

As women took on more leadership roles in teams, many found a new voice. The motherist work culture encouraged new identities. Early decisions the teams made to invoke the language of traditional femininity contrasted with their later expulsion of the department manager using the combined discourse of traditional gender norms, women's rights, and workers' rights. Women unevenly incorporated empowered attitudes within the dominant trope of traditional womanhood. They still identified primarily as mothers, but, increasingly, the inconsistency between the theory and practice of teams pushed women workers to not only resist but contest management control of the labor process. Workers had entered into a social pact with management. In the end, it was management who did not fulfill its end of the bargain, thus unleashing a struggle over the firm's future.

## CONCLUSION

This chapter explored the paradox of self-managed teams by examining the practice of control and contestation on the shop floor. The theory of modular production, as explained to workers and implemented in the firm's rules, provided for extensive worker autonomy by encouraging skilled and independent workers to make decisions pertaining to production. However, the practice strayed substantially from the theory. Worker placement on the shop floor reinforced traditional gender norms used in recruiting and training workers. Management ideologies assigned different jobs to men and women, with important consequences in terms of their wages and autonomy.

Teamwork was meant to solidify the community of fate belief, each worker helping each other out to achieve higher production levels and thus larger bonuses. Yet the policy of workers having to control each other's labor to earn bonuses wreaked havoc on social relations. Tensions resulted when team leaders experienced overwork; training increased bottlenecks, escalating interpersonal conflicts; new workers were not given the conditions to certify for new operations; and differential efficiency and quality levels pitted workers against each other. Workers responded by using a motherist work culture to enhance autonomy within teams by decreasing the length of the workday, granting mothers preferential permits to miss work, while holding managerial abuses—such as sexual harassment—in check.

Workers consented to the team system, though not seamlessly. Most workers keenly understood that teams required extra physical, mental, and emotional effort. Under teams, workers took over many responsibilities previously under the purview of managers. It was harder for workers to control their own labor, now being surveilled not only by managers but also by fellow teammates.

The contradictions of self-managed teams eroded trust in management. When the company, reeling from its growing debt with banks and creditors, started curtailing some of the teams' autonomy under self-management, workers withdrew their consent from that system. Although there had always been some resistance and skepticism about teamwork, workers had nevertheless internalized the production and quality goals with the expectation that the firm would continue to provide expanded benefits and a high wage. Difficult social relations were endured in exchange for material rewards. But when capital shortages led to changes in the incentive structure and the intrusion of advisers into teams, erosion turned into outright contestation. By incorporating new attributes of assertiveness into their work roles, women carved out spaces for independent action.

CHAPTER 5

# Lean during Mean Times

By mid-February 2001, heightened tension was palpable on the shop floor. Rumors abounded that workers would be fired because of the economic crisis. One day, rumor spread that the second shift would be eliminated. Nobody felt secure in his or her job. Even those I would have considered the best and most indispensable workers felt their livelihood threatened. It was the beginning of the end. Management changed the rules of teamwork, the social contract established with workers. In response, individual resistance rapidly cascaded into open collective struggle on the shop floor.

The events that led up this confrontation are important in and of themselves and as part of a series of incidents that gave meaning to larger social processes. For this reason, this chapter is organized chronologically to show how resistance turned into contestation.

### February: Management Cancels the Second Shift

Although managers often stressed Moctezuma's growing financial difficulties during the training modules, the first time I really understood the severity of the situation was Thursday morning, February 22, 2001. Managers had spoken of the "liquidity crisis," the shortage of working capital, since mid-1999; but workers were unclear if it was a veiled threat or reality. We would soon find out it was both.

That Thursday morning, over fifty women crowded the workspace outside the pants office. The department manager could be seen talking to the workers and advisers. I asked our team leader Luisa, "What's going on?" She could not answer. No one knew. Everyone was asking the same thing. Ana, one of the older and more vocal members of the team, spotted her sister, who worked the second shift, in the huddle. Ana found out what the commotion was about. "The second shift was terminated last night. The company told some of them to show up for the first shift today!" explained Ana excitedly. "They don't know what's going on—if they have a job or not. Everything's up in the air."

As we assembled around Ana, trying to make sense of the chaos, the union president and vicepresident stomped onto the shop floor. It was always easy to spot them: young men with loud voices, proud roosters strutting around, carrying themselves with such an air of importance. Today, they were more ruffled than usual; they were flustered, waving their hands, ordering the women from the second shift to stop talking with management. They screamed out, forcefully: "Don't accept anything from them. They didn't consult us before terminating the second shift! They can't do that. The company didn't consult us first!"

The union president Reynaldo moved from team to team, making sure the workers knew that the union had not participated in this action. Then, just as quickly as he came onto the floor, he left. We still did not know what was happening, but almost everyone dutifully made their way back to his or her workstation to commence another workday. The women from the second shift lingered outside the department manager's office, talking to managers as well as some of their friends and family already on the first shift. The next time I lifted my eyes from the ironing, most were gone.

Not much time had passed before Luisa called a meeting. I looked around. Teams all over the shop floor were huddled into meetings. Usually it was hard to hear in these meetings because one had to talk over the chatter of machines. This morning no machines were running. Luisa began in a serious tone: "The other teams want us to decide if we should carry out a work stoppage against the union to pressure them to deal with this situation differently." Much to my surprise, the workers listened carefully, in relative silence, none of them showing any real outrage at the unilateral and drastic action taken by the firm.

Worker discussion revolved around two issues: the union and movement cohesiveness. While concerned with the elimination of the second shift, many perceived that the union was not responding appropriately given the company's economic crisis. Workers believed the union cared more about its own interests than getting jobs back for workers from the second shift. One young woman complained that Reynaldo did not care about the workers, stating that he was upset that he was not part of the inner circle that made the decisions. Others agreed. Ana, whose sister was caught in this limbo, felt it was a mockery and indignity against the people on the second shift to be moved around like Ping-Pong balls. Underlying the heated conversation was an understanding that Moctezuma was facing an economic crisis and that cooperation rather than antagonism should be the first strategy to weather the storm.

Workers also decided that, prior to taking any action, they had to find out what the fired workers wanted. Of crucial importance to any mobilization was the level of commitment by fired workers. Lety, a longtime worker and single woman, remarked: "Remember last year when we walked off the line for a few hours because the company fired some workers? I went outside to support them. They were eating pizza, having fun, completely unaware of the work stoppage inside the factory and the problems we were going through for them. Let's make sure the *compañeras* want to come back to work this time. I heard some from the second shift do not even want to return." Women's voices agreed in unison. Again, Ana interrupted, "And let's make sure either *everybody* in pants participates, or *no one* does. Otherwise those that walk off the line will get into trouble."

The purpose of the proposed work stoppage came up. One woman commented: "No matter how much yelling and screaming [we do] and how many times we walk off the line, Reynaldo and the union will not come talk with us. And that's what we want . . . [to talk]. So is it really worth it?" Just as she said this, one of the advisers, Patricia, walked up to the group. She had started at the factory as a line worker over thirty years ago. Patricia spoke in her usual soft-spoken manner: "Look, I tell you this because I heard the company tell the women this morning [that] they want to hire them. They want to keep them on the first shift. They are good workers and they [management] are trying to work everything out. The company will welcome anyone who wants to return to the first shift. This problem will be solved." As my teammates mulled over the new information, we got news from the other teams.

The leader for the team next to us walked over, carrying a pair of pants in her hands, to use an iron close to where we were having our meeting. While pretending to iron, she told us that the others had decided to wait until Monday. "If a solution isn't found over the weekend, then we'll do what we have to do." What she said next proved to me that workers still understood their interests to be aligned with those of management. "We feel a work stoppage would only hurt the company, which is in a difficult situation now. We don't really want to turn against them. So we decided to wait until Monday." Our team quickly concurred. We all returned to work. The meeting took no more than ten minutes. I was perplexed that workers had so quickly decided to protect the company in spite of their indignation over the dismissal of coworkers from the second shift. While the cancellation of the second shift was a serious infraction, it was not unexpected. Rumors of this cutting of the second shift had abounded for over a month. However, it was the first sign that management would not honor its obligations to workers. Nevertheless, most workers were prepared to give management the benefit of the doubt, categorizing this event as an extreme isolated action. Shielding the company from a wildcat strike was in the workers' personal interest as they believed their future to be closely tied with that of the company. Cooperating to weather difficult times, therefore, was one of the sacrifices required of the Moctezuma family.

The union, however, was seen as only self-interested. Workers shifted their anger toward the union for reacting antagonistically without taking into account the larger picture—the economic state of the company and, thus, the secure employment of all workers. In the eyes of workers, Reynaldo's actions on the shop floor laid bare the union's true colors: self-aggrandizement. Before this incident, the union was perceived as a company union; now, it appeared opportunistic and power hungry, turning on both the company and the workers.

Ten minutes later, Luisa called our team to another meeting. I thought she was going to tell us of another job protest; instead she brought our attention to an urgent order that had to be completed that day. Everyone should put other work aside to concentrate on getting this important order through. Immediately, the team shifted into high gear. People I had never seen before started coming through the workstations, looking for bundles, passing work through. The department manager and the two advisers pulled up their sleeves to help out as well. Utility workers showed up to support us in the bottlenecked operations, and several of my teammates very patiently showed them how to perform the operations. Not even half an hour had elapsed since our heated discussions about a wildcat strike, but I looked around to see our team working like a well-oiled machine. Everyone was at a workstation, concentrating on doing the operation with speed and accuracy. Interpersonal conflicts that so often hindered the flow of work temporarily dissipated.

At that moment, I wondered why my *compañeras* were so loyal to the company that had just announced the firing of hundreds of coworkers. Not only had they returned to work after considering a wildcat strike, but when the company asked them to work extra hard, they did so with renewed fervor. Were they afraid to lose their jobs if they did not comply? Perhaps a few believed so. But the fact that I heard no complaint about working harder to meet the urgent deadline points to other explanations.[1] After careful examination of field notes and transcripts, I conclude that workers had internalized the belief that their interests coincided with those of the firm. That is, while they may have had legitimate gripes against the union and the company, workers recognized that the firm was experiencing a difficult economic period. Working hard to meet urgent deadlines, the *compañeras* showed management that they were still willing to participate in this cooperative endeavor. The workers had shown good faith, now management had to respond.

Another possible explanation for workers' support of management could be the lack of comparable jobs in the local labor market. Conversation with teammates, however, revealed that it was not the local but international labor market that provided competition for the firm. While employment at Moctezuma was considered one of the best opportunities in the area, migration to the United States had become an important economic and social safety valve for families in this central state. In fact, so many workers had voluntarily left their jobs at Moctezuma to migrate north in the past ten years that (as discussed in chapter 2) the company had instituted a policy of not hiring workers who had family in the United States.

Research on immigration from Mexico to the United States provides further evidence for this pattern of growth. Migration to the United States quintupled between 1995 and 2005, with the central state in question being one of the new Mexican sending states, moving from the bottom rank of sending states in the 1980s to the top five in the year 2000 (Arroyo Alejandre and Rodríguez Álvarez

2008; Guerrero Ortiz 2007; Lozano Ascencio 2001, 2003). Remittances from migrants had thus became a growing and essential part of family reproduction, with an estimated 35 percent of families in the central state receiving remittances in 2005 (Muñoz Jumilla 2004; Muñoz Jumilla and Del Moral Barrera 2007; Tuirán Gutiérrez, Santibáñez Romellón, and Corona Vázquez 2006).

Local employment options also existed, but they did not pay as well or provide as many benefits. Whether workers stayed or quit depended in part on their age, length of employment, and family circumstances. Older women found it hardest to find employment locally and were the least likely to migrate. Recent hires were the most apt to leave since they had not accrued seniority, which increased a worker's compensation package if fired. Women who relied on the benefits—especially health-care benefits—for their family were the least likely to leave. The choice of workers to stay at Moctezuma or leave thus depended on a series of personal circumstances as well as their perception of employment stability and managerial commitment. Women were not willing to keep their jobs at all costs.

## MID-FEBRUARY: MANAGEMENT BREAKS MORE PROMISES

Although the workers supported management and went back to work, their faith in management was conditional. My teammates expected reciprocal sacrifices from Moctezuma. During the March 2000 contract revision, workers had voted to forgo a wage increase and freeze a number of side benefits for one year.[2] The firm promised to invest the capital back into the firm. Workers knew Moctezuma was traversing difficult times. They could have chosen to reject the proposition. Instead, in good faith, they agreed to cooperate. Even by workers' estimation, these were not crucial benefits. However, the gesture of *lending* this capital, the workers' money, to the company for a year was of great importance to the workers. They had put the company's commitment to workers to the test.

The deadline for unfreezing benefits was quickly approaching. Much discussion on the shop floor revolved around the upcoming March salary revision talks. One teammate told me she was already talking to a lawyer friend in case the company reneged on its promise (which is indeed what happened at the end of February 2001). To do so would be a clear betrayal of the spirit of cooperation between workers and management. Other coworkers spoke of the recent elimination of the second shift as a negative indication regarding the reinstatement of their frozen benefits. Suddenly, the future did not look good.

### Contesting Bonuses

Even more contentious than the potential continued freeze of benefits was the issue of production-quality bonuses. In August 2000, the union and company had announced that bonuses would no longer be calculated by department but, rather, for the entire shop floor. Beginning in January 2001, however, there had not been enough production to merit bonuses. At issue for the workers was who was to blame for lower production. Management claimed that production was down, clear and simple. If production did not exceed the goal, by contract, no bonuses were given.

Workers did not dispute that production was down. Rather, they argued that, since the company failed to supply the material conditions with which they would have undoubtedly surpassed production goals, they should still receive bonuses. Several times, I participated in team conversations that ended with workers claiming something to the effect of "Well, we helped them out with the benefits, now it's their turn to help us out." In the eyes of many workers, a social contract existed at Moctezuma, the spirit and meaning of which was continually being contested.

The issue of bonuses became so divisive that the company decided to call a meeting on Friday, February 23—the day after the near-wildcat strike—to announce the *partial* reimbursement of bonuses. The union delivered the message. Six hundred pesos, equivalent to one and one-third of weekly base pay, would be given in two installments as a production bonus. Furthermore, since the ranks of the first shift had been enlarged by members of the second shift, total production quotas were going to increase to 1,900 pants per day (1,200 for the first shift and 700 for the second). So, while management was caving in on some of the workers' demands, it had also changed the rules of the game. Although the union president Reynaldo hoped this news of the bonuses would dilute discontent over increased quotas, it did not happen.

Immediately, the more outspoken women protested the new arrangement. An older woman from jackets went head to head with Reynaldo, accusing him personally of dishonesty. In her view, if the union did not represent the interests of workers, it was in the pocket of management. This skepticism was probably also a reaction to the long history of union corporatism and corruption in Mexico, where unions do not generally respond to the needs of workers (Cook 2007; La Botz 1992).

Usually, workers who stood up to the union were eventually fired by the company to safeguard against subsequent worker unrest. In this instance, the woman who stood up to Reynaldo was fired *that same day*, so were workers belonging to the opposing slate in the past union elections. My teammates thought the union was cleaning house. The union was probably making use of the exclusion clause whereby workers expelled by the union must be fired by the company. Needless to say, this further eroded the confidence workers had in both their union and, more important, their employer, which was now apparently allowing the union to wage personal vendettas.

### Challenging Team Rules

Having returned to work in our teams, we discussed who would decide work assignments. Several women had brought the issue up with Reynaldo. According to the rules of teamwork, the self-managed teams worked together to decide the work responsibilities for each member. Now that new workers were arriving on Monday, who would have the final word on where each would go? That is, who really controlled decision making on the shop floor? The existing workers' contract said it was up to the individual teams. Reynaldo had assured them it would remain so. With mounting suspicion, women remarked among themselves, "Let's see what happens." Company and union promises were increasingly falling on incredulous ears.

Monday, February 23, the day of reckoning, came and went filled with confusion and contestation, but no strike. Early in the day, Luisa called a team meeting. She had been asked to find out which machines were open. Immediately, Ana spoke up: "What I want to know is who is going to decide where the people are going to go. Is it going to be the team or are they [management] going to come in and impose a new plan on us?" Luisa threw her hands up in the air, showing even her mounting frustration. "I don't know," she said, "I was just asked to get the information." As team leader, she was once again caught in the uncomfortable position of being a coworker yet being the mouthpiece for management, too.

Impassioned exchanges continued as Luisa reported back to the departmental office. What the workers were saying was true: in reality, there were no available machines. With the exception of two specialized machines used on some higher-end models, all workstations were staffed. Crowding a surplus of bodies around every possible machine was not an efficient use of space, workers, or materials.

Despite the absence of open machines, the next day Luisa returned with five new workers. Two of them were young unmarried women, while the others were middle-aged women who had been utility workers in the second shift. The male mechanics spent most of the day squeezing in three old sewing machines from the back of the factory. The workspace became very tight. Still, two of the new workers did not have a workstation. They stood behind new teammates, learning operations by watching.

Nobody seemed especially pleased with the arrangement. Not only were there new workers to fit into the first shift, but there was also a new layer of advisers from the second shift who were roaming the shop floor, checking individual efficiencies. The work environment was tense, filled with pressure and uncertainty.

When Luisa announced later that day that people were going to be shifted around to make room for the new workers, a near revolt occurred. Carmen, a quiet, forty-something single mother, had been moved earlier in the year before she could certify her operation; she was now being asked to return to that position. She said nothing, though one could read the disappointment on her face. It was Ana who quickly stuck up for her even though they were not close friends. Angrily, she noted, "That's not fair. She was only at the first operation for four months getting up to 60 percent and then you moved her here. Now she's at

80 percent on the second operation! And you want to move her back again to the other more difficult operation? She has not had the chance to certify on either one of them!"

Again, Luisa did not have an answer. As usual, when caught in the middle of disputes or pressed to make decisions or clarify team requests from management, our leader relied on the team adviser for direction. "Let's ask Frida," she suggested.

When Frida came over, not only did the she confirm that Carmen was to be moved, but she also announced changes for two other workers. One of them had also not yet been certified on her operation. The team complained bitterly. The adviser's retort was brusque: "You've had plenty of time to certify. If you're ready, certify now. If not, move on." The implication was clear: these were not good workers and thus were expendable. Frida then moved on to another touchy subject. She said, "This is one of the most complete teams. Nobody has quit, at least not yet. All positions are filled and machines in use and you are still not getting your production out." A flood of fiery voices responded: "We are not complete! We have five new people plus three who are not certified!" Frida held her ground: "You are still one of the most complete teams. If you cannot get your production out, you only need to look inside your team for the answer."

In effect, as relations were already charged within team four, this comment detoured discussion to long-standing internal conflicts about individuals, quality, and efficiency. Knowing that the team was divided, Frida continued: "For example," pointing to one of the women, "I see her punch in early every day but [she] doesn't get to her workstation until five or ten minutes past [the start time]. Why doesn't anybody ask her why she's late? And your [two] *compañeras* who didn't come to work today? Why do you let them get away with it? Why do you let Lety [one of those absent] arrive late?" I think Frida was planting these questions deliberately, knowing exactly how the women would react. It was no secret that there were cliques in the team who detested each other.

The tension in the meeting was palpable. Then, Vicki spoke up: "Let's expel them![3] They always arrive late and never get their production out. I say we take a vote." Silence followed. Vicki repeated her request; a vote was called. However, only one other worker voted with Vicki for expulsion. Then, a friend of the ones at risk for being expelled said, "Well I think that if there is a problem we should tell it to them in person, not just expel them." After more tense debate regarding problematic workers, the adviser ended the meeting with one last comment: "You should all learn from Betty. She arrives at 6:30 A.M. every day. Everybody has to do their part." The meeting disbanded, and we returned demoralized to our workstations.

Many of us were in a state of shock: team practices had been turned on their head. The adviser had *imposed* work assignments over the objections of the team. Moreover, she was clearly manipulating internal conflicts to divert attention away from management transgressions. Had our team expelled the two workers in question, the company would have had no recourse but to fire them, making more room for the second-shift workers. While I was aware of the animosity between the two main camps in the team, I was surprised they surfaced so strongly during this period of transition toward movement building. Growing disappointment with management had showed signs of a flourishing solidarity between workers, such as Ana's ardent defense of Carmen.

Still trying to understand what had just happened in the meeting, I spoke with several teammates. First, I asked Betty why she arrived early every day. "That's the only way I can get my 100 percent out," she replied. "Besides, since I'm at the beginning of the line in our team, I like to get some work out so when the others arrive they can get to work right away." She had internalized the team concept.

Next, I asked my teammate about her close friends who had been the target of expulsion earlier. She agreed that one of the women missed a lot work, but she did it on purpose; that woman was apparently hoping to be fired in order to receive the severance package that, as per the Federal Labor Law, the company was required to pay for dismissal (even with cause). But my teammate thought that Vicki had unfairly accused Lety. It was no secret that the two women had never gotten along; both were natural leaders of their respective groups of friends. "Lety always completes 100 percent of her work, even when she arrives late," she noted emphatically. "Why did she and the others miss work today?" I asked. Shrugging her shoulders, she replied, "I don't know. We'll find out tomorrow."

Luisa called a meeting the next morning to introduce two more new workers who had come over from the second-shift jackets one line (J-1), and to discuss work permits. Both workers who had been absent the previous day asked the team to give them work permits for medical purposes. One woman, a single mother, said her youngest child had been sick. "Well," said the only other worker besides Vicki who had voted to expel her the previous day, "you can't control when kids get sick." Mocking her coworker, Ana responded, "I agree. When your kid gets sick there's nothing you can do. But isn't it funny that yesterday we were going to expel her and now we're talking about a permit? I say we give her the permission slip and discuss the other situation later." So the team voted in favor of this woman's permit. Meanwhile, Lety, who was childless, had shown the doctor's prescription for new eyeglasses as proof for her absence; however, her permit was not granted because a team can only issue one permit daily. Despite the team's interpersonal tensions, motherhood still stood out as the most important bond between workers.

### Production Problems on the Shop Floor

The following week, there was an urgent order that had to get out by Thursday. Material shortages hampered the process, further demonstrating how company capital constraints directly affected production and, thus, the ability to produce returns on investments. Our team was working at full capacity, with all machines being used, and several people were training to operate machines in other teams since we could not accommodate them. The adviser asked me to find fifteen bundles of the urgent order and to push them through the shop floor. Finding them was difficult enough, but pushing them through meant going down the line, from worker to worker, asking for priority on the bundles, standing there while the operation was performed, and then doing the same with the next worker. Although I asked nicely and was as patient as possible, I was acutely aware that my presence alone added pressure.

Pushing bundles through also meant negotiating relationships in teams and banking on my social capital to get work done. Several women said they would do the operation, just because I was the one asking. At one point, however, I asked one of the new workers if she could perform a multistep operation that required her to relocate. She looked at me and said, "Ask Vicki to do it." No one had ever dared ask anything of Vicki as she was difficult to deal with. "No," I replied, "You ask the team leader to make the change if you want but I'm not going to ask Vicki." She looked up from her ironing and said, "*You* ask Luisa." I was caught between a potential fight with Vicki and alienating the new worker. I went to Luisa, who was already overextended, and requested that she resolve the problem. After some debate, the new worker reluctantly performed the operation, allowing me to proceed to the next workstation.

Although I was supposedly doing a worker's task, I felt very much like management demanding more labor from workers. This must have been what the team leaders meant when they said they were worker-managers. In the end, half of the order due on Thursday went out on Saturday, the rest the next Tuesday. Not being able to force teams to work overtime, the advisers and employees rolled up their sleeves and stayed late to produce this rushed order.

The next day, our team was almost paralyzed because the team in front of us did not have the materials to make waistbands. This only heightened the debate on production bonuses. Advisers complained that urgent orders were not being completed. Self-confident and fiery as usual, Ana told Luisa: "It's impossible to do it because there are no waistbands. And team three isn't getting the waist-bands out because they don't have materials. So the fact that we are stuck and there is not a lot of work is not our fault." Nevertheless, management kept pressuring all of us to meet quotas.

With production halted, workers focused on repairs, piles of which seemed to appear miraculously every morning. With the second shift cancelled, rework could no longer be blamed on those workers. Workers suspected that these repairs were coming from outsourced work. (This would later be confirmed to me by a manager.) While the contract did not dismiss the possibility of outsourcing, the social pact between workers and the company held that work for Moctezuma would be prioritized for its employees, as its administrators and managers secured projects for production. However, even with suspicions of outsourcing to cheaper labor, my teammates worked hard on repairs.

## MARCH: PREPARING FOR CONTRACT NEGOTIATIONS

On March 6, union representatives called a meeting to announce that the company had appealed to the courts for portions of the collective-bargaining contract to be voided because of the firm's financial crisis.[4] Moreover, the company was proposing a new payment structure, which included doing away with production bonuses altogether. Reynaldo, surrounded by the executive committee and the business agent, made it clear that, owing to the financial crisis, workers had to accept the elimination of bonuses. In exchange, the union would request a wage raise, which would be discussed at the next union assembly, on Saturday.

After this announcement, the workers returned to the shop floor. Everyone was startled and upset by the news. Not only was the company changing the rules but doing so by going to outside authorities, without any previous discussion with the workers. If the firm was based on openness and cooperation, some wondered, why had management not spoken directly to the workers? The production and department managers stood outside the pants office and stared at the workers. I was very much aware of their gaze and fairly certain that my coworkers also knew that they were being watched.

For the first two weeks of March leading up to the contract revision, tension filled the air as work slowly filtered through the shop floor. The insertion of new workers into teams increased internal conflicts and lowered production. In the meantime, managers spread the word that clients were ready to take their business to China and Central America, where wages were lower. At one meeting, a woman asked me, "Is it true? Are wages cheaper in China and Central America?" I answered, "Yes, but wages are not everything. Proximity to the United States and high-quality work are also important issues that clients take into account."

Everybody was apprehensive. Twice, coworkers warned me to be careful whom I spoke with as there were two team members who were believed to relay information to management. One was an older utility worker with fifteen years on the job, the other was Elena. Although the women who warned me belonged to feuding camps, they did not point fingers at each other. An uneven and fluctuating sense of solidarity among the workers was growing, even in our conflict-filled team. At times, they battled each other directly using quality complaints as weapons; at other times, they expressed solidarity, contesting management's legitimacy when they acted outside the bounds of the community of fate.

On Friday, which was my last day in the pants department as I prepared to go to J-1, I asked Reynaldo for permission to attend the union's general assembly. He quickly replied, "Yes." I also asked my coworkers if I could interview them after work. Everyone agreed. I told them that I would invite them individually for a cup of coffee and then give them a ride home.

Up to this point, I had been taking the company bus into work at 6 A.M. and taking two different city buses for an hour and a half to get home in the afternoon. From this point forward, I borrowed my father's car for interviews so as to not unnecessarily extend my coworkers' day. This proved advantageous not only for the time saved but also because I was able to see the homes and neighborhoods in which workers lived. Some were government-subsidized apartments, others cardboard shacks. Twenty-five percent lived up to two hours away in rural towns. Two workers commuted four hours daily. This was definitely not the one-hour traveling time radius human resources (HR) purported to require.

As wages and bonuses decreased, the cost of travel became understandably more and more of an issue. In fact, one of my teammates who lived two hours away quit during this week. As a single mother with three kids, she said she had stayed this long at Moctezuma for the medical benefits; now she was only earning enough to cover her transportation costs. She planned to sell tamales outside her house but was not sure that she could make much money; at least she wouldn't leave her kids alone anymore, she reflected.

## DECIDING TO STRIKE

The union's general assembly was held Saturday morning, March 10, in a meeting hall around the block from the company. It turned out to be a referendum on teamwork at Moctezuma. Workers raised questions about teams and the firm's commitment to the workers. The union seemed to be playing to both sides. It questioned the firm's willingness to negotiate; however, it also accused workers of undermining teamwork. The union's approach had been to respond to a few of workers grievances while implementing larger changes requested by management.

In the Japanese model of lean production, unions play a supportive role, coordinating individual grievances with management rather than making demands on behalf of all workers. As such, they participate in consultations rather than collective bargaining. In Mexico, the character of unions had changed from corporatist government-controlled to company-centered; so, the Japanese model fit well. Historically, Mexican unions have excelled at parsing out paternalistic favors from both the state and (now) companies, in order to secure a base while at the same time pocketing large sums of money.[5]

At Moctezuma, the company provided the union with funds to furnish sports uniforms and put on cultural and social events, as well as the "many concessions" in the contract such as cloth for soon-to-be newlyweds, cash for new babies, and money for family deaths. The union, together with the company, incorporated itself into the social world of workers by being there at every crucial moment of their lives.

However, under serious capital constraints, it was no longer possible for the company or the union to respond in the paternalistic ways of the past. The union, caught between pleasing the company and the workers, was in an especially difficult position. There were no more bonuses or gifts to exchange for the workers' consent to teamwork.

The meeting began with Reynaldo presenting both the union and the company's proposals for the upcoming contract negotiations. In essence, the company requested a decrease in benefits with a modification to the wage structure and elimination of production-quality bonuses. Meanwhile, the union asked for substantial increases in benefits and base pay.[6]

The details and discussion of each proposal led to several conclusions. First, the union was open to negotiation on the bonus and wage structure on the condition that wages and benefits would be increased, not decreased. As Reynaldo put it: "If we can't raise something, at least we don't want to lose anything." Second, management had no use for an incentive structure given the difficulty in providing workers with materials to reach daily quotas. Moreover, incentives proved counterproductive since they opened up an arena for continual contestation by workers.

Workers did not respond positively to the company proposal. At first, the union appeared to support the workers' discontentment. The union president and other executive committee members echoed the fighting words coming from the workers. Reynaldo asked, "A very high price has been paid, the loss of 500 workers. Are you willing to make half of what you're making?" Vicki, sitting next to me, was quick to answer: "No! Not *even* what we're making now!"

One comment yelled out by a worker was especially poignant. She said, "The company doesn't guarantee us work. It can go broke at any moment. We can't trust them. So why are we even discussing the production incentive scale if we have no job security?" Another woman stood up, adding, "Either we accept a base salary, fight for a fixed amount, or we go on strike. We either have something or nothing!" Yet another yelled out, "I don't even know what I'll eat tomorrow. Our wage isn't enough to buy anything anymore." Loud applause followed.

The union stood silent on stage. Now, a week before the yearly contract revision, workers challenged the union executive to stand up to the company, to be "real men" and declare an actual, legal strike.[7] Some women hurled insults at the union president. "Reynaldo!" shouted an older woman, "Stand up and fight [for us]! Show us what you're made of—show us your character!" With this, she tauntingly grabbed at her crotch, implying that even she had bigger balls than him. Another woman screamed out to her *compañeras*, "Let's not forget [that] we're single mothers!" Speaking to the workers, another said, "We need worker unity!"

As such, women used their shared sense of identity, predominantly as single mothers, to call for a strike, questioning the manliness of a union leadership that seemed reticent to lead. Workers cleverly used their subordinate status as women to turn the tables on the male leadership. The message was that the so-called most vulnerable of the women workers had the courage to stand up to the company, but that the union, marked as male, did not. This gendered language of workers as female and union as male continued throughout the labor unrest, underscoring how the union did not truly represent the workforce.

Not all workers in the general assembly supported a strike, yet few voiced their disapproval. One worker said, "What the union proposes is better than nothing but it's not so good." A *companera* stood up: "Don't let yourselves be deceived by radicals because they're only interested in themselves, not the source of income." Not voicing a direct opinion on the strike, a woman reminded everyone that it was a serious decision: "The same thing could happen here that happened a year ago at the ammunition company. For a minimal difference in wage, there was a thirty-day strike," she remarked. "The company fired and compensated everyone and began to contract back at lower wages and benefits." Her warning was well taken; many knew of that struggle.

But the momentum toward a strike was building, with dissent to a possible strike mostly discouraged. The dynamics in the large assembly turned so that disagreement was censured; workers who opposed a strike faced jeering. Nevertheless, some workers were dissenting, arguing that the firm's survival was the issue at hand, not their apparent betrayal by the company.

For most, an altered understanding of events reinforced solidarity among workers in opposition to management. The women increasingly interpreted management's deeds—cutting the second shift, imposing workers into teams, refusing to unfreeze benefits, filing a motion with labor courts to rescind parts of the collective-bargaining agreement, eliminating incentives—not only as grievances but, moreover, unfair actions. Management had underhandedly changed the rules of the game and broken the social pact. While, at first, managerial changes seemed logical reactions to the financial crisis, most workers now understood them as exploitative. The moral outrage expressed a budding class consciousness I had not witnessed previously. Steven Vallas found a similar situation at AT&T, where managerial violations of "workers' conceptions of dignity, fair treatment, and other normative constructs" led to increasing levels of class consciousness (1987, 253).

Other studies of strike mobilizations have found comparable dynamics where discontent quickly turned into what Rick Fantasia calls "cultures of solidarity" (1988). Examining three strike mobilizations in the United States, Fantasia found that, when unions block worker dissent, workers often find alternate forms of organizing where dissatisfaction and anger can explode into emotional outbursts of class consciousness. Other scholars claim that, although chosen as a means to elicit consent, participatory work methods (such as teamwork) can often increase solidarity and heighten a sense of workplace injustice (Hodson et al. 1994; Vallas 2006; Zetka 1992).

In the case of Moctezuma, the union's stonewalling and the company's breaking of promises help explain how most workers quickly shifted from supporting the firm's increased labor effort to ardently pushing for a strike. Many workers, especially those who had believed that Moctezuma was a special kind of family as espoused in the community of fate belief, now felt betrayed by management, and that anger cascaded into a call for a strike.

At the union general assembly workers and union representatives debated the truth about the company's financial problems. A woman spoke up from the middle of the room: "I don't understand. They've been saying they're in crisis for two years. We froze our benefits. I bet they were planning on cutting the second shift since then, but instead asked us to freeze our benefits." A man near me whispered: "Such a crisis, that's why you see all those big cars in the parking lot." Workers openly questioned management's sincerity in pushing the community of fate ideology.

In response, Reynaldo assured workers that the company was indeed in financial crisis. He explained that the company would not even able to compensate recently fired workers until April 27. "The company has no money!" echoed another union delegate. Heated arguments continued: "The union told us to lend the benefits, and then at the next negotiation—" said one woman, breaking off. "Let's see where you shove your benefits!" Discontent fueled disbelief and anger.

Immediately, the discussion turned into a referendum on modular production. The union defended the company, accusing the workers of undermining the system. Reynaldo remarked: "The company *had* responded. They retained 252 *compañeros* from the second shift. You say you want guaranteed work but fewer variations in models. But you worked under the old piece-rate system and know that those who work harder, earn more. Let's not scorn variation." He continued his speech:

> On average 2,000 suits were made [per day] last year with 1,432 workers. We didn't reach the 2,300 and we had plenty of workers. But the teams would say they had bottlenecks, so more workers were sent in to help. In the year 2000, the plant worked at 70 percent. So everybody here is to blame. All sides failed to respond, some more than others.

Immediately workers countered that, in 1999 and 2000, they had each received a bonus of $320 pesos on average; this translated to having produced around 200 extra suits daily. So, how was it possible that they were not reaching their quota? Once again, many workers argued that material shortages—not their lack of effort—were the main cause of suboptimal production levels. As one worker put it "The system started to fall apart, when [work] pieces did not appear on the shop floor."

Bolstering his position, Reynaldo pointed out the many ways workers subverted teamwork. For example, he said, "The *compañeros* in the finished products department wouldn't process more than 3,000 suits [per] day because it didn't garner an incentive. So they went to the other extreme. That's where the problem started." He continued: "Or what about doling out permits that weren't needed. You would say, 'We're self-managed,'" he said with a tone of slight derision, "and gave permits to go see the girlfriend. Teams gave out more permits, [which translates into] more [lost] work hours than ever before."

The union president was pointing out how workers contributed to the company crisis; he persisted: "Let's not complain about what we had a hand in making."

Although Reynaldo included the union in this final admission of shared guilt, his examples and presentation implied that it was mostly the workers' excesses that aggravated the company's financial crisis. Yet his examples show just how out of touch he was with the workforce. While he repeatedly used the male pronoun and form for workers (*compañeros*) and used examples of male workers taking time off to see their *girl*friends, most workers' requests for permits concerned family issues. In reality, permits were mostly requested by and given to mothers so that they could attend to children's health or education.

The meeting ended when Reynaldo pronounced that, on Wednesday, March 14, they would decide whether "to go on strike over soap and towels" or if they were going to fight over wages. Lost benefits and broken promises, he implied, were not legitimate reasons for a strike. He also forwarded a message from the company: they had a limited amount of capital. If workers were not in agreement, the firm was considering closing the factory and beginning negotiations over severance compensation. A resounding "Yes!" was heard. Vicki leaned over to me and said, "For what we are making now, yeah!" The expectation that if workers were fired they would be compensated lowered the perceived cost of striking.

This brought Saturday's assembly to a close. Another assembly was scheduled for the following Wednesday. Throughout the week leading up to that day, my new teammates in the J-1 department, who welcomed me despite the tense situation, kept warning, "Keep your guard up. Careful today." "Careful of whom?" I asked. Their answer: the union. The workers were going to call their bluff and demand a strike. To do so, they had to remain united, stand their ground.

As I had been completely involved in the evolving situation, I followed my new teammates to the union meeting. This time, however, I was turned away at the door by Reynaldo. "Sorry," he said, grinning, "I have no problem with you coming in but it's against the rules. You're *not* a worker." His smile was utterly unconvincing. My new teammates, with whom I had already become close, complained but to no avail.

Early the next morning, María, a neighbor and coworker with whom I took the bus to work every day, gave me a blow-by-blow account of the meeting. With her permission, I taped the conversation. María had become a good friend, a key ally, and an invaluable source of information.

Apparently, the decision to strike was relatively uncontested. María explained that the workers were ready to call a strike with or without the union. At the start of Wednesday's assembly, Reynaldo relayed the message that the company had nothing to give. The response from the women, according to María, was to strike. "How long did it take to reach that decision?" I prodded. "Seconds." "Seconds?" I marveled. "How did you get the union to go along?" Maria recounted the events. The union, challenged through reason and insults, did not have a choice. In fact, after the union made their introductory comments, the workers would not let them speak. They were silenced with gendered hoots and jeers. The union lost control of the meeting.

Still in disbelief, I asked María how things happened so quickly. "We decided seconds after entering [the meeting]. We gave no more thought to it. What happened is that all the workers were so furious—since two weeks ago and before [that]," she said. "[Those] from the pressing department already had red shirts on."

The cutting department, however, was not ready to go on strike. The few voices of dissent heard were from them. When I asked María why this was, she responded this way:

> One girl [sic] from cutting spoke and said she wasn't in agreement with the strike. Then we all answered, "Okay, you're not in agreement with going on strike because you earn [more] than we do." We, who are in teams, are making $150 or $200 [pesos per week]. Well, the truth is that it's just not in our interest; not at all. And we kept going at it until, in the end, people just kicked that girl [sic] out. They told her to leave. And that if there was a strike she had to support it in spite of what she said. She said she was a single mother with two kids. "You're better off than us. At least you make more, whether a single mother or not," we all said.[8]

I spoke to other workers who confirmed María's version of events. Her recollection of the heated exchange at the union meeting points to several important matters. First, one of the key issues that convinced workers to go on strike and to suspend their consent was that those who worked in teams were, at this point, earning very low wages, while those still at piece rate were taking home considerably higher amounts of money. Although cutting had theoretically been scheduled to be the last department to change over to teams, it had not yet occurred.

No matter the reasons, the fact that cutting was still doing piecework, yet earned more money, had the unintended consequence of radicalizing those in teams. Those organized in teams did take home sizable paychecks at one point, but this was no longer true. With wages now so low and management taking drastic and unilateral steps to curtail the autonomy of workers, it was clear that the company had no intention of guaranteeing a better source of livelihood, as promised.

The second point raised from Wednesday's assembly relates to the discourse around single motherhood. As discussed previously in chapter 2, the firm recognized that workers would have children at some point, so they hired women—married or single—who had family support for dealing with childcare. In general, the women hired either lived with family or close to family. Nevertheless, management consistently reminded workers that, according to HR, 70 percent of them were so-called vulnerable single mothers in need of everyone's help.

The worker files that I examined painted a different picture. Of the 913 women employed during the fall of 2001, only 270 were single, divorced, or widowed mothers. This means that only 30 percent of the women at Moctezuma were indeed single mothers (See table A.1 in Appendix A). This breakdown is similar to the composition in the two teams I worked in. Although the jackets team had an unusually large number of male workers, only 14 percent of team members overall were male. Of the women, 35 percent were married with children, 23 percent were single and childless, and 38 percent were single mothers. Only one was married without children.

Yet there was great variation among single mothers with whom I worked. Of the ten single mothers in the two teams, three young women had young children and lived in extended households; three were older women with teenage children, who took care of themselves; and one lived alone with her young children. The latter case is the only one that even approached the image of defenselessness. Although ten cases are not sufficient to draw any conclusions, they suggest that single mothers were not as economically desperate as proclaimed by managers and some workers. The term *single mothers* masked a great deal of variation in terms of economic and living situations.

In Mexico more generally, single female-headed households represented 21 percent of households in 2000 (Chant 2007). Mexican gender ideologies depict single mothers as the most vulnerable members of society, living in extreme poverty, and responsible for the next generation's stunted mobility (Ariza and de Oliveira 2001; Nehring 2005). Research, however, shows that the poorest households are those headed by men who are chronically unemployed but follow cultural conventions that prohibit wives and daughters from working outside the home. Female-headed households, in contrast, often include extended family and multiple-wage earners, which decreases the dependency on any one person. Moreover, while single female-headed households may have fewer resources, women have greater power to decide how those resources will be distributed (Chant 2007). Comparing female- and male-headed households during the 1990s economic crisis in Mexico, González de la Rocha found that the female-headed households were better able to protect the nutritional and health priorities of families, which exhibited less drastic change in diets, less violence, and more equal distribution of responsibilities (2006).

Managers employed the term *single mothers* to reinforce the ideology that women's primary responsibility was to the home. In the case of Moctezuma, in drawing from larger Mexican gender conventions that mark single mothers as the most vulnerable and weak members of society, the firm portrayed itself as their paternalist benefactor. The message given to all workers, but especially to single mothers, was that they should be thankful for having such a munificent employer. Given the kindness of the firm, then, it was incumbent on the rest of the workers to protect Moctezuma's survival in the name of the family's so-called weakest members.

While women internalized the same gender ideologies, a process of contestation began to take shape as some workers strategically used the term "single mothers" to their benefit. I witnessed interactions in which workers described themselves as single mothers to extract demands from management. That is, they made the case that *because* they were *mostly* single mothers, workers deserved special economic considerations such as bonuses and paid vacations. Comments included things like "They [the firm] have to pay us more. The single mothers among us can't survive without [this increase]." While management constructed the workforce as single mothers who needed protection, workers turned the construct around to demand material benefits.

The discourse around single motherhood became an ideological battleground between workers and managers, each vying for a moral high ground to justify their demands. Workers appropriated the term to contest management's power and to point out the discrepancy between the promises of a good family job and the reality of decreasing wages. Vallas similarly shows how workers at pulp mills who partially converted to teamwork used the rhetorical framework of participation to contest managerial authority (2003a).

The use of *single motherhood* as a discursive form of resistance was problematic. The term was utilized by workers to mean different things. For some it conveyed the need to focus on work, not organizing. For others, single motherhood expressed the strength and principled stance of women against management. By using the term, these workers made the point that management's treatment of workers had been so immoral, single mothers—the most vulnerable in the factory—had found it necessary to fight back. Both uses, however, reinscribed motherhood as women's primary role. Yet this identity revolved around shifting individual and collective demands that provided a weak basis for collective action (Hossfeld 1990).

While I understood the anger and sense of betrayal on the part of workers, a strike still seemed a risky proposition to me. Thus I continued to prod my friend María. Nearing the factory, I asked her, "Do you really think the company is going to negotiate today?" Her response was very telling:

> The truth is we don't know what the company will do. As someone said, the same could happen to us as at the ammunition factory: that they fire us all, have to pay severance, and begin hiring new personnel again. We are risking that. But the union told us that, in this case, [the company] would compensate at 100 percent. That's what they said, that they would fight for that. And if the company wants to hire people, I guess it will be at the lowest possible wage. . . . As far as I understand, the company is in debt with everyone. They haven't paid INFONAVIT [the National Workers' Housing Fund] nor IMSS [the Mexican Social Security System]. As a [matter of] principle, we're going to fight for everything. But, as Reynaldo said, if the boat sinks, we all go down. Let's see what happens.

While going on strike at first appeared irrational given the lack of good jobs in the area, workers were actually making a cost-benefit analysis, interpreting the costs and benefits from their particular vantage point as working mothers.

If they accepted the company's proposal, they would make less (already a meager sum in their eyes) and lose leverage to negotiate with the company. If they went on strike, the outcome was uncertain. However, knowing pertinent portions of the Federal Labor Law, workers were cognizant that the company had to liquidate all its possessions to pay severance compensation to workers. According to bankruptcy laws, the company could not just close its doors. As such, it was really a choice between two poor options: keep an increasingly difficult job or at least receive compensation and look for another job.

The crux of the matter was their interpretation of managerial actions. Most workers expected management to share the costs of keeping the company afloat. But managerial disorganization, as well as underhanded tactics to cut workers wages and benefits, eroded their trust in management. As Moctezuma's community of fate unraveled, workers came to see that, despite the discourse of family and shared responsibility for company success, the firm cut into workers' wages whenever it encountered economic difficulties.

For my teammates, it was their worst fear confirmed: management had been wolves in sheep's clothing all along. The sense of personal betrayal was palpable. The team leader from J-1 expressed it this way: "They fucked us over. I don't care if I lose my job; I'm going to get back at them!" There is no doubt that workers believed that the firm mismanaged the company. However, now that workers personally experienced management's duplicity, retracting their consent was not enough. A strike went beyond resistance to confrontation.

The likelihood of a strike meant that I needed to make some decisions of my own. Management had given me access to the factory to conduct my research, but, given both my identification with workers and my personal politics, I was unwilling to cross a picket a line. This was the end of my study, I thought. I told María about my dilemma. She said, "Just tell the managers you need to continue your study." Other coworkers suggested the same.

I was on my way to the HR office when I met Belinda, the director's assistant, in the hallway. We huddled into a corner of the hallway to talk. "I have a dilemma," I explained. "You know that I'm studying how workers experience teams." She nodded. I continued, whispering nervously, "Well, they're going on strike today. And I want to go out with them but I'm afraid that the company will then lock me out." To my surprise, she had an answer ready for me, as if my presence on the shop floor had already been discussed by management. "We know. You go out with the workers and then maybe you can give us more information later." My face must have turned red because my cheeks felt like they were on fire. I muttered, "But you know that all of my interviews are confidential." She was asking me to snitch, which I would not do. "Yeah, that's okay," she replied. Our conversation ended with this ambiguous response. I do not know if she still expected me to give her information, but I knew that I had at least bought myself a bit more time at the factory. I went back to my team and continued ironing.

## CONCLUSION

This chapter explains how the breakdown in the social pact between management and workers at Moctezuma led to a strike. While most workers agreed to exchange augmented effort for increased wages and benefits, consent was not unconditional. Workers' consent was based on the expectation of reciprocal obligations.

At the end of February 2001, management broke some key rules: they unilaterally fired the second shift, encroached on team autonomy by placing second-shift workers into the first shift, eliminated production-quality bonuses, refused to unfreeze loaned benefits (offered in good faith by the workers), and, finally, they began legal proceedings to void parts of the workers' contract without consulting workers. These actions undermined management's efforts to cast Moctezuma as a family.

By recounting the details of worker deliberations and organizing strategies, I have made three interrelated arguments. First, teams offered an established communication and decision-making network used effectively by workers for their own interests when deciding mobilization strategies. In addition, the act of organizing by team strengthened solidarity and helped create a new identity from which women mobilized.

Second, in the process of rallying against management, women workers' perception of their own interests and relationship with the firm changed. While previously women tended to identify primarily as *mothers who worked*, their fight against management's injustice shifted their identities to *workers who were mothers*. As mothers, their role was to provide for the family; as workers, to defend their right to work under fair conditions. As they knew all too well, children could not be fed and clothed without a decent job; the two were inseparable.

Third, this chapter demonstrates the importance of gendered language as a terrain of struggle. Management and the union marshaled gendered images and language to support their role as patriarchal benefactors and that of workers as vulnerable women needing protection; however, workers strategically used their status as women both to extract benefits and to subvert relations of power. By underscoring the prevalence of single mothers on the shop floor, women workers asserted the righteous nature of the struggle and the inherent solidarity and strength of mothers; in doing so, they also questioned the masculinity of unjust male union leaders and managers.

In the month leading up the strike, grievances took on new meaning as workers reinterpreted managers having used the economic crisis of the firm and global competition to change the rules of the game in an unjust manner. Moral outrage and feelings of betrayal transformed individual resistance into collective action, which rapidly coalesced into a strike and worker mobilization.

CHAPTER 6

# The Strike

## FROM MOTHERHOOD TO WORKERS' RIGHTS

On March 15, 2001, at 3 P.M. sharp, the workers of Moctezuma walked out on strike. The strike committee, a group of men and women chosen at the last union assembly meeting before the strike, rallied workers at the loading dock. They told workers to guard every entrance and exit so that machines could not be taken out, to go and "defend our turf." Some machines, which the firm likely destined for work outsourced to workshops during the strike, had already been removed during the lunch break. I joined my new team in the back of the factory. Production managers were making the rounds of the empty shop floor, cordially greeting the few of us standing guard inside. By 6 P.M., we all gathered back outside for an update. There had not been any resolution yet. It was decided that workers should stay outside by the front gates, with smaller groups standing guard at entry points.

Administrative personnel were relocating from the Moctezuma offices, moving desks and filing cabinets to the building next door, the sister textile firm, Italia. Ana and other workers from pants stood in their way; my teammates put up a fight while yelling that the administrative personnel had no right to remove things from the factory. I overheard Belinda, the human resources (HR) recruiter, who was my liaison with management, say to a group of workers: "It doesn't have to be this way. We both want to win, but we don't want to be against each other." A top manager from the HR office, known for his aggressive manner, began to take pictures of the workers hovering around the firm entrance. Workers wondered why he needed pictures, telling each other to be careful.

In the meantime, other workers debated the correct procedure for declaring a strike. A brief scuffle occurred as some workers hung up a red-and-black banner on the gate and the aggressive manager pulled it down brusquely. Workers did not seem to know what to do, but they all agreed that management should treat them with respect. The mood at the factory while the strike committee, union, company, and state arbiter met at the local conciliation and arbitration board (LCAB) was tense but hopeful.

142

Discussions about putting up the flag continued. Some workers had called friends that worked at the nearby large Japanese auto plant. The word from their union was that what "our" union officials told us was wrong; the red-and-black flag *had* to be raised. Then a man's voice over the loudspeaker instructed pregnant women to go home. The remaining women would be allowed to leave in the evening; the men would stand guard over the factory all night. An informational meeting would take place at 7 A.M. the next day. We waited in the parking lot, between the two factory gates. Several workers who had only now heard of my study approached me. Some were wary of my presence; others thanked me for being there.

The next morning, workers were organized into guard shifts that would be covered by different teams. Assignments streamed over the megaphone: "Team one, guard HR; team two, go to the back entrance, team three, the warehouse." One of my new teammates grabbed my arm, "C'mon," she said, "that's us." I protested, uncertain if I could or should participate. She replied, "Well, you *are* part of our team, right?" This was enough to convince me, though I was nervous when we had to show our company identification to pass the first gates. My I.D. badge, which I always wore around my neck like everyone else, specified "employee"—not worker—on it. As employees were either middle management or administrative assistants, I did not expect to pass beyond this point. But the guards allowed me to enter.

## UNDERSTANDING THE STRIKE THROUGH WOMEN'S WORDS AND ACTIONS

Our post was immediately inside the gates. Ironically, I found myself guarding the doors to HR, the very authority that had given me permission to conduct research. I shared the irony with my teammates. During the *guardia* (guard shift), the ten of us—all women—sat underneath a palm tree and talked about our lives, hopes, scary stories, jokes; anything we could think of, really, as twelve hours was a long time. I had the digital recorder used for interviews with me and asked if I could record the conversations. Although I had only been with this team for five days, my sense of belonging was already strong enough that I dared ask. They readily accepted and spoke freely. The discussion centered around four issues: the law and state involvement, reasons for the mobilization, preferred outcomes of the strike, and solidarity.

### Deciphering the Role of the State

The shift began with discussions of the law: what was necessary to declare a strike? Several of my new teammates had called lawyers; others were in contact with the strike committee. Still there was no agreement. Irene, a utility worker who would later be elected to the new democratic union, was in contact with a strike committee member who was at the LCAB. He told her that the state arbiter called the worker's actions a work stoppage, not a strike. The arbiter said that, if negotiations were not successful, a notary would be called in to declare a strike. However, the deadline for negotiations kept changing, and that made workers nervous.

The role of the LCAB was also unclear. Irene gave us updates from her friend Miguel in the strike committee: "[He] said Conciliation [shorthand for LCAB] is trying to make the company see their actions are mistaken; this is a contract revision not a salary negotiation." Fernanda interrupted, "That's what my lawyer said. They [the company] should negotiate." Irene continued: "The governor's second in command, the undersecretary for labor, has arrived [at the negotiations]. The government doesn't want a strike because it would affect many families. Their job is to encourage employment, not unemployment; that is why they want the firm to settle." One recently married coworker said, "If the company will not give us anything [severance pay], Conciliation will help us." Importantly, the women believed that the labor authorities were protecting workers' interests; the LCAB was on their side. Many workers noted how they had voted for the center-right National Action Party (PAN) government, which had broken seventy-one years of uninterrupted rule by one party at the national and local level. They hoped this government would be different.

### "We Fight for Our Children"

At this point of the worker mobilization, one day into the strike, the company and union were seen as the enemy. This was reaffirmed when the majority owner of Moctezuma came to check on the factory installations. Everyone in my team and a couple other workers nearby swarmed him, leaving me behind to guard the door to HR.[1] My teammates challenged him assertively: "What the company gives us [wages] is not enough for anything! It's not even enough for our kids!" To this the majority owner, a tall and heavyset blond man with blue eyes, abruptly responded: "I like to be spoken to face to face. Who is talking to me?" My *compañeras* proudly recounted how one of them pushed her way to the front and said "I am!" The women laughed when they told me this.

They continued telling me about the encounter with the owner: "Then, another woman asserted, 'I'm not begging for anything but demanding what's *rightfully* mine. How much money do you spend on gasoline? I bet you spend more than our entire salaries! We don't want money for our car. We want it to provide for our children.'" Taken aback by the women's combativeness, the owner responded that talking would be a more appropriate way to negotiate than taking over other people's property. With this, he left. My teammates were not convinced by his argument. Once back with the team, one woman joked, "I *do* want it for gas, [only] for my kitchen—I don't have any left!" Uncontrolled laughter followed.

For the women, this exchange articulated precisely why they were striking: the right to earn enough to provide for their children. They deployed their identity as mothers to convince the owner that their work grievances were real and fair. Back on the grass, keeping guard over the HR entrance, I recorded the following conversation between Fernanda and Chela:

> FERNANDA: I bet he [the owner] spends thousands of pesos on gasoline and restaurants. But we're only asking for 300 pesos. Three hundred pesos disappear quickly. And the kids? They don't understand. They need food, clothes, shoes to go to school.
>
> CHELA: Yeah, my little one . . . knows we keep the milk in the fridge. So he goes to the fridge and says, "Milk, milk." He doesn't know there isn't any milk.
>
> FERNANDA: What are you going to tell him? That there isn't money? Kids don't understand. We just want what is just for the worker. No more, no less. Only what is just.

Both Chela and Fernanda were mothers, but their opinions were not unique. Chela and her two-year-old son lived with her parents. Fernanda and her husband, who fixed shoes on the street earning a quarter of her salary, lived in his parent's apartment with their two kids, his parents, and his brother's family. Just like their teammates, their families depended on the wages they brought home. The inability to fulfill their motherly duties transformed Fernanda and many other women into fervent advocates for their rights as workers.

As time passed that day with no word from the strike committee, the distrust of the union grew, further fueling discontent.[2] Both the union and the strike committee were at the LCAB, with the business agent acting as their legal adviser. This worried workers. One worker commented how the strike committee, also in contact with the union leader of a nearby Japanese auto plant, had already discovered that the business agent was providing contradictory information. In fact, the auto plant leader straightforwardly said, "He [the business agent] is telling you lies."

From our vantage point on the inside of the factory gate, we could see the rest of the workers milling around the parking lot, awaiting word on the negotiations. Several times workers voted on issues, such as what to do next, by a show of hands (see figure 6.1). During one of the votes, an older woman in her sixties called us over to the fence. Two *compañeras* went over to see what she wanted. She had brought boiled eggs, hot tortillas, and rice for our team. "Just a little food for you; it's all I have," she said. Our team was touched by the gesture, energized by the show of solidarity by the *abuelita* (grandmother).

Late in the evening, jackets two (J-2) broke up into teams to take over the next guard shift. Then it was our turn to mill around the parking lot. As the sun set, people huddled into cars for warmth; others laid blankets on the concrete to sleep. María had told me to come prepared, so I had; like others, I had brought blankets. I spent that night with several of my pants teammates, talking and joking as we awaited resolution to the strike. Since I had my recorder, I was also able to tape conversations after obtaining permission from individual

Figure 6.1. Decision making during the strike: voting through a show of hands, March 16, 2001. Photograph by author. Photograph taken with permission from top management at Moctezuma.

workers. A feeling of camaraderie filled the air. Music blasted from cars; some women danced. The carnival atmosphere belied the fact that workers had taken over the factory. However, this is not that unusual; euphoria is a common feeling among those involved in collective action (Zolberg 1972). I spent most of the night talking and joking with coworkers.

### Preferred Mobilization Outcomes

As we sat on the cold asphalt of the parking lot, I asked Silvia, a married worker who lived in government housing, her opinion of the union. She replied, "Well, I don't think the union is going to back us up. In fact, they already gave in. It's as if there were no union. . . . The business agent has already shown he's with the company. In reality, workers are on their own. Really, we are alone." Lupe added, "I think they're afraid, or I don't know what is wrong with them. They are like kids who are playing around. For them this is a game." Over and again that night, women workers portrayed themselves as responsible parents and the union as immature children.

As discussion continued, it was apparent that most workers' preferred resolution would be for the company to fire workers and compensate them according to the law. Then, if the company wanted to hire anyone back even if at lower wages, workers could decide what to do. From the women's point of view, then, both workers and the company could move on. At one point, a quiet young single woman said, "I just want them to fire us and give us our severance pay. That's all. I can't endure any longer at this wage." Another responded: "We're in this fight now, whether to win or lose. I hope we win but I'm willing to lose. The only thing that worries me is that we're sacrificing our families. I haven't seen my baby in a day and my husband is angry at me. And we might not get anything in the end, not even our savings." To this, I noted, "But, by law, you have to be compensated." Her reply spoke volumes: "Yeah, the law—who respects the law?"

### Building Solidarity

As the night progressed, several men who worked at the Moctezuma's sister company, Italia, stopped by to show support. One of them was Silvia's neighbor. The conversation when they arrived had been on decreasing wages and paycheck deductions. Right away one of the men, who was drunk, said, "Many people don't understand the deductions and payroll tax. You're confusing matters. You're including all your deductions and complaining about paying $4.50 pesos for cafeteria." To this, one of the younger female workers retorted, "Yes, but *you* make $2,000 pesos." "No," he replied, "I make $4,000 pesos [around U.S.$450] monthly." The women gasped; the men made twice as much as they did. Another male worker added, "You don't understand. The company isn't dumb. It's going to take away bonuses not wages."

Interrupting the conversation, a female voice over the loudspeaker asked the striking workers: "We have a question. Should we accept [a deal]?" "No! No!" was the general response. The woman's voice proceeded: "I'm in agreement that we shouldn't lose what we have fought for, but compensation talks can take a long time. It could be months, even years. We have to keep up the guard shifts all the time. We have to take turns. We have been here without bathing, without seeing our kids and some already want to go home. Are you ready for this?" The workers emphatically yelled, "Yes!" "Then we have to be organized. We can't start fighting each other. It's not going to be easy. It could be years. We'll organize by department teams. Raise your hand if you want to continue?" At this point, workers were shouting, "We are a majority! All of us!" The women I was with yelled out, "Yes! Yes!" Then different teams were called up to the front to start organizing more guard shifts. For the rest of the evening, my teammates and the other workers nearby discussed the details of striking.

### The Strike Is Broken

Around seven o'clock in the morning workers received the news that the union had signed a contract with the company at 3 A.M. on Sunday, March 18. By that time, workers had taken over the factory grounds for fifty-seven hours through rolling shifts—though, for the last thirty-six hours, everyone had been asked to stay. The strike committee arrived at the factory to inform striking workers how the union and company signed a contract against their wishes. Then, the same labor arbiter who had been pushing for negotiations declared the strike illegal: either return to work or be fired.

Half awake, cold, and hungry, the workers loudly protested as the union president explained the new contract. While vacation and *aguinaldo* stayed the same, there would no longer be bonuses, suits for marriages, or money for babies; moreover, the company would provide $85 pesos (U.S.$9.44) toward savings accounts, marking a reduction from the old contract for most, where the company provided 13 percent of wages toward savings accounts. More important, he said, there would be a base weekly wage of $482 pesos (U.S.$53.50), but the company would pay $800 pesos from now until June 2001. However, if workers reached production goals in May and June, this higher wage could remain. The company's offering of such a high wage, in spite of a purported financial crisis, points to how regaining control of the workers was of primary interest to the firm at this time.

Workers booed the union, yelling that they had sold out. Disillusion and anger spread as workers said that they would come back to work the next day but the fight against the company was not over. The first thing to do was to change the union. I later found out that many workers spent that Sunday networking with other unions, calling labor lawyers to question the validity of the new contract, strategizing for the next steps. What the workers did not count on is that the state would side with the company, breaking local, state, and federal laws as it "arbitrated the dispute."

## THE IMMEDIATE AFTERMATH: BEYOND THE FIRM

March 19, 2001, was the first day back at work after the failed strike. Top managers stared down workers as they showed their I.D. badges to enter the factory. Inside, there was a hum of voices as workers reflected on the weekend's events. One of the older women in my new team said, "We have no pride, we came back in with our tails between our legs." Another responded, "We lost the benefits but nothing else has changed." Chela, a single mother who lived nearby in her parent's home, said she wanted to quit but refused to give up her severance pay; she had worked at the company for seven years. She was willing to pay for a lawyer in order to leave with her severance package, even if he claimed 20 percent of the amount. After these fighting sentiments, she stated, "I feel defeated inside." Lupe, one of the older women in the group who traveled two hours daily just to get to work, vocalized a feeling many later expressed, "It was worth it just to see the people so united, but we got nothing. You can't pay the bus with food coupons. You can only buy food and, in a year, they'll take that away too!" Juan, the team leader chimed in: "Now it's not just against the company but also against the union."

Most workers wanted to continue the fight. The issue that resonated most with my teammates in jackets and pants was how to topple the union, which they believed had sold them out. For this purpose, meetings were called almost every day after work to discuss how to decertify the union and install their own independent democratic union.[3] Labor lawyers often arrived at these meetings; they offered their services, promising quick results.

### Mobilizing Dissent Inside and Outside the Factory

On that first day back, a massive meeting took place after work at a nearby park. With the strike committee as the movement leaders, it was decided that everyone would work at 50 percent capacity to protest the agreement made by the firm and the union. The next day, handwritten notes were passed from person to person, spreading the word about this new strategy. Notes also included names of the people believed to be on the company's side; they were to be left out of the loop.

Management was quick to respond to the work slowdown. Several of my teammates received reprimands for low efficiency. Advisers moved frantically on the shop floor, demanding workers to produce at 100 percent efficiency. When this tactic failed, workers were called individually into departmental offices, where they faced managements' questions: Did they not understand the repercussions of stalling production? Why did they insist on ruining the company? Were they willing to risk their jobs? Workers understood that they were being intimidated.

Team leaders were responsible for enforcing the work slowdown. They assiduously watched over production numbers and pressed workers to participate. Juan kept a close eye on each worker, congratulating them for working at 50 percent or cussing them out if they exceeded this level. While Juan's style was on the aggressive side, all team leaders monitored production on the shop floor and achieved widespread compliance from workers—a fairly remarkably feat given the increase in managerial threats. Workers sustained the work action for eight weeks.[4] While supply shortages contributed to lowered production, it was workers' solidarity that prolonged the labor action.

Throughout all of this, the workers' organizing of meetings continued after work. At one of these meetings, only two days after the strike, a coworker asked me to tape the lawyer who had come to offer his services. This turned out to be a decisive moment in my time as a participant-observer. Since I was conducting interviews after work, my teammates knew I carried a digital recorder. Caught up in the movement and camaraderie, I began taping. Another worker looked at me and noted, "She's not a worker. Why is she taping?" "She works for the company!" charged another. I heard others say, "No, she supports us! She's *not* a company spy." One of the strike committee members requested that I leave; as I complied, a shouting match ensued between those that wanted me out and those that knew me to be loyal to the workers. Despite my labor sympathies, the workers' mistrust was well founded: there were company spies everywhere. At that moment, I had transgressed the ambiguous line between participant and observer.

Getting myself kicked out of the meeting that day changed the way I conducted research. I left the meeting under the big jacaranda tree in the supermarket parking lot. Tears of frustration, sadness, and shame overwhelmed me as workers fought over my true allegiance. Two women from pants came over and hugged me, assuring those around us that I was carrying out a study for an educational degree. Elena, who only had a grade school education, shouted at the doubtful: "She's just trying to improve herself! Isn't that what we all want to do?" During this tense time, my presence seemed to aggravate relations between workers and hinder mobilization efforts. Thus, I decided to continue to go to work every day, but I no longer participated in any meetings outside the factory or worker mobilizations.[5] Despite this wonderful show of camaraderie, work on the shop floor became more and more difficult as increased pressure and control by managers further fractured the solidarity among workers.[6]

### Electing a Democratic Union

A week after the strike, on March 22, workers overwhelmingly voted to install a new union, composed now of the leaders who had emerged during the strike.[7] The majority of the new union was male, with women holding subordinate offices. However, workers commented how the new union president, Pedro, was completely different from Reynaldo. He worked in final pressing and, during the strike, had spoken with such emotion about the unjust character of management actions that he had cried in public. He asserted what others were feeling: "We're not rebellious people. We're just defending our rights!" His tears evidenced a different form of masculinity, a heartfelt solidarity with women workers that Reynaldo lacked.

Electing new union leadership was the first step in representing the newly aligned workers. But, at this juncture, it proved very challenging to officially replace the existing union; they refused to convene an assembly in which workers could vote in favor of a new union committee. In response, the workers marched downtown to the labor authorities' offices to demand the change, but to no avail. Day after day, workers would march three miles after their long workday to the state capitol to make their plea. On their own initiative, a group of women workers went to a local morning radio show on March 27; there, they denounced the union for "selling out" to the company, and noted how the LCAB was dragging its feet in certifying the new union. When these workers returned to the factory, the company fired them. Several of the workers labored in J-2, which began a work stoppage that spread to the whole shop floor.

Finally, on March 29, under pressure from workers, the discredited union called a general assembly. The old leadership was ousted and the new union ratified while fifty police officers stood outside the assembly hall. By this time, the democratically elected union had also selected a new business agent, Mr. Ramos. He had been the only labor lawyer who had agreed that mobilizations could complement legal procedures to fight the company. (Interestingly, the new business agent had been one of the previous auto union leaders fired during the 1970s wave of independent unionism in the area. After being elected general secretary, he had ruled the auto union with an iron grip for over a decade. During that time, he had favored improving his membership's economic position over participating in the larger independent union movement; see Martínez Cruz 2000; Rendón Galicia 2008.)

The following day, the new union and business agent began the legal process to demand the union's registration with labor authorities. They attempted to enter the factory grounds to consult with workers, but the company refused them entry. Now, running from one state agency to the other, the new union circumvented management's forced segregation from the workers by contacting key team leaders through cellular phone calls. Although not permitted, these team leaders ducked under tables or into bathrooms to take the calls, passing information through team networks. When the shift ended that day, over seven hundred workers (of the nine hundred left at the factory) marched downtown, where they demanded to speak with the governor. The new union committee, which was not affiliated with any formal union, sat down to negotiate with top state leaders. The governor's assistant sent a formal request for the deposed union committee to step down. It was ignored. Nothing happened.

### Using Teams to Organize Mobilizations

Team structure was a key, effective tool for communication and strategizing during this period. Team leaders and utility workers, whose job description allowed them to move around the shop floor, were used to communicate and plan events. For example, the day the new union was locked out of Moctezuma they asked team leaders to collect workers' signatures and I.D.s for the union to be certified. Juan coordinated the retrieval for the jackets one (J-1) department. The democratically elected union then went to the labor authorities with more than the requisite two-thirds of union members' signatures necessary for certification, but still the authorities refused to acknowledge them as the official union. It should be noted that more than three-fourths of the workforce supported this action; this show of support was undoubtedly enhanced since the petition circulated during team meetings, where dissent was made public.

Team structure was also used to both mobilize and solve the free-rider problem in marches. Just as with guard shifts, marches were organized through teams. Team leaders passed down information to their team members. The team leader collected worker I.D.s, which would then be returned at the end of the demonstration. If workers did not stay until the end, they could not use their I.D.s to enter the factory the next day. This, together with workers' indignation at management's unjust treatment since the strike, secured a strong show of force during the many street demonstrations.

### Stopping Traffic to Talk to the Governor

Meanwhile, management persisted with its intimidation of workers on the shop floor, calling them one by one to the office to discuss efficiencies and political activities, at times officially reprimanding workers for "insubordination" (see Appendix C). Talks with the labor authorities were going nowhere. The newspapers reported that the secretary of labor, the official in charge of all labor matters for the governor's office and to whom the LCAB president reported, had until recently sat on Moctezuma's board of directors.[8] Outraged with the conflict of interests of state negotiators and the improper denial of union certification, workers decided to block one of the main city avenues when the shift ended.

Figure 6.2. Blocking traffic to demand a meeting with the governor, April 4, 2001. Photo by Tizoc Cuellar, *La Jornada*, April 4, 2001.

That day was April 4. Workers demanded that the governor and labor arbiter meet with them to certify the newly elected union leadership. Instead, the governor sent in over 250 military police, local police, and federal judicial police—each force armed with clubs, dogs, and tear gas—to break up the sit-in protest (see figures 6.2 and 6.3). A dozen people were hospitalized, including a pregnant woman; another dozen were arrested. The governor never showed. Marta, whose experience that day later inspired her to become a movement leader, explained the sit-in:

> It was a spontaneous action. We didn't have any signs ready. We just decided to do it. I was with Pedro [new union general secretary]. The patrol cars were there. They told us to move. We said we wouldn't move. [The police] said they would hit us. Pedro and Mr. Ramos wanted us to move. But I said, "No, they'll have to kick me out."

When workers returned to work the next morning, over thirty military police in full riot gear lined the company entrance. That morning, my mother insisted on taking María, a neighbor and coworker, and me to the factory. Lots of other parents were there; husbands, too. We had to walk between two rows of military police holding batons and shields and wearing gas masks just to pass through the

Figure 6.3. State repression of workers' sit-in, April 4, 2001. Photo by Tizoc Cuellar, *La Jornada*, April 5, 2001.

outside gates. Workers waited in the parking lot between the two gates until 7 A.M., when the shift began. Confused, we lined up, showed our I.D. cards, and entered the factory gates; as we passed, again, the HR director stared each one of us down. Parents and husbands returned home.

On the shop floor workers checked on each other, sharing stories of how they escaped the attack and finding out who was missing and hurt. We learned that a group of workers had kept the new union leaders and the business agent out of harm's way, keeping them in hiding all night for fear of more reprisals. The rest had stood up to the police, all the while singing the national anthem. Later that day a group of women workers went to the state congress, asking the left-center Democratic Revolution Party (PRD) to support their cause.

### Repression Opens New Doors

This event marked a turning point for the workers' mobilization for several reasons. First, the print, television, and radio coverage widely publicized details of the strike, harassment by management, and state complicity.[9] Among the details made public was the secretary of labor's close connections with the firm. Moreover, it was made known that the majority owner of the company, the man my teammates had confronted during the guard shift, had been the beneficiary of $168 million pesos in a government bailout for another failed business. The combination of police aggression, together with news of government-business complicity and corporate malfeasance decidedly turned public sentiment in favor of the women workers. For example, headlines in the business-oriented newspaper accused the firm of "intransigence" as the cause of the labor dispute. Articles claimed "civil society" was outraged at the violence hurled at "defenseless women and children."

Second, workers took advantage of the publicity to mount a public relations attack on the state and company, invoking collective notions of justice and gendered morality. Symbolically, workers made use of their relative powerlessness as women and workers to underscore the exaggerated and immoral repression by the powerful, the (male) governor who would not meet with them and instead sent riot police. In this way, the workers' wielded symbolic leverage to make moral and material claims (Chun 2009).

Third, the sit-in marked a change in movement strategies as workers capitalized on their notoriety to forge relationships with politicians. A day after the police repression, a group of women visited the PRD in the state congress, lobbying them to support the movement to certify their democratically elected union. In response, both the PRD and the Institutional Revolutionary Party (PRI) openly chastised the LCAB and the company. A week later, both parties proposed a bill to force the LCAB to recognize the workers' union. Although the center-right PAN, which held both the national presidency and the governorship of the state, blocked the bill at first, a weaker version passed unanimously a week later. Throughout the next months, the PRD became an important ally of the workers' movements, providing office supplies, photocopying for leafleting, and a presence at marches.

Fourth, the attention garnered by the workers' bold moves helped build relationships with nongovernmental organizations (NGOs) and local independent unions. The day of the violent retaliation by police, a local human rights group sought out movement leaders to offer support. Several of the female leaders quickly accepted this gesture of solidarity. The close working relationship that developed hinged on a shared experience: one of the founders of the human rights group, Laura, had previously been a worker at Moctezuma and participated in the 1972 strike.

This human rights organization became a bridge between the workers and the larger, independent NGO movement. From this moment on, one of the women from the democratically elected union was designated to attend local weekly meetings of the Civic Coalition, an NGO bringing together sixty organizations.[10] Other studies of women workers in industrializing areas have found that exposure to a politicizing organization is key to transforming acquiescence to resistance (Peña 1997; Young 1987). Participating in the Civic Coalition radically transformed several of Moctezuma's leaders, who moved from focusing on primarily work-related issues to demands for justice for women, workers, and citizens. Nancy Fraser terms this a shift from redistribution to recognition and representation (1997; also see Dahl, Stoltz, and Willig 2004).

Fifth, the police repression radicalized women workers. Most women had previously considered themselves conservative and had voted for the PAN in the recent governor's race. This was the case for Irene, one of the members of the strike committee and a utility worker from my team in J-1. She had been at the factory for thirteen years; her husband worked at the company's textile mill, Italia. When I asked her about her experience with state agents during the strike, she said:

> At first we went to the LCAB, and everybody treated us wonderfully, promising to help us. But they never fulfilled one promise. . . . I voted for the PAN. Now I realize it's not convenient for the governor that there be a strike at a local company, or that it [the company] go broke or disappear. No one will want to invest in the state anymore, so they are watching out for their interests even if that means screwing over workers. Almost all of the politicians are businessmen. [They're] hard on the worker; they think and act like businessmen.

Most workers shared Irene's disappointment with the state's unyielding support of the company. In our conversations, it became clear they had supported the conservative government in the last elections and had expected their support against the company. Yet the stonewalling by labor authorities transformed the viewpoint of the women workers, radicalizing them as they struggled to protect their rights from management's encroachment and the state's complicity with management.

However, public sentiment and local support was not enough to convince state labor authorities to recognize the newly elected union—a recognition needed to officially represent workers. After having been thoroughly criticized in the state congress for inaction, the LCAB promised to certify the union within a few days. A week later, on April 11, the same labor authority officially denied the union recognition. It claimed that the vote to elect union representatives had not been carried out according to union statutes, with the necessary two-week notice, during a prearranged scheduled general assembly, with previously announced slates. In response, seven hundred workers took to the streets, staging a one-and-a-half-hour-long sit-in in front of the government palace. Local human rights groups and other unions joined in.

### Continued Intimidation of Workers on the Shop Floor

Back on the shop floor, management increased worker harassment. The deposed union began a campaign to discredit the workers' movement. They began by accusing two foreigners—myself and the Calvin Klein auditor—on a popular local radio show of being foreign agent provocateurs. At this point, I decided it was best for me to stop working on the shop floor. (I had already been considering this, given the tension caused by my presence.) The Calvin Klein auditor also left.

Everyone knew the company had spies to keep tabs on worker mobilizations. Some workers from other teams thought I was one of them. One day I had to go the cutting department to exchange some articles of clothing. On my way back hisses and insults were hurled at me. I could not help it; tears welled up in my eyes. Several of my teammates from pants saw this and ran to my defense, hugging me and insulting the hecklers back.

On another occasion, when I was assisting Juan at the ironing press, he said, "Let's go drink water in the back." I protested, commenting we had a closer water station. "I want to introduce you to the guys in final pressing. They think you're a spy because they don't know you," he explained. "I told them they're wrong." As we walked to the back of the factory, Juan put his hand on my shoulder as he greeted the other workers by name. As we slowly drank water, we were scrutinized by the workers. Several approached us, and Juan introduced me as a friend and supporter of the movement.

These were difficult and emotional times for me, but, more important, they were disruptive to workers. My teammates from both pants and J-1 went out of their way to defend me instead of concentrating on their own work and movement objectives. My desire to have as little impact on my teammates and other workers was clearly failing. I decided to end the participant observation portion of the study.

At this point, rumors spread that the company would soon close; workers feared Moctezuma would declare bankruptcy in effort to do away with the labor dispute. Not expecting to get a positive response, I asked the top managers if I could have access to production and personnel files. To my surprise, they said yes. On April 9, I worked my last day on the shop floor, although I was still conducting interviews in the afternoons. Since I was doing research in the offices, some workers continued to suspect me as a spy, looking on me with scorn. Others believed me to be an ally, prompting them to come in to chat and update me on the mobilization. Once again, this reflected how divided the workforce remained throughout this period.

One of the utility workers, Raquel, had been elected to the strike committee. I had gotten to know her while we worked in the pants department together. One day, she came to talk to me about what was happening. I learned that the workers had decided to continue working at 50 percent efficiency to protest the lockout of the workers' chosen union. The director of HR had gone out of his way to talk to Raquel while she worked. She wrote down his words so she could tell me what had happened. "Why don't you tell your friends to stop this? I hope you're more intelligent than them. This isn't the way to get something," he said to her. In her typical poised manner, she asked him, "Well, what is the way, sir?" "Working harder; that's what they do in Japan." She responded, "Well, we're not in Japan." With this, he walked off in a huff. Clearly, the manager's frame of reference as to how teamwork should function was the Japanese experience and, most likely, the managerial version of Japanese lean production. But, as discussed earlier, even in Japan, consent was negotiated through stable employment and good pay for core workers.

Days later Raquel phoned me at home to give me an update. She told me that on Monday, April 30, at 3:45 P.M., the entire workforce had been called down to the cafeteria. All levels of managers stood around the perimeter of the cafeteria. The general manager told the workers that the company was upset that a few workers who did not want to work were taking the company under, that anyone who did not want to keep working at the factory should give their names to the managers in the back of the room. Yet even without any workers coming forward to resign, managers were writing down names or pretending to do so. The general manager also accused the independent union of corruption and claimed that the company wanted to negotiate directly with the workers, without any intermediaries.

Then workers were sent back to the shop floor. Immediately, individual workers began to be called over the loudspeaker, summoning them to the departmental offices. Around fifty workers were fired that day—among them Raquel, the entire new union leadership, and the strike committee. Mexican labor law forbids the firing of union leaders, but the state did not castigate or reprimand the firm. Workers found themselves fighting the company and the state without union representation.

### Standing Up for Workers on May Day

The next day was May 1, a holiday where, historically, in Mexico, corporatist unions parade through downtown singing the praises of the government and the 1910 Mexican Revolution. Once before, in 1974, the women of Moctezuma had led a protest march fighting for an independent union. So it was again on May 1, 2001. They led the march with banners accusing the company and the government of repression and corruption, followed by other groups who supported their struggle. Importantly, not only were they given the highly visible and symbolic role of being the first union in the parade, but they were also referenced in many other groups' slogans and banners. Although new to the arena of union struggles, the women quickly became the face of the growing local social movement unionism. (See figure 6.4, one of many marches after work to protest managerial and state complicity.)

Back at the factory the next day, the fired workers were not allowed to reenter. In defiance, over eight hundred and fifty workers embarked on another march downtown. However, this time, approximately one hundred workers broke rank with the protestors and went inside the factory to work. Among those was a teammate from pants, an older worker who had come over from the afternoon shift and who had recently been rotated into the team leader position. In retaliation for going in to work instead of protesting, my teammates from pants harassed her to the point where production was halted. The company fired her. Frida, one of the department advisers, then took over the team leader position. She later complained to me that there were too many details to keep straight; she could barely keep up with the work.

Figure 6.4. Marches after work to demand recognition of independent union, May 2001. Image used in a Human Rights newspaper supplement, titled "Where Are the Women Workers?" Photo by Tizoc Cuellar, *La Jornada*, May 7, 2001.

I learned all this as I sat around a long table with fifteen other *compañeras* as we celebrated Mother's Day at Vicki's house. It was an amazing occasion. Here I was at a party with my teammates from pants who, only a few months earlier, hated each other so much they would not even speak. Now we toasted ourselves as mothers and workers and strategized ways to get the union recognized.

The experience of mobilizing to fight the state and company had transformed many of these women. While it is true that some, like Vicki, had already been more inclined to voice their complaints, others who had not had that self-assurance blossomed. Throughout the months of mobilizations, many discovered they had a voice and strength that they did not know they possessed. My coworkers now expressed a sense of empowerment, an ability to make strategic choices they could not have envisioned earlier.

## Fighting Corporatist and Protection Unions

The sense of empowerment was tested as workers faced new threats, this time from other unions. A month after the strike, the Confederation of Mexican Workers (CTM), one of the strongest corporatist unions, had offered to represent workers given that the LCAB had denied the elected union's petition to be certified on April 11. Two days later, the women voted in an assembly to reject the proposal, citing the CTM's lack of historic interest in the working class.

On May 19, the new union—still locked out—scheduled a general assembly. The day before, members of the CTM leafleted women workers at the end of the shift, trying to dissuade them from going to the general assembly. Moctezuma's management also intensified their intimidation campaign, threatening workers with dismissal if they attended even though the meeting was outside of working hours, on a Saturday. Some workers made it known that the company had offered them $500 pesos (U.S.$55) as a bribe to stay away.

The scheduled election took place with special care, following the statutes to the last detail. In order to counteract any claim of illegality or irregularity, the director of the Department of Labor and Social Welfare and two inspectors were invited to witness the elections. Transparent urns from the 2000 national presidential elections were used to contain the votes. Although ample time and encouragement had been given for an alternate slate to form, none had. The election results were 618 votes in favor of the poststrike leadership, 3 against, and 2 null votes. Meanwhile, harassment continued at the factory. And, the following week, four more workers were fired.

Six days later, management announced that the LCAB was going to certify a union to be headed by a woman worker known to be an ally of the firm. Although there was no vote to elect her and no one else was listed on the executive committee, management intended to install her as the union representation. A march was scheduled for May 31 to protest the firm's imposition of a fake union. Again, management threatened to dismiss any worker who attended. Workers told newspapers of telephone death threats. The uproar that ensued, coming from both workers and social movement organizations, impeded the sham union's certification. Moctezuma workers, accompanied by the Civic Coalition and workers from other factories, staged an overnight sit-in at the labor authority's offices. Even the Housewives Association marched with pots and pans in support of workers. In the end, the LCAB did not file the needed paperwork for the fake union. Management, however, continued trying to install its own union delegate at the factory. By this time, sixty-six workers had been fired since the strike.

Although workers had meticulously followed LCAB and union statutes, state labor authorities continued to block the independent union's certification. A newspaper article quoted a worker commenting in frustration, "Now what's missing?!" Yet another worker was quoted, saying in exasperation, "All we want are our rights" (García Flores 2001).The now twice-elected union, supported by the workers and local social movement groups, redoubled their public protest, staging sit-ins in front of the LCAB offices, marching through downtown streets, and making pronouncements in the media. While workers took to the streets, the director of the Department of Labor and Social Welfare, who had been present at the union election, attempted to fracture worker solidarity by claiming that the union's business agent was advising them incorrectly.

State officials also redoubled their efforts to control the Moctezuma workers as the nearby auto plant's (male) workers threatened to strike over stalled contract negotiations. Fearing the region would lose foreign investment if it appeared to be a site of radical unionism—as happened in 1972—the state clamped down on union struggles even more. With state officials and the company refusing to accept the union democratically elected by workers and continued police intervention, the movement at Moctezuma began to lose strength. Slowly, the number of participants waned; fewer marched downtown, and even fewer showed up at the union meetings.

On June 1, three and a half months after the strike, the newly elected union called a meeting at the electrical workers' offices. Only two hundred workers showed up. After all this time spent fighting both the company and the government, the majority of the members of the new union leadership decided their participation hindered rather than helped the movement. Another slate, chosen from inside the plant, would have a better chance of getting certified, they said. Marta told me how the union leader Pedro cried when he told workers he was stepping down. He said his family begged him to quit; they were afraid for his safety. Unmarked cars followed him everywhere. He had received multiple death threats. This was the last union meeting that took place.

Several of the women from the executive committee refused to give up. Together with other fired workers, including Marta, they formed the resistance committee in struggle (*comité de resistencia en pie de lucha*). They convinced the PRD senators to take their case to the national senate, which they did. On July 3, the resistance committee, supported by thirty Moctezuma women workers, the Civic Coalition, the PRD, a taxi drivers' union, and environmentalists, blocked the entrance to the governor's office. In their interviews to the press, the women leaders sought to frame the decline in activity in a positive light: they explained that the union leadership was taking a needed break to reassess movement strategies and that more workers were not present because of harassment by management.

The resistance committee also made known the attempt by management to install a phantom union from Mexico City. Workers were being taken one by one to the main offices to sign a document supporting the phantom union under threat of dismissal. Other workers reported having been taken to Mexico City to visit the offices of a protection union confederation.[11] Protection unions proliferated in the northern border in the 1970s to provide maquiladora assembly plants with legal union registration without worker representation.

They are usually established without worker knowledge and furnish the contract and union registration required by law. The key function of a protection union is to prevent workers from forming their own union since the legal requirement for union representation is already fulfilled by the protection union, and workers cannot form their own union without contesting the entitlement (*titularidad*) of the collective-bargaining agreement already in place between the company and the protection union.[12]

Moctezuma succeeded in imposing a phantom union, Protejer, which was certified by the LCAB on July 19 but not made known to workers until September. Workers who had demanded a democratic union and fair deal from the company were incensed yet again. The injustice of the state's certifying a phantom union was not lost on the workers. A resistance committee member declared: "The governor must stop protecting the company because the working class is in its legitimate right to demand justice because we pay taxes too" (Calvo Elmer 2001a). These women had shifted from seeing themselves primarily as mothers to identifying themselves as citizens.

The LCAB's certification of the phantom union was all the more egregious because the resistance committee and several corporatist unions were contesting representation. The resistance committee continued the legal process to obtain certification. In early July, one of the women workers in the resistance committee entered an injunction with a higher court to protest the LCAB's refusal to grant recognition, while the resistance committee continued to mount pressure on the labor authorities. In early July, the resistance committee traveled to Mexico City to present their case before Pre-Congreso Ciudadano, an organization made up of sixty NGOs, which unconditionally promised support.

The resistance committee also initiated a campaign to follow the governor to all of his public engagements until he met with them and put an end to the firings at Moctezuma. The negative public attention garnered by the women's presence forced the governor to sidestep events, enter through back doors, and increase police presence. But he did not meet with them. The firings, not directly under his control, continued. By mid-July 2001, once Protejer had received recognition by both the LCAB and management, 126 workers had been fired since the strike.

Besides the resistance committee, three other unions competed for the workers' support in July and August. Despite having been turned down after the strike, the CTM continued its attempts to woo workers. The Revolutionary Confederation of Workers and Peasants (CROC), which has been historically linked to the ruling PRI party, offered support in exchange for representation, and the Confederation of Mexican Workers and Peasants (CTC), considered more of an employer-dominated union, offered to open a state office affiliated with the textile industry in order to represent the women. These unions promised to fight management to reinstate fired workers and renegotiate the collective-bargaining agreement, although they proposed only slight changes.

In general, their record in the central state and elsewhere in Mexico indicates that they would have maintained a compliant workforce and provided only the minimal representation needed to satisfy legal requirements. Their interest in such a high-profile case was more likely geared toward enhancing their tarnished images as defenders of the working class, in addition to collecting union dues.[13]

By the beginning of August, the resistance committee and other groups of workers had turned down the three contending unions, though all persisted until October. The competition to represent workers at Moctezuma, however, was a moot point. Without the knowledge of workers (or the other unions), Protejer had been awarded a protection contract. No longer were there union offices in the parking lot building, nor were workers chosen to be delegates as they had been under modular production. Around September, when I was still collecting data from the HR office, a woman with no knowledge of the garment industry came to town from nearby Mexico City for one day, every two weeks. She sat in the HR office waiting to see if any workers wanted to talk to her. Not many did. She turned out to be the union representative. She never addressed her "members," and few were aware who she was or why she was there. The fact someone from the union even came to the factory, however, points to management's need to appear as if it was abiding by labor rules and, thus, acting in the interest of workers.

Two months after the concealed recognition of the protection union, the information was accidently leaked by a manager. Angry workers confronted management. The response was further termination threats. In fact, throughout the summer and fall, a small but steady stream of firings continued. Workers, in turn, persisted with their denunciations of the company in the media. Knowledge of the agreement with the protection union also reignited the CTC's interest in Moctezuma. The CTC contested Protejer's title over the collective-bargaining agreement at the LCAB offices by demanding a recount of the union's membership. The CTC claimed to have the signatures of over 50 percent of active and fired workers. In mid-October, a new head of the LCAB board divulged that the former head had ordered the contestation order by the CTC to be "lost." Again, the CTC demanded a recount, now asserting they represented over 60 percent of active and fired workers at Moctezuma.

Nothing came of the CTC demands. Protejer continued to be the union legally registered at the LCAB to represent the workers at Moctezuma. Management had successfully installed a protection union that would shield the company from both the workers' and outside union's attempts to renegotiate the collective-bargaining agreement.

### Taking on a New Strategy

The lack of state response to the many demonstrations and the continued threats at work were taking its toll on workers. Groups of workers embarked on new strategies. Some lodged suits for unjustified dismissal to obtain severance pay. Others joined the PRD in sending a letter to the national secretary of labor informing him of the irregularities in the LCAB's actions, asking him to take the side of the "defenseless women" (Bucio 2001b).

The trope of vulnerable femininity and, especially, of single mothers, a core belief in Mexican gender ideology, was used in newspapers to construct an image of weak women who needed others to intercede on their behalf. Sometimes, women workers strategically invoked this image to garner support. At other times, they really believed that single mothers were victims. Ana from the pants department told me: "The difference between my sister and [me] is that she's a single mother. She doesn't have anyone to help her with the kids, she earns less; she's all alone. I have my husband to help me out."

The ways disparate groups—including workers, managers, unions, political parties, and newspapers—discussed single motherhood points to it being a terrain of ideological struggle. Devon Peña writes that "ideology is both a force for social control and social change. In either case, ideological conflict takes place as a struggle to control the terrain of public discourse, to define what the 'real' is" (1997, 132). Within the firm, management had a long history of using single mothers as a justification for increased effort: producing more meant helping out desperate single mothers who counted on their jobs to feed their children. Policies and discourses that furthered the image of the firm as a family, with the owner as the benevolent patriarch, was an attempt at social control.

During the strike, women began to reinterpret the meaning of single motherhood. Many workers developed an oppositional consciousness by "claim[ing] a previously subordinate identity as a positive identification, identify[ing] injustices done to their group, [and] demand[ing] changes, . . . and seeing other members of their group as sharing an interest in rectifying those injustices" (Mansbridge 2001, 1). For an oppositional consciousness to emerge, subjects need to cast off dominant ideas that normalize their subordination. When the strike committee member underscored her status as a single mother on the day of the strike, she laid claim to her inherent dignity and called out management for their unfair treatment of workers.

The revindication of single mothers as strong and deserving of rights, however, was uneven. While women spoke of themselves as resilient, they often made use of the trope of vulnerable femininity in the media to highlight management's dishonorable actions. This was especially true after the police repression of workers on April 4. Local media picked up on this discourse and recast the labor dispute as a matter of dishonest employers taking advantage of powerless women. Thus, although workers successfully made use of the trope of single mothers to further the movement demands, they reinforced rather than challenged women's inferior status.

After the majority of the new union stepped down in June, the resistance committee was the main group pressuring the state, including a suit for failing to certify the democratically elected union. Around seventy of the fired workers entered legal suits against the company for their unlawful termination and reinstatement, but there were no more mass mobilizations. Not only was the union tired, but solidarity had been fractured on the shop floor. The high levels of mobilization were not sustainable, especially in light of overt state support for management—via repression of workers and failures to certify the new union.

The triple shift of working, mobilizing, and taking care of the home took its toll on women workers. Aside from being physically exhausted, many faced tensions at home. Some workers complained that costs related to the marches were eating up their already diminished take-home pay. Others criticized the pressure they felt from coworkers to participate in mobilizations.

Workers were demoralized. The larger worker movement at Moctezuma, understood as widespread support visible through marches and work slowdowns, was all but dead. The resistance committee, however, remained active for years. Mostly made up of fired workers and a few of the elected leadership who did not step down, it continued to wage a war against the state and the firm through the courts and the media.

In March 2002, the resistance committee wrote an open letter to the workers still laboring at Moctezuma, prodding them to use the first anniversary of the day that the governor sent two hundred and fifty police to repress them as a moment for reflection and action. The letter reads:

## One Year of Dignity in Moctezuma [*Un Año de Dignidad en Moctezuma*]

A year after our governor sent antiriot police to beat us for being "social destabilizers," we, the fired, are still fighting to defend our right to reinstallation. And you? Have you resigned yourselves to working on your knees, being humiliated and abused, giving up your pride and dignity just because of the beating they gave us?

Are you willing to lose all that other *compañeros* and *compañeras* have earned with difficulty and courage through the strike? Wake up! Organize and fight for your right to recuperate our former benefits and wages! And if we can support or help you in any way, we will, so that the same errors are not made, so that the white union bought by the company does not take your dues without doing anything for you.

We who are left are only a few, but we [are not willing to] allow ourselves to be defeated. We demand our rights and do not accept alms like our *compañeros* and *compañeras* who have desisted and have betrayed us. Because of this and all that you know about how the company and government have mocked all of us, let us do something so that this April 4th is beneficial to many and to not feel humiliated and defeated. *Compañeras* of *Moctezuma*, be brave like you were before and defend yourselves!

Signed, The Resistance Committee [El Comité de Resistencia][14]

Both the tone and words chosen by the resistance leaders in the open letter denote a radicalization of their position. Borne out of repression and a deep sense of injustice, the stance of these women against the firm and state hardened. The resistance leaders would not settle for less than what they were owed by the company, and anyone who did so—even out of economic necessity—became a traitor to the movement.

In 2002 and 2003, the resistance committee led the May Day march as the women from Moctezuma had done in 2001. Their fight against the state and firm had become emblematic of the working-class struggle. For this reason, one of the movement leaders was invited to read the independent unions' manifesto, where she called for a rejection to the proposed labor law reforms, an end to the destruction of national industry, cessation of union repression, solidarity with indigenous movements, and improved state relations with Cuba and Palestine, among other things. With this resistance leader reading the demands of the labor movement, the ways the women workers had entered into larger public debates and become the voice of the movement were now evident. Other participants in the march commented that Moctezuma women were modern-day Adelitas, referring to the women who followed their husbands into battle during the 1910 revolution and ended up commanding soldiers in the field. In much the same way, workers at Moctezuma—who had begun their journey as mothers—were transformed into citizens defending the rights of workers.

## CONCLUSION

This chapter highlights how larger structural pressures and internal dynamics culminated in a break of the social pact between workers and management at Moctezuma. In examining the buildup to the strike and detailing the process used by workers in deciding to strike, I note several points. First, the justification for the strike was not purely economic, though it played an important role. Prior to the strike, the firm managers claimed for years that the firm was in economic distress, citing Chinese and Central American competition. Workers understood the constraints of a highly competitive global economy and gave management the benefit of the doubt, supporting them with increased effort during emergencies. But management did not respond with shared sacrifice. Instead, it canceled the second shift and went behind the backs of workers through the courts to rescind portions of the collective-bargaining agreement. The final straw came when the company, during the yearly contract revision, refused to return the benefits workers had "lent" them the previous year to help capitalize the firm. Workers saw this as a slippery slope leading to deteriorated wages and working conditions; management could not be trusted.

Second, most workers believed the union would not defend their interests, either. During the period preceding the strike, the union took contradictory stances, taking vigorous positions for and against management. Usually the union backed up management's policies, with union delegates stressing the benevolent character of management and chastising workers for not giving their all. However, upon the cancellation of the second shift, the union took an antagonistic stand against management—not because management eliminated the second shift but because management didn't consult with the union first. In response to the inconsistent positions taken by the union and their air of self-importance, workers increasingly distrusted them. The union tried to play both sides and lost the little legitimacy it had with workers.

Third, workers subverted the team structure and used it in the service of their own interests. Teams trained workers as leaders and provided a communication network for shop-floor level decisions to be made quickly. When the second shift was cancelled, the entire shop floor broke into team meetings where they, first individually and then collectively, decided to not go out on a wildcat strike. Teams also provided a mechanism to increase solidarity and discipline dissenters during the strike.

Resistance, however, was not based on team organization only. A fourth point is how a new consciousness emerged as workers decided to fight management. Workers' identities shifted from being primarily that of mothers who worked to workers who were mothers. The difference is important. At the beginning, women workers saw employment as a means to provide food, shelter, and education for their children. But as management began to change the rules of team operation, workers coalesced to protect the pockets of autonomy they had created. The more management tried to cut bonuses and benefits, the more workers fought back. A feeling of betrayal underscored the sense of injustice most workers experienced. It was at this point that employment ceased being a means to earn a living and became an end in itself—a right worth protecting. During the long hours guarding the factory throughout the strike, the women spoke of the economic hardships they would now face. But their anger at the indignity of being, in their words, "used" by the company was the greater issue, and the company's behavior needed to be addressed.

Fifth, the process of workers' transformation was gendered in nature. Although the primary identity of women workers shifted, they were no less concerned with their motherly duties. The difference, however, was the understanding of those responsibilities. While, before the strike, children's needs were used as a reason to work hard and not make demands on management, now the needless suffering of their children became the motivating factor to fight. To be a mother meant more than providing food; it also meant standing up for your rights and the rights of your family.

The mobilizations also proved to women that they could stand up to management and to male union leaders. Preceding the strike, women strategically marshaled their subordinate status in society and at Moctezuma to illuminate how the firm had broken its social pact with workers. They challenged the union's masculinity for having turned its back on workers. Then women workers turned around and used this same subordinate status to convince higher-paid male workers in the cutting department to go on strike. If the most "vulnerable"—single mothers—had the courage and strength to fight management, so could everybody else.

In the next chapter, I show how management fought back by reorganizing production and making use of its influence with the state to block workers' lawsuits and maneuver the bankruptcy courts.

CHAPTER 7

# "We Lost Control of the Shop Floor"

## FLEXIBLE TAYLORISM AND THE DEMISE OF THE FIRM

After the labor authorities colluded with company management to declare the strike at Moctezuma illegal, workers had no choice but to return to work. However, most women and men returned with a renewed fervor to fight for their rights as workers. In response, management intimidated, harassed, and fired workers while it installed a phantom union that was quickly rubber-stamped by the labor authorities. Although public demonstrations ceased after three and a half months, some workers still discussed how to elect another democratic union or make especially harsh managers pay for their excessive pressure. Still dealing with resistance on the shop floor, the top production manager said to me in exasperation, "We lost control of the shop floor." To deal with this, key elements of lean production were changed, leading to a new production system I call *flexible Taylorism*. The new system combined heightened worker control with increased quality imperatives.

### CHANGING THE ORGANIZATION OF PRODUCTION PIECEMEAL

The first step taken by managers in late May 2001 was to eliminate the team leader position in the most disruptive teams. Although teams still existed, advisers—whose ranks were now doubled with supervisors from the cancelled second shift—became team leaders in the most rebellious teams. Team leaders had played an especially important role in organizing resistance against the state and the firm; they had been crucial in sustaining disruptive actions. By eliminating the team leaders who had been most vocal and effective in generating dissent, management hoped to cut communication and mobilizing networks.

The second step management took to control workers during this time of increased mobilization was to revert to paying workers by the piece in June. Piece *rate* now, however, had a different meaning than it did five years previously. If workers did not reach their efficiency requirements, they were verbally penalized. If they produced more than their quotas, however, there were no longer any bonuses. At this point, the tension and antagonism between workers and managers on the shop floor were extremely high: the company accused workers of sending death threats to managers; workers charged that the company had hired thugs to beat workers in their homes. Whether these accusations were true or not, the atmosphere on the shop floor was filled with intimidation and hostility. The company did not even bother to offer incentives as a way to increase production. They saw direct control as their only recourse.

The third step taken by management was to seek out new contracts to make up for clients lost during the strike and the ensuing period of decreased production. The firm began producing uniforms for two Mexican airlines and added women's suits to be sold in national department stores. These contracts were domestic, thus requiring lower quality than high-end garments for export; this was important since workers had difficulty with different techniques and operations needed for women's clothing. While it was not difficult to produce men's airline uniforms, the new women's uniforms and suits complicated production lines enough to stop them altogether.

It was the task of the industrial engineers, advisers, and multiskilled utility workers to figure out how to organize the lines for women's clothing, which required different sewing and pressing operations to produce a distinct shape. Unlike men's suits, women's suits required more delicate, curved stitching, and minute deviations from the curvature resulted in visible puckering. This issue was especially relevant since most women's suits were not made of wool cashmere but synthetic fabrics that were more difficult to manipulate. Moreover, the company did not own the specialized pressing machines needed to set the curved stitches. Thus the work was more demanding and required workers' ingenuity to produce the cheaper, lower-quality suits.

Production problems also rose from changes in the workforce. This led to the fourth change. The company needed to replace workers who had been fired or who had quit. But the firm did not want to be saddled with the financial responsibilities of hiring new employees, such as paying for government medical services or higher severance pay resulting from accrued seniority. At the beginning of April, management began hiring new workers through a temporary employment agency to skirt union and benefit requirements.

Management also controlled costs by harassing workers to the point that, increasingly, they left of their own volition. Without having been fired, workers were not entitled to receive any indemnity. The company's harassment tactic further soured an already inhospitable environment. Chela described it as "being treated like slaves." In one case, my neighbor María realized that she would never get fired because she performed three key operations at 100 percent efficiency. She missed work several days in a row, incited fights with managers, and insulted other workers—anything to get fired. She was not. After months of making barely $200 pesos weekly (U.S.$22) after deductions—too little to make ends meet, and unable to get fired, she quit. She had been at the factory for five years. Had she been fired, she calculated she would have received $5,000 pesos (around U.S.$550) in severance. Utility workers, who earned the most, saw their wages cut in half.

Another worker shared her frustrations with the compounding pressures—from managers to produce and from workers to keep going to marches and demonstrations. She spent a good portion of what little she did make in transportation and food at protest events. This young woman decided to immigrate to the United States with her family. A man from her government-subsidized apartment building specialized in taking whole families over the U.S.-Mexico border, which cost steep fees: U.S.$1,500 per adult, U.S.$1,200 per child. Relatives already in the United States would lend her the money, which she would pay back once she was working in the North.

By May 2001, workers' spirits were the lowest I had seen. It seemed like more and more workers were trying to get fired or were quitting. Production was hampered not only by the tensions with management and the low morale of workers but also the increased number of new workers who had to get up to speed quickly. As I had learned in *la escuelita*, sewing was not as easy as it appeared. It was even more difficult to make women's suits since there were no instructions. Each worker had to sort things out along the way. New workers did not have the experience or knowledge to do this.

By June 2001, the situation at Moctezuma deteriorated further. During June and July, six of my teammates stopped showing up for work; another six were fired. Of those who remained, Lupe wanted to quit but needed medical benefits for her family, and Juan, the team leader who had been so active during the first months of mobilizations, had become an assistant to the adviser, looking for bundles on the shop floor. (My teammates cursed his name, as he was believed to have become a spy.) Three different coworkers were considering making the dangerous trek to the United States to look for work. They had looked for work locally, but anyone who had worked at Moctezuma was summarily rejected for employment. Workers were blacklisted, just as they were in 1972.

## REORGANIZING THE SHOP FLOOR, AGAIN

Five months after the strike, the company again reorganized its production lines. In mid-August 2001, the factory closed for a few days to make physical changes to the shop floor to reflect new rules. Piecemeal changes were made permanent with the addition of a few new rules. Teams were eliminated. Without teams, there were no team leaders who could freely roam around the plant talking to other team leaders. Without teams, there were no more meetings excluding management from worker decisions. As it had been previously under Taylorist work organization, every worker would be individually responsible for his or her quota. However, the base wage was no longer supplemented by incentives or bonuses. Instead of being advisers, middle management reverted to being line and area supervisors with greater authority over workers' labor. An enhanced hierarchy of supervisors would now assure smooth running of the now traditionally organized line.

The only remaining sign of lean production was the emphasis on quality. While each worker was still responsible for her or his own and previous workers' quality, with task sheets to direct the flow and display each person's action on the product, a new layer of quality supervisors was set up. In effect, the new organization—a hybrid between modular production and the progressive bundle system—retained elements beneficial to company goals while discarding features that allowed worker autonomy.

Compared to the previous modular production organization, the shop floor under flexible Taylorism combined assembly lines with modular layout in order to best respond to production requirements. Some areas remained the same, while others changed in ways that made linear assembly possible. Production was still pulled with kanban cards and used a modified just-in-time (JIT) inventory system. Close communication with suppliers continued, but without resources to keep working with input producers that had the highest quality and fastest turnaround times, Moctezuma reverted to stocking some inputs from less able suppliers. However, issues of supervision and hiring practices starkly reverted to Taylorist principles.

### Managerial Control

Under flexible Taylorism at Moctezuma, direct control returned reinforced. A parallel system of quality supervisors was added to the recently augmented production management staff. Thus, instead of the three supervisors previously in place in the jackets department, there were now six production and three quality supervisors, in addition to the department manager, totaling ten supervisors for the jackets one line. Moreover, management set up quality checkpoints along the line, spending their days in the midst of workers instead of in the offices on the shop floor-perimeter. Supervisory control was physical, visible, and antagonistic. The only area where management presence was reduced was at the top level. Previously there had been one general production manager and one quality manager who oversaw the shop floor; now only one production manager called the shots.

Quality supervisors roamed sections randomly checking quality, returning bundles with errors, and ensuring that all workers followed the correct work method within the standard allotted minutes. With greater numbers of quality supervisors, more of them concentrated on performing statistical process control (SPC), a labor-intensive task. It entailed meticulously evaluating and measuring a certain percentage of all operations, graphing even the minutest digression from the product specifications. The goal was to ensure quality at each step, recording which operations (and thus workers) caused problems. As Jane Collins has shown, requiring SPC of manufacturers is a critical component of branded buyers' increased control of the production process (2003). Importantly, it is not only quality that is closely surveilled but also workers.

While quality managers were preoccupied with SPC, production supervisors took over many responsibilities formerly performed by team leaders, such as following the flow, dealing with absenteeism and turnover, and anything else that would affect the final product leaving the line. By this point, the company had lost most of its international clients given that it had not been able to keep to delivery schedules or quality imperatives while dealing with labor unrest, capital shortages, and new unskilled labor. Making quality products remained important to retain higher-end national clients, but JIT delivery was impossible to guarantee. Although several clients had signed industry codes of conduct to ensure that the manufacturers' upheld corporate socially responsible practices, it is not clear these had any effect. Moctezuma handled delivery and quality problems, and circumvented the implementation of corporate conduct codes, by subcontracting out work.

While control was exacted by all levels of management, not all management lent their support to the changing relations on the shop floor. Top managers seemed the most aggressive and were responsible for most of the harassment and intimidation. In contrast, line supervisors tended to shy away from overt pressure. As I witnessed, they encouraged workers to not give up the fight, which they reasoned was right. At one point, when supervisors were forced to ask workers to go to the departmental offices and sign for a phantom union to be installed, some were careful to not threaten workers. Instead, at least two supervisors I know of went up to people who they thought would not mind signing, and asked them to "please sign" if they felt comfortable with the action.

Midlevel managers knew that their jobs might be on the line if they were seen to be sympathetic to workers, so they disguised their sympathies for worker struggles through professional behavior. Supervisors during this period were extremely conscientious, zigzagging in and out of the line to check quality and production without interacting much with either workers or higher-level managers. Although this retraction to "objectively measuring" work may have seemed neutral, it pressured workers to produce more. Work pace was thus regulated and augmented by amplified supervisory presence. I later found out that managers' pay was often two to three weeks late during this period, explaining why they might have covertly supported workers' continued mobilization.

Other forms of control extant during modular production also persisted. The white boards that recorded production and quality remained. However, instead of being posted at the outer boundary, where each team had been previously, they were now placed strategically over key, difficult, or bottleneck operations. Whether workers were reaching their production and quality goals was still visible to all. Yet without any shop floor–wide bonuses to aim for, the white boards exerted less peer pressure.

## Redesigning the Layout

The layout of the shop floor also contributed to increased surveillance and control of worker movement and labor. Under flexible Taylorism, low buffers still allowed for maximum visibility. However, the new layout provided a more linear design with more space between workstations, making communication more difficult. The departmental offices were relocated to the shop floor periphery. Given the enhanced levels of supervisory control, it was no longer necessary to have offices in the middle of workers. The workers' expenditure of effort could be clearly seen, and production and quality managers roamed the shop floor everywhere.

A further change was the addition of a "stock" area—essentially, a larger version of what had previously been the local supply station—in the middle of the shop floor itself. Under JIT production, the cost of storing inputs was externalized to suppliers. By August 2001, Moctezuma no longer had the economic resources to coordinate supplies with high-quality producers who could work under JIT. Instead, lower-quality suppliers who could not guarantee the product on tight schedules were used. Thus stock had to be secured within the factory grounds to keep production flowing.

## Hiring Practices

Whereas Moctezuma had previously recruited and hired women (and some men) of all ages, preferably with experience and high school education, management told me they now actively and exclusively sought young women between the ages of eighteen and twenty-five, with no previous work experience and low levels of education. Finding that kind of female worker, however, was not that easy. New workers, hired through a temporary agency, told me they earned a third less than previous hires. According to company records, from April to October 2001, ninety-one workers were hired, of which seventy-six were women. Of these female hires, nearly 50 percent were between the ages of sixteen and twenty-five, and only 12 percent had no previous work experience. But, interestingly, 30 percent had formerly worked at Moctezuma, and another 20 percent had been employed at a sewing factory or workshop.[1] Therefore, despite mangers' stated preferences, new workers were a combination of seasoned and inexperienced workers. Hiring practices most likely responded to production imperatives requiring knowledgeable workers and the availability of new workers in the labor market willing to work for low wages.

Comments made by management at this time point to them perceiving young women as more malleable and docile. Furthermore, past experiences led them to believe that, since young women often leave when they marry and start families, they would be a transitory workforce—which, importantly, is less likely to organize. Thus management's desire to hire young, inexperienced women for their compliance and docility was balanced with rehiring an important number of experienced workers.

### Trading Unions

The last significant adjustment made under flexible Taylorism was a change in union representation. Under Taylorism and modular production, Moctezuma had boasted a close relation with a union friendly to the company. But workers ousted this union after the strike. For months the democratically elected union had pressured the local conciliation and arbitration board (LCAB) to certify it, to no avail. By mid-July, as described in the previous chapter, management had successfully installed a protection union, Protejer, from Mexico City. The labor authorities quickly certified that protection union, making it the legal representative of workers at Moctezuma. Importantly, the imposition of Protejer effectively put an end to legal battles over representation by other unions and organized workers. Management had won.

## The Complicit Role of the State

The center-right National Action Party (PAN) government consistently took Moctezuma's side in the labor conflicts. Given that the state would not certify the newly elected independent union or do anything to curtail the firm's illegal actions, workers increasingly viewed government as complicit with management. At first, workers' complaints were specific grievances about unfrozen benefits, reneged wage increases, and elimination of bonuses. However, as their protests fell on deaf ears, workers gradually identified first the union leadership and then the government as allies of an untrustworthy employer.

State support for the firm can be explained in part by the election, in 2000, of a PAN governor who had elevated business interests in state policy. A revolving door of local businessmen into state agencies existed. In the case of Moctezuma, this was particularly evident and detrimental to worker demands, as the state secretary of labor was an active member of the firm's board of directors throughout 2001. Moreover, in 2002, the governor appointed the director of Grupo Mexicano as secretary of the economy, where he lobbied policymakers to bailout the company. Importantly, LCABs fall under the purview of state secretaries of labor, making them highly politicized judicial venues. The ambiguous nature of labor law provides LCABs with inordinate power without clear rules, and the secretary of labor used that power to benefit Moctezuma—which he still legally represented.

It is important to understand the role played by the state in supporting the company's interests. To this end, I discuss how workers interacted with the state through the courts, how state agents and the protection union shielded the company from bankruptcy, and how state officials and peak business organizations used this case to weaken worker protections.

## Fighting Back through the Courts

From the very beginning of the labor dispute in March 2001, the labor authorities, backed by the governor's office and the state secretary of labor, had supported Moctezuma management, forcing workers to resort to new strategies, including lawsuits. Through several law offices, over three hundred fired workers sued to obtain their severance pay.[2] Of those seeking legal recourse, around seventy women, many of whom belonged to the resistance committee and worked with an independent human rights groups, also demanded reinstatement. Both of these groups lost members along the way, unable to keep up with the interminable bureaucratic delays or frustrated by the lack of results. One of the women from the democratically elected union, who had not stepped down in June, filed a suit, along with the business agent, against the LCAB for denying union certification.

All three types of suits were delayed through manipulation of technical requirements of the law. First, labor arbitration cases require that all parties be present. Yet the LCAB did not compel the company, which repeatedly failed to show, to be present. Second, it is the responsibility of the LCAB to provide all parties with timely citation notices for meetings to take place. However, the LCAB continually failed to announce the meetings, resulting in delays. Thus, by May 2002, arbitration meetings between the company and suing workers had been postponed ten times. No talk had taken place, which meant legal cases were stuck in limbo.

Workers who had taken legal action against the company in 1972 had similar experiences. Gaby sued the company for reinstatement after she was fired in 1974 for supporting the independent union. She told me, "I sued the company for violation of my rights, and after eight years, I won the case. The very next day my file was lost at Conciliation [LCAB]." She cried as she recounted her story. Laura also filed a suit against the company and the medical branch of the Mexican Social Security System (IMSS) since she was pregnant when fired in 1972. Although she won a small amount of money, enough to buy some clothes, she said it was like "David fighting Goliath." As a member of the independent human rights organization advising the resistance committee after the 2001 strike, Laura commented on the judicial process: "Many women bet on the judicial system. But it's a bureaucratic labyrinth where most become disillusioned and lose hope."

There were so many irregularities with the LCAB suits that, in May 2001, resistance committee workers, through the lawyer at the human rights organization, petitioned a federal district court to compel the LCAB to hear their case. Four months later, the federal district court requested the LCAB's case files, which they refused to provide. In response to repeated requests, the LCAB claimed the case files had been lost. By June 2002, the district court ruled that the local labor authority was incompetent to hear the women's cases and made a judgment in their favor.

The resistance committee attributes their success to the continual pressure placed on the courts and the participation of the human rights lawyer. Although work and family responsibilities made it impossible for all the women to attend court hearings, they organized so that a few were always present. Some women found employment through personal networks in small food preparation and sewing workshops. Quite a few became home workers, taking in garments to sew at home. While this work allowed them the flexibility to attend hearings, it also entailed the longest work days and lowest earnings, averaging $100 pesos per week (U.S.$9 in 2009).

In addition, fired workers seeking reinstatement sought out letters of support from international human rights groups like Amnesty International, Americas Watch, and Lawyers without Borders. Notably, this strategy was facilitated by their collaboration with the local human rights group, which understood the political landscape and had contacts with national and international nongovernmental organizations (NGOs) and movements. Thus workers' continued presence at the court proceedings, combined with international scrutiny, led the case to be decided in the workers' favor in spite of the state government's attempt to railroad the process.

Such support was not available for the case of the union representative who had remained with the business agent as her lawyer. The business agent's refusal to accept support from local social movements and opposition political parties isolated him to the detriment of the case. In August 2001, a federal district court decreed her case against the LCAB to have merit. When the federal court requested the case file from the LCAB, however, it arrived with pages missing and the 2000 and 2001 collective-bargaining agreements modified. A month later, the LCAB presented affidavits showing that two executive officers of the democratically elected union had retrieved the certification petition before stepping down in June 2001. Movement observers find it difficult to believe the legitimacy of the statements given that they would have been used earlier by the labor authority to deny recognition. Nevertheless, these documents nullified the case. Without local support, the union leader no longer pursued the case.

### The Economics and Politics of Bankruptcy

While fired workers' cases made their way through the courts, workers back at the factory were experiencing furloughs and cutbacks. In September 2001, the company stopped making contributions to the national housing institute (INFONAVIT), although it kept collecting workers' deductions. By December, IOUs were distributed instead of savings accrued throughout the year. Managers' wages were delayed by a month.

In December 2001, Moctezuma's owners began bankruptcy proceedings. The company continued to operate under court protection, although it became increasingly difficult. In March, the firm was unable to pay creditors the three billion pesos owed. By June 2002, the company stopped paying workers. During a furlough, with workers gone, management took out machinery and raw materials to set up informal workshops around the city.

The degree of state support for the company became evident in July when one hundred and fifty employees, composed of office workers and midlevel managers, were fired. The secretary of labor, still operating as an executive on the board of directors, offered fired employees—but *not* workers—$1,000 pesos monthly (U.S.$109) in the form of federal training scholarships, along with a small payment, *provided* they did not file suit against the company. Most refused, and a new wave of legal suits ensued. This undue use of influence by the secretary of labor was roundly criticized in state congress and the media.

Nevertheless, the state congress debated whether to save the company from bankruptcy. The majority owner intervened in the discussion. He pointed out how the company, employing one thousand workers, was the biggest taxpayer in the state, and its demise would harm banks, leading to larger repercussions. The governor came out publicly in favor of the bailout, as did the secretary of the economy. However, the Democratic Revolution Party (PRD), NGOs, and workers ended the debate with swift opposition.

A month later, the federal bankruptcy court decreed a precautionary embargo on the company's assets.[3] The Protejer protection union, which had been present at the company since July of the previous year, declared a strike at Moctezuma, which by law halted all bankruptcy proceedings. Within another month, at the end of September 2002, 340 male workers at Italia, the textile mill next door belonging to the same owner, also declared a strike. Renewed debates on saving the company resurfaced in the state congress. The governor made a plea for local entrepreneurs to form a group to purchase the company or to find new investors; federal and local state support was promised. In addition, PAN representatives made the case in the federal Congress that the firm deserved help to restructure its debt, claiming it had been hit hard by the effects of the 1997 East Asian financial crisis (known in Mexico as the Tequila Effect). The petition was turned down.

### The Politics of Striking

The strikes at Moctezuma and Italia differed in important ways. First, since Italia was a textile company, its workers belonged to a Confederation of Mexican Workers (CTM) industry-wide union, which ruled under a master contract (*contrato ley*). The Italia case was heard by the Federal Conciliation and Arbitration Board (FCAB) and was thus less subject to local influences. After the strike, it was made known that Italia's union had postponed the strike fourteen times. Moreover, in January 2002, it had agreed to take a 50 percent wage cut to help capitalize the firm and, in May, to only receive benefits. Notwithstanding the diminished working conditions, the CTM union claimed the strike was not a labor dispute but a financial matter. The act of striking ended any precautionary embargoes ordered by the courts as labor disputes take legal precedence. Given that Italia workers were covered by a master contract and that local union decisions were most likely made in conjunction with the national leadership, the lack of worker revolt at Italia is not remarkable.

Protejer's level of union involvement in Moctezuma, however, was surprising since protection contracts rarely involve physical presence and much less collective resistance. Strikes entail workers' physically keeping guard at facilities. It appears that Moctezuma's union, unlike Italia's union, had not been planning a strike until notice of the precautionary embargo was made known. At the time of the strike, 360 women and men were actively laboring, with 220 of them on furlough. Given that the strike helped only Moctezuma's management, many current and fired workers described the strike as "fictitious."

Soon after the strikes were declared, a Mexican investor showed interest in the two companies. Negotiations stretched from September 2002 to March 2004, with the state extending the bankruptcy hearings multiple times. Negotiations were hobbled by finance creditors, especially Citibank Banamex and GE Capital, which actively pursued legal cases—each claiming they should be the first to receive payments from the company. Other problems arose, including the investor's trouble raising capital, the majority owner's reticence to sell, worker lawsuits in multiple courts, and Protejer's demand for full compensation for severance pay and lost wages before commencing work under new ownership. The latter cannot be interpreted as support of workers' rights; rather, it was a stalling tactic.

In fact, in August 2003, the workers at Moctezuma accepted the investor's proposition to work at the same wage levels, including seniority and productivity bonuses. Wages lost during the strike, a common demand, were voluntarily forfeited. But the Protejer union refused the deal. The majority of women vowed to go back to work anyway, ending the strike. In the wee hours of the next day, women workers broke the chained locks placed on doors by the union and began to work. They had summoned a judge to witness their terminating the strike. In response, the union leadership petitioned to the LCAB to declare the workers' action invalid and the strike still in effect. The LCAB complied.

This case of the protection union is important for two reasons. First, it lays bare how protection unions do not represent workers' interests yet have full support from state labor authorities. Second, it was the basis for a successful complaint made in 2005 to the International Labor Organization (ILO), alleging violation of the right to strike. The Protejer leadership entered a petition to the regional ILO offices claiming that "a group of people foreign to [Moctezuma] together with ex-workers came onto the company's premises so that representatives of the state could 'witness' that there was no strike" (ILO 2005).[4] The people "foreign to the company" were the women trying to begin working again. By 2008, the ILO had sent a recommendation to the government to investigate the case (ILOGB 2009). Importantly, it was a Mexican government representative who decided which complaints were to be forwarded from the regional ILO offices to Geneva for further study and recommendation. The Protejer case was advanced.

The resistance committee had also lodged a complaint with an international governmental body. However, having no standing as a union, it could not seek redress—even if only symbolically—from the ILO. Instead, in conjunction with a national worker's rights group affiliated with the independent union, the Authentic Labor Front (FAT), the resistance committee entered a complaint with the Inter-American Human Rights Commission of the Organization of American States (OAS) in 2004. The case claimed that the company had not respected the collective-bargaining agreement for having cut benefits and changed bonus structure in 2001 and that the LCAB had violated the right to strike by not recognizing the democratically elected union (CEREAL 2009).

Although the workers knew that the case could not be heard at the OAS until all judicial proceedings concluded in Mexico, the case represented a denouncement of the injustices they were experiencing. Thus both the ILO and the OAS cases were mostly symbolic since the international organizations could only make toothless recommendations. In the meantime, fired workers were embroiled in a complex web of legal suits.

In March 2004, the company officially declared bankruptcy. At this time, Protejer entered suit against the company in the name of its 360 workers. Under bankruptcy law, the workers were supposed to be the first in line to receive compensation from the sale of Moctezuma's assets. One year later, the property was sold at half price to a sole bidder. However, further sale of assets was delayed by injunctions obtained by GE Capital and Bancomext, the state development bank. In February 2010, Protejer, the last to enter suit against the company, obtained $38 million pesos for workers' compensation, little of which workers received. Italia workers collected a portion of their compensation in March 2010. Since neither union has received full reimbursement, the strikes by Protejer and CTM are still ongoing (as of January 2012). There have been no more sales of company assets, and thus, no more worker compensations. In March 2011, ten years after the original strike and the first wave of lawsuits for unfair dismissal, workers with private law firms received compensation, although below expected levels. By lawyers' calculations, Vicki was owed $200,000 pesos. The LCAB settlement provided her with $75,000 pesos, which amounted to $58,000 pesos after paying legal fees. With the money, Vicki completed a second story to her father's home, where she lives, and now rents out the first floor. The resistance committee, whose case was the first to be decided in their favor by the federal courts, is still awaiting compensation.

### Business Organizations and the Politics of Labor Reform

While worker cases proceeded through the courts, state government officials and business organizations used the case of Moctezuma to heighten the call for labor law reforms. In May 2001, the local chapter of the peak business association, the Entrepreneurial Coordinating Council (CCE), blamed "old unionism," referring to social movement unionism of the 1970s, for having taken over the company. In addition, they faulted hardline unionists with scaring away investments, which "certainly could have generated the bankruptcy of the company" (Bucio 2001a).

Starting in July 2001, five other large companies in Mexico, including several transnational corporations, suffered economic difficulties and labor disputes. Small businesses and productive workshops were going under by the hundreds; migration to the United States rapidly increased. Government officials blamed economic problems on the U.S. recession, Chinese dumping, and both radical and corporatist unions, stating that their demands scared away investment.

In this context of economic crisis and growing unemployment, the CCE and the CTM union proposed pacts to save jobs. The only way to do so, they believed, was to allow companies to furlough workers and reduce wages by 40 percent, with the understanding that when conditions improved, wages would go back to their previous levels. In addition to wage cuts, official unions proposed "to generate a strategy with entrepreneurs to be able to guarantee the certainty required in the state to attract investment" (Morales 2001b).

Days later the CTM, CCE, Mexican Employers' Confederation (COPARMEX), and state government signed the Pact for a New Labor Culture to "face the urgent need to overcome the challenge of globalization, which implies a real struggle for markets, and the phantom of labor instability" (Morales 2001a).[5] The governor reiterated that the new labor culture was only possible if irresponsible union leaders stopped pressing workers to commit illegal acts and instead turn toward conciliation in order to reach "real peace and harmony" (Morales 2001a). As a signatory of the pact, the secretary of labor, who was also an executive at Moctezuma, called for both workers and capital to be respected in this effort to stabilize the state economy. To the women workers at Moctezuma, his words must have rung empty.

Thus official unions, business organizations, and the state privileged providing conditions of capital accumulation to domestic and foreign firms at all costs over protecting jobs. Implicit in this stance was an understanding that the underemployed and unemployed would seek better opportunities in the United States. In October 2001, the president of the local CCE sent a message to migrants in the United States who might want to return to the central state during the U.S. recession. He said, "The best that you can do . . . is to remain in that country" (Bucio 2001c). There was no room for returning migrants in the local economy.

## THE DECLINE OF GRUPO MEXICANO

While Moctezuma's new owners took energetic steps to sell their products in the global market, financialization and their own organizational structure hampered their economic stability. Neoliberal structural reforms, following the demands of the International Monetary Fund (IMF) and the World Bank, had prioritized fighting inflation. However, in order to lower inflation, interest rates had to be increased, which made credit more expensive domestically. Further reforms lifted constraints on capital markets (stocks and bonds) and decreased barriers to the movement of capital across borders; this made the Mexican economic system more vulnerable to global financial instability, which is what instigated the 1997 Asian financial crisis (Babb 2005; Garrido and Puga 1990; Morera Camacho 1998).

Moctezuma's initial investments—sunk costs made to transform the firm into a lean factory and full-package producer—in the end debilitated the firm's capacity to respond to market fluctuations and worker unrest. That is, the expenses that the firm had to take on in order to do business with the high-end buyers were irrecoverable and set the firm on a path from which it was difficult to deviate (Barham, Bunker, and O'Hearn 1994). The added expense of training—and, at times, taking over, or verticalizing—local suppliers to ensure quality and timely delivery, as well as the expanded corporate welfare programs established to create a community of fate belief, added to the debt. Mexican firms did not, and do not now, operate in a framework of accessible capital and support structures (Maxfield 1990; Tirado 1998).

By 1998, financial problems had begun to surface at Moctezuma. Failed diversification into the international restaurant sector—an investment of U.S.$13.9 million—did not issue returns and instead led the company into a lawsuit against those hired to manage it. Moreover, when Mexican ownership took over Moctezuma and Italia in 1994, large amounts of capital were invested in upgrading the factories. The expenditure to establish the state-of-the-art acetate textile mill extracted additional capital. One top manager at Moctezuma commented that, at the beginning, "the new owners improved the factory and invested many millions of dollars—[to the tune of] U.S.$50 million—and they thought the market was going to absorb everything we produced." But sales projections to wholly cover firm-upgrading investments did not materialize.

To make matters worse, in 2000, Grupo Mexicano received news from the Italian investors who had retained controlling interests in the U.S. distribution center that, to continue using its services, it had to be purchased outright. When Pérez had bought the conglomerate, it came with a five-year contract to the distribution center, which held the contracts with retailers and was thus crucial for utilizing the all-important U.S. market. When the five years were up, the terms changed: either purchase the distribution center or be cut off from its services. The same top manager explained the outcome:

> We had to buy it. It was an investment of . . . U.S.$122 million. Then this led to businesses that did not work according to [our] expectations of growth. . . .
> And on the other hand, the acquisition of this U.S. company led to debts,

[to our] having to pay these debts and not having liquid capital [assets readily converted to cash] around. Moreover, the banks here in Mexico are not lending money.

These large investments in the distribution center in 2000 forced the already cash-strapped firm to take on further short-term debt to cover past loans.

Specifically for Moctezuma, cash-liquidity problems affected production expectations in the form of material shortages on the shop floor. When asked about the lack of materials, department managers said there was not enough money to pay suppliers. Evidence of this can be found in the firm's 1999 and 2000 economic reports that were made public during bankruptcy hearings.

At my request, an international auditor, John Hepp, and a corporate accountant in Mexico, Carlos Alfredo Torres Moreno, reviewed the balance sheets. In their estimation, the company began experiencing liquidity problems in 1997, progressively and irrevocably, which led to the crisis in 2001 (see table 7.1).

Beginning in 1997, there was an increase of short-term loans that were disproportionate to the operating costs of the firm. This in itself is not that surprising given the way the privatization of the Mexican banking system favored industrial groups and provided perverse incentives to make large loans to them and others. The use of short-term debt as a form of capitalization is congruent with the practices of many economic family-based groups like Grupo Mexicano (Garrido Noguera and Ortiz Guerrero 2009). Long-term loans were then being used to cover short-term bank debts—that is, through debt and refinancing of debt, banks came to own majority shares in the enterprise. Journalist accounts confirm this process, reporting that, in July 2000, Grupo Mexicano restructured short-terms loans for another four and a half years, having loans

TABLE 7.1

MOCTEZUMA'S PROPORTION OF WORKING CAPITAL TO DEBTS,
1996–2001 (IN MILLIONS OF PESOS)

| Year | Liquid Capital | Debts | Ratio of Liquid Capital to Debts |
|------|----------------|-------|----------------------------------|
| 1996 | 344,478 | 145,609 | 2.36 |
| 1997 | 638,831 | 401,510 | 1.59 |
| 1998 | 635,830 | 641,279 | 0.99 |
| 1999 | 788,352 | 873,158 | 0.90 |
| 2000 | 612,621 | 656,550 | 0.93 |
| 2001 | 411,067 | 1,045,114 | 0.39 |

Source: Compiled by author from company's public financial records.

worth U.S.$3.8 million with Dresdner Bank, U.S.$12.5 million with Citibank Mexico, and U.S.$7.5 million with Inverlat.

The balance sheets also show that, although sales remained steady, the operating costs rose, cutting into the company's profit. In 1996 operating costs were 27.4 percent of sales; by 2001, they were 42.2 percent. In 1998, the effect of carrying a high level of loans and high operating costs resulted in the firm using 70.5 percent of its profits to pay debt interest. As a result, working capital was drastically reduced, and the company was self-liquidating, selling off licensing agreements, brands, and reducing its workforce. In 2000, the company sold its high-end retail store for $13.9 million pesos and stopped the market launch of two brands in the United States and Canada. At that time, it was also expecting a loan from GE Capital, which did not materialize.

An alternate explanation for Grupo Mexicano's economic difficulties could be a steep drop in sales for men's suits, which would have seriously affected any clothing firm. However, national statistics do not support this theory. The export value of the men's dress sector increased 20 percent from 1999 to 2000 (INEGI 2002). Thus, it is more likely that the drop in sales is more a reflection of client dissatisfaction with quality and delivery time of the product than a change in the market.

Moreover, continued drops in 2001 cannot be attributed purely to market decline. According to economist Huberto Juárez Nuñez, the effects of the U.S. recession hit the Mexican garment sector in March 2001 (2003). This is corroborated by the total value of exports and production, as well as the number of jobs in the textile and apparel industry, which dropped significantly from 2000 to 2001 (INEGI 2002, tables 2.126, 2.215, and 3.229). However, given the data in the company's economic report, it is clear that the company was on life support even before the forced purchase of the U.S. distribution center in 2000 and before the strike and effects of the U.S. recession in March 2001.

While Grupo Mexicano benefited from export promotion policies and possessed close ties with state officials, it did not hold controlling interests in privatized banks, as did some of the larger, more successful family-based industrial groups. Capital outlays for industrial upgrading, failed internationalization investments, and slower growth sales than projected were exacerbated by the institutional environment in Mexico, whose weak financial institutions were vulnerable to global fluctuations and provided fewer credit opportunities at high interest rates and with shorter payoff turnaround times (Berensztein 1996; Dussel Peters, Ruiz Durán, and Piore 2002; Jiménez 1999).

In 1998, the effects of East Asia's 1997 financial crisis and Mexico's policy of monetary restriction further increased interest rates on both consumer and corporate loans. Moreover, as oil prices fell (below U.S.$10 dollars a barrel), the government was forced to restrict its line of credit through development banks. While the state lent less capital for export, the private lending institutions pulled back even further. Private credit decreased 25.4 percent from 1996 to 2001, while state (development) credit increased 488 percent in an effort to make up for the lack of available capital for investment. For the same period, defaults on commercial bank loans by textile and apparel industries increased by 73 percent. Defaults on state bank credits also increased, but only by 34 percent for the same period (INEGI 2002, table 4.1; Jiménez 1999).

In December 2001, Grupo Mexicano initiated bankruptcy proceedings. Major creditors included GE Capital, Citibank Banamex, Scotia bank Inverlat, as well as the state export promotion bank Bancomext. Bankruptcy documents reveal that Grupo Mexicano owed over $430 billion pesos (close to U.S.$47.25 million dollars) in debt with assets short of $54 billion pesos (just under U.S.$6 million dollars). While close ties with national and local state agents did not translate into financial solvency, they did assist Grupo Mexicano in fending off creditors and fighting workers' attempts to install an independent union. The fact that two Grupo Mexicano executives held government positions—director of the secretary of labor and secretary of state—helped enormously. The state governor and labor authorities preferentially implemented labor laws at the LCAB to deny the workers' independent union's legal standing and then certified a company-imposed protection union.

Moreover, state agents facilitated the delay of bankruptcy hearings by extending deadlines to find investors and impeding the liquidation of assets multiple times. When potential investors did arise, in 2003 and 2004, majority owner Pérez turned down their proposals as insufficient. While state agents could have legally obliged Pérez to accept, they did not. In the end, Grupo Mexicano was declared bankrupt in 2004. The factories stand empty today, machinery gathering dust inside. One hundred and eighty workers who sued the company for unlawful dismissal with one particular lawyers' office received partial compensation in 2010. The rest are still waiting.

## Understanding Moctezuma's Failure in Comparative Perspective

### National Firms and Industrial Upgrading

Moctezuma's bankruptcy brings up the question, Would the company have failed had it not invested in modular and full-package production? I cannot answer that based on one case study. Ethnographies are better suited to answer questions of process, such as *how* the firm struggled to deal with a changing global environment, rather than alternative outcomes. But studies on the Mexican apparel sector and organizational change provide some insight.

Moctezuma's bankruptcy does not mean that Mexican firms cannot be successful or that the transformation to modular production caused the firm's failure. Participating in the global market is a highly competitive and risky endeavor—one that was worsened in 2001 by the U.S. recession given Mexican firms' dependence on U.S. markets. Many other large exporting firms—national and transnational—also failed during this period (Garrido Noguera and Ortiz Guerrero 2009). The area near Tehuacán, Puebla, alone lost between fifteen thousand to twenty thousand apparel jobs in 2001. When the economy began to recover in early 2002 many firms relocated to rural areas and hired first-time workers under short-term contracts or no contracts at all (Juárez Nuñez 2003; Maquila Solidarity Network and Human and Labour Rights Commission of the Tehuacán Valley 2003). Between 2001 and 2003, an estimated two hundred fifty thousand apparel and textile jobs throughout Mexico were lost (Harvey 2005; Maquila Solidarity Network and Human and Labour Rights Commission of the Tehuacán Valley 2003).

Investing in industrial upgrading to increase competitiveness likely affords Mexican firms an advantage during economic crises. Gereffi, Martínez, and Bair's (2002) study of jeans production in the northern city of Torreón demonstrates that full-package producers were better able to weather the U.S. recession than assemblers or maquiladoras. They argue that a key component of success was forging close relations with American firms that could assist with credits, know-how, and access to the U.S. market and combining that assistance with the Mexican firms' local knowledge, capital, and entrepreneurial spirit. Nevertheless, they point out that Torreón fell short in its attempt to become an industrial district, despite ample state support. A study of apparel producers in the state of Puebla also found that the largest exporting firms tended to be full-package producers that were organized around modular production (Juárez Nuñez 2003). Yet despite proximity advantages, the Mexican apparel sector in general *still* cannot meet quality standards, produce in large enough volume, or fulfill delivery schedules necessary for export; lack of credit and reliable suppliers are the biggest problems (De Coster 2007; Dussel Peters, Ruiz Durán, and Piore 2002). Competing internationally is extremely difficult.

If anything, Moctezuma, as a national firm with established networks with state agents and national suppliers, might have been more inclined to tough out the economic downturn than transnational garment and textile firms. Andrew Schrank's research on the garment, textile, and footwear industry in the Dominican Republic sheds light on the differences between national and transnational capital. Using firm-level mortality data, he argues that "domestically owned firms [were] significantly more likely to survive the vulnerable period between the implementation of NAFTA and the arrival of NAFTA parity than their foreign-owned counterparts" (2008, 11). He found that foreign firms were more likely to respond to economic downturn by leaving the Dominican Republic. In contrast, domestic firms that were locally embedded tended to rely on their social capital and knowledge of local conditions to pursue alternative strategies, including firm expansion and full-package production.

Something similar might have occurred in the city where Moctezuma was located. Several high-profile U.S. and Canadian garment firms located at a nearby industrial park, which was set up at great cost to the local state, closed their operations in 2000 and early 2001. According to a manager who had been employed at one of these U.S. firms, delivery times and quality were problematic and annual worker turnover topped 90 percent. Although U.S. management had planned to implement modular production to produce pants, it never did so. Faced with these obstacles, the firm opted to move to China. Viewed this way, Moctezuma may be an example of a domestic firm making use of local knowledge of the labor market and suppliers, as well as its ties to regional political and economic elites to weather difficult economic times—at least for a longer period of time than their foreign counterparts.

### Organizational Change

Scholars note that, in order to decrease uncertainty, firms tend to emulate successful organizational forms, leading to isomorphism, or similarity in structure. This organizational form then becomes the benchmark for success, the example to follow (Abrahamson 1991, 1996; DiMaggio and Powell 1983). Moctezuma experienced isomorphic pressures to upgrade from state policies and management fashion setters, such as regulation bodies and consulting firms. These maintained that Japanese lean techniques were not only helpful but necessary to capture value added in a highly globalized economy. At the same time, branded manufacturers and retailers provided coercive pressures when they demanded JIT production, increased quality, and turnaround time.

But the question remains: Did the company's flawed implementation of modular production cause the economic crisis? While the new owners were inexperienced in garment production and their actions during the strike demonstrated they cared more about controlling workers than enhancing quality, the partial and piecemeal implementation of modular production was not out of the ordinary.

Some organizational theorists suggest that the bundling of organizational practices is more successful than individual adoption (Appelbaum et al. 2000; Pil and MacDuffie 1996). Others argue that the transfer of organizational innovations is almost always a departure from the ideal since organizations exist within institutional environments that cannot be easily reproduced; firms must adapt to local circumstances (Damanpour and Evan 1984; Florida and Kenney 1991; Kenney and Florida 1993). Moreover, emulating organizations may have imperfect and incomplete information, reproducing formal rules while ignoring crucial informal practices and norms necessary for organizational effectiveness (Westney 1987). It is also difficult for an established firm—a brownfield site like Moctezuma—to overcome organizational inertia, to depart from formal and informal practices that have been internalized by managers and workers (Hannan and Freeman 1984; Sydow, Schreyögg, and Koch 2009; Vallas 2003a).

Another obstacle to organizational change is resistance from managers (Prechel 1994; Smith 1990; Vallas 2003a). At Moctezuma, some midlevel supervisors lost their jobs with the reorganization to teamwork; all lost authority vis-à-vis workers.

It would not be surprising if they half-heartedly implemented new rules. Managers at all levels spoke of the financial crisis of the firm, stressing the "millions of dollars" that were "wasted" on the international consulting agency. They perceived this as having been a bad and unnecessary investment. Whether their perception was correct or not, it points to the resistance by management to change and the questioning of decisions made at the highest levels concerning the direction of the company.

Organizational change can lead to contradictory effects. Under globalization, teamwork is often adopted for its competitive system of having multiskilled workers who can quickly respond to market changes. At the same time, however, teamwork is considered a normative strategy of increased responsibility accompanied by greater worker autonomy. These competing logics can result in uneven managerial practices and workers experiencing teamwork as both empowerment and coercion, which can have detrimental effects on organizational effectiveness (Hodson 2001; Vallas 2006).

Tensions between human resources (HR) and the production department pointed to the existence of such competing logics. The HR department focused on social relations, on how to manufacture consent. Meanwhile, production managers privileged the techniques and outcomes of teamwork. The competition between the HR and production department leadership resulted in uneven and confusing managerial dictates.

Vital to any organization are social norms that demarcate appropriate behavior. Respecting these norms—on recruitment, promotion, training, work practices, compensation, and grievances—bestows legitimacy to management. Hodson argues that managers must be good citizens in the workplace in order to develop the trust of their employees. Managers are good citizens when they "[abide] by norms concerning the treatment of employees and [provide] a workable technical system of production" (Hodson 2001, 93).[6]

Management's violation of social norms can have serious consequences, especially under lean production practices, which are premised on trust. If managers do not follow their own rules, mistrust and managerial incoherence can follow, making it difficult for workers to achieve their work objectives. Organizational effectiveness and managerial legitimacy decrease, which in turn can lead to workplace chaos and managerial abuse (Juravich 1985; Roscigno and Hodson 2004). Mistrust can also turn into resistance, especially when workers have created a sense of cohesiveness and solidarity (Hodson et al. 1993; Vallas 1987, 2003a).

Organizational disarray can lead to individual or group resistance. Individual resistance in the form of turnover is the most common. Organizing as a group against the firm occurs less often in flexible participatory organizations because employee involvement schemes often increase worker loyalty, careful worker selection weeds out more militant employees, and teamwork lateralizes conflict (Crowley et al. 2010; Hodson 2001; Vallas 2003b, 2006). The disjuncture between the rhetoric and practice of participation, however, may mobilize workers' resistance (Milkman 1997; Pollert 1996; Vallas 2006). Empowered workers can then use the citizenship skills they learn at work to mobilize fellow workers against the firm. This is *precisely* what workers did at Moctezuma.

## Conclusion

Management attempted to reestablish control on the shop floor by reinstating Taylorist work organization with elements of lean production—what I call *flexible Taylorism*. Management had noticed how workers subverted the team structures to organize and sustain mobilizations. Hence, they reorganized the shop floor to remove the empowering aspects of teams while retaining control and quality-enhancing elements such as whiteboards and quality auditors. The changes were accompanied by continual firings of movement organizers and their replacement by mostly young, inexperienced women. Moreover, management installed a protection union to put an end to calls for authentic worker representation in the workplace.

However, this was not enough to contain workers' resistance; the conflict had moved into the public eye through marches, petitions, and increased media scrutiny. In the process, movement participants increasingly defined themselves as *citizens* waging a fight for *fundamental rights*. The firm fought back, using its influence in the state government, mounting its own media campaign, and firing movement leaders and supporters.

In the end, the garment firm could not produce the quality garments it had promised without skilled workers; this prompted its petitioning for bankruptcy protection in December 2001. For the next nine months, the company hobbled along until the courts called for a precautionary embargo of company assets. At this time, the presence of the protection union, Protejer, proved beneficial; they declared a strike, which automatically halted all bankruptcy proceedings. What followed were years of political wrangling as business entrepreneurs and government officials sought ways to bail out the firm, including pumping in money and finding investors. Although federal courts did rule the firm bankrupt in 2004, injunctions in favor of national and international banks halted workers' compensation, who started to receive partial payment only in March 2010.

This chapter has also highlighted the ways that state agents and companies have exploited the purposeful ambiguity in labor laws to favor capital over workers. Providing an environment that promotes investment conditions has always been important to the state. But under increased global competition, it has become the primary role. Controlling labor unrest while promoting favorable conditions for business interests creates the illusion that investments will be secure and development will follow.

# Conclusion

## "WE ARE WORKERS, NOT BEGGARS"

What does the case of Moctezuma tell us about development in the age of globalization? How did globalization shape women's struggle in 2001? And how do women's actions inform the concept of agency? Moctezuma is an important case to study because it represented a high-road model for local development premised on empowered women workers, high wages, and organizational innovations. As a full-package producer, it offered, according to Gereffi and Martínez in a paper prepared for the World Bank's *World Development Report 2000/2001 on Poverty and Development*, "better opportunities for development by accelerating technology transfer, creating high quality jobs with better wages, and providing opportunities for local entrepreneurs, correcting some of the exploitative characteristics of the maquila[dora] production system" (1999, 2).

State development planners had devised an apparel and textile industrial district around the long-established and internationally known firm. Moctezuma and the accompanying textile mills were considered successful examples of national firm upgrading; Grupo Mexicano, the parent company, controlled 20 percent of apparel and textile export markets. It was not a fly-by-night assembler. So, how do we make sense of the firm's collapse?

### UNDERSTANDING GLOBALIZATION

The case of Moctezuma demonstrates that globalization affects firms and workers in multiple ways. How local institutional circumstances and practices constrain and enable change, however, is historically contingent. Place and time matter. Globalization had an effect on Moctezuma in six important ways. The first three deal with inducements to adopt particular organizational forms. First, Grupo Mexicano grew out of state neoliberal reforms that shaped corporate behavior in favor of adopting organizational innovation and expansion based on short-term debt, resulting in undercapitalized firms. Second, as one of the twelve strategic economic sectors targeted for growth by the state, the garment and textile industry benefited from state policies that promoted the adoption of total quality management, lean production, and full-package production. Third, international management consultants also offered lean production as the best way to compete internationally.

Three more events highlight the shifting and precarious nature of global integration for firms in a Third World context. First, at the same time Grupo Mexicano was adopting Japanese-style production, the concentration of power in the global apparel industry translated into increased demand from brand-name clients to produce more high-end suits for less cost and lower turnaround time; global firms did so by requiring organizational innovations like just-in-time production, statistical process control, and teamwork. Second, the opening of Mexico's capital markets made the country more vulnerable to global financial crises, such as the 1997 East Asian financial crisis, which tripled interest rates and increased the firm's debt load. Third, China's entrance to the World Trade Organization (WTO) and the provision of North American Free Trade Agreement (NAFTA) parity to Central America and Caribbean countries enticed producers away from Mexico just as the U.S. recession decreased total consumption (Dussel Peters 2005; *just-style* 2005a; *just-style* 2007).

Given the convergence of these factors—pressures to adopt expensive organizational innovations under worsening conditions of global competitiveness and production—Moctezuma's fall from grace is not that surprising. However, that is only part of the story. The reorganization of production also shaped social relations on the shop floor and affected how women interpreted their relationship with managers.

## THE CHANGING NATURE OF SOCIAL RELATIONS
## ON THE SHOP FLOOR

The organization of production affects how both workers and managers experience work. Piecework and teamwork at Moctezuma shaped the labor process to include positive and negative aspects for workers; it was not a simple zero-sum equation. In general, women said they preferred piecework because they controlled the pace of work and thus the amount of money they provided their household. The familial work culture stressed women's family roles above all else. The factory layout, with piles of bundles around workstations, allowed them to either slow down or speed up according to their needs. If there weren't enough materials, workers used their time-out card so their efficiencies and pay would not be negatively affected. Partnered women and single mothers reported that they were more likely to self-exploit, consistently operating at a frenzied pace to earn large bonuses. Young unpartnered women preferred to work leisurely and socialize, earning the base wage.

Under piecework, however, women labored under the watchful eyes of multiple hierarchies of supervisors. Although they could wield a big stick with workers, supervisors were also beholden to workers to produce results to show to upper management. Piecework essentially pitted workers against supervisors. Control was direct and antagonistic, a competition between workers using their discretionary power and supervisors their direct power. Given the emphasis on quantity over quality, piecework was an inefficient production system.

Modular production promised the increased quality required to compete in global markets. Significantly, Moctezuma attempted to compete globally through high wages and benefits instead of cheap labor. Although managers still carried gendered ideologies that marked women as the best suited for detailed and meticulous sewing work, workers' skill was rewarded. Retaining skilled workers was of such importance that, when teamwork was implemented in 1996, the firm entered into a social pact with workers whereby enhanced benefits were traded for worker loyalty.

Management constructed a belief in a community of fate that reflected and reinforced specific gender expectations. Geared specifically to the mostly female workforce, management offered workers access to a family clinic, dental and reproductive health campaigns, and weekly coupons exchangeable for food at the supermarket. In addition, management used posters and special factorywide celebrations to portray itself as a benevolent patriarch.

The social pact was required, moreover, because lean production changed the experience of work. In effect, women and men became worker-managers charged with controlling each others' expenditure of effort to increase quality and volume. Under modular production, self-managed teams and an open layout that made all actions visible became the operating forms of control. Productivity and quality bonuses pushed workers to continually pressure and supervise each other, while reduced inventory and white boards with updated production data made individual autonomy difficult. In addition, new rules on quality obliged workers to return poorly made garments to preceding workers, resulting in interpersonal animosity and tension. Nevertheless, workers understood that they had exchanged amplified control for greater benefits.

This begs the question, Did the increased cost of labor make the company uncompetitive in today's highly globalized apparel market? The answer is no. In the niche market of high-end suits, quality and turnaround time are key. These were obtained not *in spite* of the increased cost of labor but *because* of it. Many of the women I met while I was working on the shop floor had previously worked at other transnational garment firms in the area; they had left because of the low wages. Moreover, the Calvin Klein auditor, present at the factory every two months, told me that Moctezuma was the only firm in Mexico that could produce suits to their high-quality specifications. High wages and good benefits that tied experienced workers to the firm made this possible.

## THE STRIKE(S): UNDERSTANDING WOMEN'S AGENCY

I understand *agency* to be social action that emerges when individuals and groups create meaning out of everyday life experiences that occur within historically contingent constraints of social, political, and economic structures. That is, choices made by women workers are negotiations between their particular life experiences and the larger context, whether that is the family, the workplace, or society.

How, then, do we explain the workers' strike of 2001? If working at Moctezuma was such an exceptionally good job, why did the women rebel? A brief examination of the 1972 strike highlights the role of globalization and teamwork in the 2001 mobilizations.

I argue that, in the case of Moctezuma, women's agency was shaped by the confluence of external factors—the effects of globalization, increased migration, heightened national social movement activity, and perceived democratization—and internal factors—breaking of the community of fate belief, development of leadership experience in self-managed teams, and increased autonomy through the motherist work culture. Women workers' identities and perceived interests were transformed as the workplace changed. No longer content to see themselves solely as mothers, women built a collective dual identity—as mothers *and* workers—who had the right to participate in both public and private spheres.

The struggle for dignity at work is at the heart of women's agency. Work is composed of instrumental and ideal elements, providing livelihood and meaning for workers; both are important in creating dignity at work (Hodson 2001). When either is lacking, workers may be dissatisfied. But grievances, although endemic, are a necessary but insufficient condition for the emergence of collective action. Social movement scholars posit that certain enabling contextual conditions make collective action more probable. When shared grievances disrupt everyday activities, are interpreted as a matter of injustice, and occur within a political context vulnerable to organized challenge, mobilization is more likely to flourish (Klandermans, Roefs, and Olivier 2001; McAdam 1982; Meyer 2004). The availability of resources such as leadership, physical space, material supplies, networks, and cultural repertoires increase the likelihood of emergence and success (Edwards and McCarthy 2004; McCarthy and Zald 2002; Tilly 1995). Last, repression is likely to invigorate collective action (Almeida 2008; Goodwin 2001; Moore 1978).

Under piecework, the familial work culture shaped women's outlook so they tended to see their jobs as a means to fulfill their familial responsibilities, whether as daughters or mothers. High turnover, atomized work arrangements, competition over easy work, and a slack labor market generally dampened mobilization. While the catalyst for the 1972 strike was the firing of 110 workers whose temporary status had expired, the mobilizations that occurred then are best explained by external factors—the presence of a strong social movement unionism in the area. This labor movement, supported by progressive sectors of the

Catholic Church, had set up a school for workers in which some of the fired workers had previously participated (Basurto 1989; Mackin 1995). This network of union leaders and university students, together with Marxist, Troskyist, and Maoist political party members, was the source of class consciousness among workers. In addition, the school was key in activating a wave of industrial protest that prompted the state to pressure the company to rehire the workers. Participation in politicizing organizations is the best predictor of women workers' mobilization and best explains the 1972 strike (Pangsapa 2007; Peña 1997; Staudt 1987; Young 1987).

Significantly, the 1972 strike occurred in the midst of the developmentalist state's industrialization phase, which had created a working class that clamored for representation. Given the recent shift from an agricultural to an industrial economy, official unions were weak. The ruling party's need for legitimacy made it more open to worker demands. The state in turn pressured the company to resolve the labor dispute. The industrial action occurred under conditions of hegemonic regime, where state intervention mediated labor relations between capital and workers (Burawoy 1985).

The political opportunity structures during the 2001 strike were very different. Faced with mounting foreign debt and accountability to international financial institutions, the main focus of the neoliberal state was to secure the conditions of capital accumulation to attract foreign direct investment (FDI). Sixty percent of FDI in 2000, 79 percent of which was American, occurred in the textile and apparel sector (Juárez Nuñez 2003). While lax labor law enforcement and the composition of local conciliation and arbitration boards (LCABs) meant that the state historically sided with capital, large industrial groups in 2001 were the most likely to attract FDI through full-package production; thus, they were key allies of the state. A revolving door between big business and government leaders solidified the shift in industrial policy toward exports. In Moctezuma's case, the alliance between business and government was evident.

Meanwhile, on the shop floor, managers told workers that clients would take their business to China and Central America if they did not work harder and for less money. The company's financial crisis, explained by management as a result of global competition, was used to justify dismissals, wage cuts, and the cancelling of the collective-bargaining agreement. It was hegemonic despotism— the race to the bottom—used to threaten workers (Burawoy 1985).

The 2001 strike was not precipitated by any one managerial action; rather, it was caused by a series of events that were, increasingly, interpreted as unjust. Workers were bound to the firm through a social pact whereby workers exchanged augmented effort for increased wages and benefits. While at first many women believed managerial promises of mutual respect and shared interests, managerial incoherence and uncertainty in payment incentives chipped away at workers' trust. Yet most continued to participate in the team system, which many workers experienced as coercive peer pressure, because they saw their interests as coinciding with those of management: continued firm success ensured their employment.

Workers' consent, however, was based on the expectation of reciprocal obligations. Recognizing the cutthroat nature of global competition—which was constantly broadcast on the news and radio everyday as Mexican domestic markets and agriculture slumped after enactment of NAFTA—women workers voted in 2000 to "lend" the company a series of benefits for one year to capitalize the firm. Just before the year was up, the firm betrayed the social pact in three ways. First, the firm cancelled the second shift, firing hundreds of workers while retaining supervisors. Workers were upset but did not turn on management, believing they could still work together to save the company. Second, management announced that loaned benefits would not be restored and wages would be cut. For most, this was a turning point—irrefutable proof that management could not be trusted. And third, management entered a petition with the LCAB to rescind portions of the collective-bargaining agreement without discussing it with workers. With this, workers erupted in a shared moral outrage.

The increasing feeling of betrayal convinced workers to reevaluate their relationship with the firm through not only gender identities but also class-based identities. Management's actions were interpreted as procedural injustices. Moctezuma's management could not be trusted; managers would continue, in the words of one teammate, to "bleed the working class in their search for profits." A female utility worker put it this way: "When [management] changed the [collective-bargaining] agreement, that was the last straw. Workers were not willing to put up with anything else. We were willing to fight to the end, even if they fired us. . . . We're not willing to put up with any more exploitation." The social pact between workers and managers was finally breached.

While women workers understood the company's financial difficulties, they no longer believed the firm would honor its contract. Previously, many women workers had described their employment as "a good job for a mother." Now women claimed their job was not worth keeping because management would inevitably push for lower and lower wages with more cuts in benefits, the proverbial race to the bottom. Although women still identified as mothers, they increasingly interpreted their interests as also class-based and antithetical to management's interests. That is, the meaning of work was redefined as women saw themselves not merely as mothers (and thus willing to accept worsening conditions of work for the sake of family income) but as workers *and* mothers (who deserved a job with dignity and a living wage, which could no longer be obtained at Moctezuma).

Unlike the 1972 strike, the key resources for mobilization took root inside the factory. The most important resource deployed by workers emanated from self-managed teams: a sense of solidarity and shared identity, as well as an effective network for communication and decision making. Although teams pit workers against each other much of the time, the motherist work culture increased worker autonomy and facilitated an emergent solidarity based on shared experiences, ideas, beliefs, and feelings. In this way, feuding women united within teams to demand rights in the name of motherhood.

Emboldened by their experience of active participation in self-managed teams, women workers saw the strike as a line in the sand. The reassessment of their relationship to the firm was facilitated by the experience of leadership and authority gained through teamwork, where workers played a role in solving production problems, coordinating with supervisors and other teams, adjudicating permits, and disciplining inefficient workers and rogue supervisors. Being forced into active roles in teams empowered women to refuse management's imposition of new work conditions. Marta credits self-managed teams with her new sense of confidence: "I learned to relate to men, how to speak up in groups, and [speak] with the bosses around. The bosses no longer intimidated me."

While self-managed teams did not produce collective action, they facilitated a process of reinterpreting the meaning of work that, together with a growing sense of solidarity, breached differences of gender, age, skin color, and marital status. Moreover, increased wages and benefits had lowered turnover and increased the costs of leaving the firm since workers would lose significant compensation based on seniority if they left voluntarily. Voice rather than exit was the predominant response by workers to worsening work conditions and managerial betrayal of the social pact (Hirschman 1970).

The lack of free spaces, however, negatively affected the maintenance of worker participation. Once management clamped down on teams and team leaders, there were no communication mechanisms between the democratically elected union and workers. Without a union office or a social movement organization that offered a meeting space to leave messages or coordinate strategies, the union leadership resorted to standing outside the gates and spreading the word to workers individually. While the resistance committee found a home with the independent human rights groups, most workers—who had voted for the conservative National Action Party (PAN)—were wary of left-leaning groups like the human rights groups. Thus, in 2001, workers lacked the organizational resources, such as local social movement support or space, that had been critical for success in 1972.

The decision of workers to stand up to the company was also influenced by several external factors tied to the social, rather than economic, effects of globalization. First, several national movements—the Zapatista uprising in southern Mexico and the university student movement in Mexico City—dominated the press during this period, highlighting the possibility of contestation. Second, news media consistently portrayed NAFTA and globalization as detrimental to national interests, validating women's interpretation of globalization as a race to the bottom. Third, immigration to the United States from the central state where Moctezuma was located had increased dramatically in recent years, providing workers with a difficult but real labor market option. Fourth, a democratization process flourished in 2000 as the center-right PAN was elected to power after seventy-one years of Institutional Revolutionary Party (PRI) rule. Many workers had voted for the PAN and expected increased access to the state. Together, these four aspects of globalization provided workers with a social imaginary, demonstrating that there were possibilities other than toiling at Moctezuma under worsening employment conditions.

Women workers had few connections with local social movements until the governor sent in riot police to violently remove their sit-in at a major highway two weeks after the strike. The media coverage exploded into public moral outrage; solidarity poured out from many different nongovernmental organizations and labor groups. This was a crucial turning point. The governor's exaggerated response radicalized many workers who now energetically took on not only the company and the union but also the state. Moreover, as women marched down streets and lobbied political parties in the local congress, they forged ties with human rights groups, women's organizations, independent unions, and other local labor struggles, learning and reiterating class-based arguments for labor mobilization.

Women's entrance into the political arena, moreover, convinced many of the need to move beyond the struggle at Moctezuma, demanding that the state be more inclusive of worker concerns and open to grassroots democratic voices. As one of the movement leaders stated: "We want to remind the governor that it was not the rich employers who carried them [PAN] to power, not a group of privileged people, but the poor people" (*MRN1* 2001).

For some women, the experience of struggle and solidarity garnered in fighting Moctezuma pushed them to see themselves as citizens, as part of a larger community demanding rights and political inclusion. When asked why she joined the resistance committee, Marta explained that she had never been involved in politics before. If anything, she was conservative because her family voted for the PAN. Before the strike, she only left her house to work and then went straight home. But management's breach of trust changed that; she said, "I worked hard. I didn't even go to the bathroom. That's why I was so angry when they said we were bad workers!"

After the mobilizations subsided in June, Marta continued fighting the company and the state through the independent human rights group. Together with other women in the resistance committee, she sued the company in federal court. I asked her what she thought could be achieved with this. She responded:

> I want the company to recognize that they unjustly fired me. I don't know if I'll get any money but what I want are better laws to protect workers. I want there to be less corruption and more just laws. . . . I am disillusioned with the PAN because they only wanted my vote and nothing else. Before, I worked

and then went straight home. Now, I go to the PRD [Democratic Revolution Party] meetings. I know myself better. I participate in my neighborhood. I joined AMLO [Andrés Manuel López Obrador] and got to know him.[1] They even offered me political training! My husband and I are in a brigade to defend AMLO. All this enriches me as a person. Now, I have something to tell my grandchildren.

Marta credits the experience of leadership in self-managed teams with her transformation from a mother to a citizen.

The great majority of workers actively supported the strike and ensuing mobilizations. Of the thirty-eight workers in the two teams I participated in, only three workers openly opposed the strike, and four felt ambivalent, offering only passive support. While the team dynamics discouraged dissent, most workers expressed support in multiple ways that led me to believe that participating in the strike was both a personal and group decision. Workers embodied agency as they acted in favor of their own perceived social and economic interests in a process that compared the experience of work—either contrasting teamwork with piecework or previous employment—and took into consideration how the changing social context provided new opportunities.

Many transferred their newfound sense of self-determination from the shop floor to their homes and work lives. Participating in social movements often strengthens women's ability to resist patriarchal relations at home (Morgen and Bookman 1988; Tiano 1994; Young 1987). Notably, this empowerment assisted many single women in navigating the labor market and life decisions after the firm closed. For example, one coworker, Rita, who had been single during the mobilizations and later quit because of the pressure to participate in the mobilizations, learned to be more self-assured.

After working at Moctezuma, Rita held several sales and cashier jobs, becoming manager of a retail store. In a conversation at the end of 2009, she said, "I loved the job [at Moctezuma] but hated the pressure of teams. But [the experience] gave me more confidence in myself. Now that I'm more experienced and responsible, I'm not afraid. You know, I'm in charge of a whole store [now]. But I couldn't have done that before." Later, Rita commented: "Guess what, I'm a single mother now." When I asked if the father helped out, she replied, "I decided on my own that I wanted to be a single mother." Her mother and brothers helped her with expenses while she stayed home, but she could not wait to get back to work. "I'm tired of being taken care of by my mother and brothers. I want what's mine. I want to work, to have an occupation. I'm really good at sales." While most women did not undergo occupational mobility after the strike (they did not find better jobs or improve their social class standings), the experience of teams and mobilizations—in spite of her eventually resenting the continued demands of mobilization—affected Rita's perception of self-efficacy and spilled over into her personal life.

Married women reported more contradictory effects. In general, husbands did not respond well to women's new sense of self-reliance. Several of my married teammates experienced domestic violence and separation when they tried to change the gender division of labor in the home. Others experienced full support from husbands, particularly if they were factory workers as well. This underscores that a theory of agency has to be culturally and historically contextualized to understand the operation of multiple structures of domination and how these affect different women (and men) in distinct ways.

## WHERE HAVE ALL THE WORKERS (AND MANAGERS) GONE?

After making several visits back to the area, I was able to determine what happened to some of the workers and managers after the factory closed. Workers experienced downward occupational mobility, which can be explained by two trends. The first is that local factories and some sewing workshops blacklisted anyone who had labored at Moctezuma well into 2006. Several women told me that, as soon as employers heard that they had worked at the firm, they were summarily turned down. Another did not disclose the information, but the factory somehow found out a week later and fired her. Therefore, women experienced long-term consequences for participating in the mobilizations.

The second trend was the continued economic decline in Mexico in the summer of 2001, due to the effects of the U.S. recession. The apparel industry was especially hit hard as U.S. markets contracted and orders for production dropped. Local jobs diminished, with a shift to medium and small sewing workshops, which often operate outside the law—not paying taxes or providing the legally sanctioned wages and benefits to workers.

Both of these trends affected the women and men who left Moctezuma, whether they quit or were terminated. In general, older women were not able to find formal employment. Most withdrew from the formal labor market completely, taking care of other people's children or selling food on the street. One coworker in her fifties noted, "What can I do? No one will hire me. I'm too old. I do odd jobs for neighbors and they give me a little something."

An important number of young women and some of the highly experienced older women workers were able to find jobs in informal sewing workshops. However, many of these jobs afforded no protection from unscrupulous employers; they also consisted of continual speedups, long hours, poor working conditions, and low wages.

One coworker I visited, Doña Ana, who had been a utility worker for over ten years with knowledge of over fourteen different operations, was laboring in a workshop on the outskirts of town. Several other former Moctezuma workers were also there, including an older woman who had been an adviser. The workshop was a converted small family storefront. A metal door opened up to a cement room where three women operated industrial sewing machines.

Connected to this room was the family kitchen, which led to a small, barren dirt yard. Women were cutting cloth on the kitchen table; outside under a tar roof propped up by poles, more women were ironing and washing clothes. Behind the makeshift work area was an outhouse made of recycled metal sheets and cardboard. I asked Doña Ana how she was doing. She shrugged her shoulders, smiled, and said, "At least I am working." (See figures Con.1 and Con.2.)

Most of the other women I spoke with had jumped from one informal activity to the next trying to make ends meet. Vicki finished the evening beautician courses she had been taking while still at work but never set up her beauty salon for lack of capital. Instead, she pieced together a living by providing a series of services to neighbors. When I visited her in 2004, her typical day started at six in the morning when she opened her juice stand, just outside her father's house. Along with juices, she sold fruit and other *antojitos* (snacks) until noon, when she delivered meals she had made the night before to teachers at a local grade school. In the afternoon, she picked up her son and another child from kindergarten and watched them while she cleaned house and made meals for her family. She also often delivered or picked up payment for the catalog clothes she sold or went to people's homes to cut their hair. By eight or nine at night, after her son was in bed, she prepared food to be sold the next day.

When I spoke to Vicki at the end of 2009, she still lived with her father. However, the income from the fruit stand proved to be insufficient. Having built

Figure Con.1. Sewing workshop, Doña Ana in the middle, 2006. Photograph by author.

Figure Con.2. Sewing workshop, 2006. Photograph by author.

up her clientele for homemade meals, she concentrated on that work instead and delivered the meals in the afternoons to the teachers at the grade school and three times per day to construction workers at a nearby municipal building site. In addition, Vicki continued to sell catalog products and cut hair. When I asked her how much she made, she replied that she was not sure but not much. However, working from home afforded her the ability to watch her son. Occasionally she was called in to the local megamarket as a sale representative for special products. "It helps make ends meet," she said.

Vicki was one of the workers who had sued the company. Although the national labor authorities had ruled in favor of workers in 2004, bank creditors had impeded compensation payments to workers. In March 2010, she received a portion of her compensation, which she invested in building a second floor onto her father's house.[2] Although the second story is incomplete, missing floors and doors, she moved upstairs and rented out the first floor, securing a steady income. She also returned to working full-time at a local beauty shop to hone her skills, even though, by the end of October 2011 she was making only $600 pesos a week (U.S.$44). Jobs are hard to come by these days, she says, so she will remain there. She still dreams of setting up her own salon one day.

My neighbor and coworker María also labored in the informal economy. She worked for several sewing workshops, but work was unstable, did not pay well, and she got home very late, having to leave her baby with her eldest teenage daughter. So she borrowed money from a friend (my mother) and set up a fruit and vegetable stand in her front yard. Every few days she took the bus down to the main market to restock the fruit and vegetables. According to her, she could only charge a few extra pesos, but that, on top of what she could earn by cleaning people's houses and combined with her husband's earnings as a bus driver, was enough to get by. After a particularly bad beating from her husband in 2003, she fled with her baby in the middle of the night to the United States, leaving her two eldest children, both married, behind.

Today María lives in California, cooking and busing plates at a Mexican food restaurant. She has encountered several Moctezuma workers in California. She says they reminisce about the time they fought back against the boss. To her delight, her little girl speaks flawless English and does well in school. While she is increasingly fearful of being deported by U.S. Immigration and Customs Enforcement, which increased raids locally after passage of Arizona Senate Bill 1070 in 2010, she continues to drive to work and takes her daughter to the nearby park. It is María's deepest hope that, by growing up in the United States, her daughter will have more opportunities than she did.

The few men at the factory that I was able to contact after my time in Mexico had an even harder time finding employment. One of the few jobs available for men was that of taxi drivers, although most did so without the required papers, risking fines and incarceration. Juan, the team leader from jackets one, drove such a gypsy taxi. José, the young man in the pants team, was a stocker at the local Woolworth store.

The precarious employment experienced by women and men who had worked at Moctezuma suggests that one of the legacies of globalization is the feminization of the labor market: women encountered greater job opportunities than men. However, this does not mean that women's labor market opportunities improved; rather, it underscores how men's options were so dismal. Leslie Sklair found a similar pattern after the 1980s economic crisis (1993).

I also tracked down several managers to their new places of employment. June 2001 was the beginning of managerial exodus at Moctezuma, when the firm's owners demoted the top echelons of managers. These men were then wooed by competitors. Managers certainly knew the depths of the economic crisis. Top male managers tended to land on their feet, working for other garment firms—some national, some transnational—in surrounding states.

Interestingly, of the three top managers I reinterviewed, two went on to work at firms that had previously been competitors of Moctezuma; one was located in Mexico City, the other in the countryside in a nearby state. The other four midlevel managers I visited found employment in new subcontracting assembly plants that had just opened up in the countryside. In these factories, the workers had been peasants only months ago, the wages were very low, and there was no union. The former Moctezuma managers raved about using teamwork with new workers who did not complain like those at the old firm.

The two female managers I interviewed had a different experience. One was the female adviser from J-1. After having been fired from the company in 2003, she found employment in the local apparel industrial park at a European factory. As a supervisor, she made $1,000 pesos per week (U.S.$90), overseeing workers who were paid $450 pesos per week (U.S.$40). That year she met a documented migrant who had returned home from Texas to visit his family. After they married, he returned to the United States, hoping to save enough money to send for her and their new daughter as soon as possible. They now live in Houston.

I also spoke with the instructor from the training center, *la escuelita*, where I had begun my participant observation. Since leaving the company, she had worked at several large workshops. She even went to another state looking for better work. However, in spite of her experience and position at the factory, her age limited her to workshop employment. She could not have been older than forty-five years of age. When I asked for her opinion on the labor disputes at Moctezuma, she just said, "I'm sad it closed. It was a good job. I saw my kids through with that job."

By following managers after the close of Moctezuma, we can see a process of deindustrialization and precarious work employment. Factories have relocated from the cities to the countryside to take advantage of people without prior factory experience, low levels of education, and few labor market opportunities who will accept just about any working conditions provided. Importantly, systems similar to flexible Taylorism were installed, using some aspects of teamwork while incorporating quality-at-the-source rules requiring everyone to supervise everyone else's work. Instead of upgrading, a process of reinscribed control with selected innovations and cheap labor ensued. Thus, the case of Moctezuma is also important for the ways managers have spread flexible Taylorism as a form of upgrading through low-road development.

## The Case of Moctezuma and Mexico's Prospects for Development in the Age of Globalization

Although Moctezuma produced for a niche market, its trajectory represents a larger pattern for apparel firms in Mexico. Dynamic export growth in apparel occurred after NAFTA was signed in 1994, with total apparel exports increasing from U.S.$1.9 billion in 1994 to U.S.$8.1 billion in 2000 (Bair and Gereffi 2003). Especially important was the yarn-forward rule that allowed yarn from any of the three signatory countries to be used in exports without the imposition of tariffs. Many believed this would increase the incorporation, and thus growth, of textiles produced in Mexico. Large textile mills from United States, such as Gilford Mills, Burlington Industries, Gayley & Lord, and Malden Mills, rushed to Mexico to set up full-package production and take advantage of cheap labor and state incentives to relocate (Bair and Dussel Peters 2006; Bair and Gereffi 2002).[3] But textile companies in Mexico were unable to compete with a glut of

Asian textiles on the world market that cost half as much to produce. In addition, Asian textiles and apparel that were transshipped illegally through Mexico to avoid U.S. quotas severely undercut Mexican production.

Beginning in the year 2000, there was a marked decline in Mexican textile and apparel exports, with concomitant deterioration in participation in the gross domestic product (GDP), number of workers employed, and wages. Compared to 2000, by 2004 textiles and apparel GDP dropped 24 percent. From 2000 to 2006, employment fell by 35.9 percent, with wages falling from above the national average before NAFTA to 90 percent of the average. However, decreases in employment and wages were accompanied by increasing worker productivity, denoting the worsening conditions of employment (Dussel Peters 2008).

An important portion of this decline is attributed to China's increased participation in exports to the United States as the Multi-Fibre Arrangement (MFA) quota system was gradually being dismantled. In 2000, Mexico was the largest apparel exporter to the United States with almost 20 percent of shares. By 2003, China had surpassed all countries, representing 71 percent of imports in textiles and apparel to the United States. Mexico's participation had dropped by 5 percent. Another important cause of this change was the U.S. recession, since 95 percent of Mexican apparel exports are destined for the United States. Chinese products, in contrast, are exported to most regions of the world and cover a larger variety of products (Dussel Peters 2005, 2008).

Most observers expected China's 2005 entry into the WTO, and thus the end of the MFA, to eviscerate Mexico and Central America's textile and apparel industries (*just-style* 2005a; *just-style* 2010). While the decline in Mexico's share of imports in the United States has continued, U.S. safeguard provisions against particular Chinese products, together with more advantageous turnaround times from Mexico and Central America, have slowed China's predominance in U.S. markets.[4] By the middle of 2009, Mexico was still the largest Latin American exporter to U.S. markets in textiles and apparel and was the fourth in the world after China, Vietnam, and India. However, in 2009, the effects of the 2008 U.S. recession, and predominance of illegal clothing in the Mexican market, had already resulted in the loss of 68,000 jobs and 666 companies in the textile, apparel, and leather sector—a 14.7 percent decline in jobs and the closure of 5.3 percent of firms compared to the previous year (Cruz Campa 2009; Maquiladora Solidarity Network 2008).

What does this mean in terms of development? The economist Enrique Dussel Peters describes the textile and apparel industry in Mexico as disconnected from the larger economy, providing low potential for overall development (2005). There are two reasons for this. First, production is concentrated in a few areas, where fewer large companies are supplying to a reduced number of international clients (Maquila Solidarity Network 2008). Second, and most important, these Mexican large exporters are utilizing state temporary import programs, as Moctezuma did, to obtain production inputs to the degree that imports almost equal exports in the textile and apparel sector.

Therefore, although the Mexican government selected the textile and apparel industry as one of twelve strategic industrial sectors because of its employment potential, state policies have had unintended consequences that do not bode well for Mexico's development. State export promotion programs, and the preference of international lead firms to work with fewer and larger apparel firms, have fostered a dynamic exporting sector based on temporary imports, which is delinked from national suppliers—thereby decreasing the possibility of domestic value-added activities, organizational learning, or other positive economic effects in the local economy (Dussel Peters 2008). This has serious ramifications for workers given that, in mid-2009, the apparel, textile, and leather products industry generated over 300,000 jobs, or 2 percent of total employment, with 70 percent of them being women (Maquiladora Solidarity Network 2009).

As a result, the polarization between large exporting companies and medium and microenterprises is growing. Firms like Moctezuma, which have achieved upgrading through full-package production, are the motor for the industry but are disconnected from the larger local economy. This explains how, when Moctezuma closed, the highly skilled workforce could only find sewing employment in apparel assemblers, workshops, or doing homework. All three options entailed an increasing drop in wages and worsening work conditions, as underscored by my former coworkers' experience.

## Mexico: Doomed as Only a Source of Cheap Labor?

Given the experience of Moctezuma and the present crisis in the apparel industry, it is easy to be pessimistic. This case has shown that development entails more than firm upgrading. But it has also demonstrated that state policies matter in shaping the possibilities of industrial development and constraining worker organization. The lesson of Moctezuma's demise should not be about the failure of the high-road option to development; rather, it points to the importance of state involvement in blocking low-road options and facilitating industrial upgrading based on high wages and skill.

The stories of the women workers of Moctezuma have also shown that workers and social movements matter in shaping social policy and strengthening democracy. The example of the women still legally fighting the state and the company against all odds provides some instruction. Through mobilization, they were able to forge stronger relationships with local social movements and other progressive unions. This solidarity translated into both moral and economic support as well as activism to bolster democratic union movements and oppose draconian reforms to the labor code.[5] Faced with a daunting adversary—the state, which promoted exports to compete globally at all costs—the women followed the double strategy of going local and global. As Nobel laureate

Amartya Sen has argued, what is needed to combat the global race to the bottom is stronger democratic institutions so workers of the North and South can demand more just institutional arrangements (2002). Building strong local social movements is necessary for then building vigorous global civil society coalitions (Evans 2008; Seidman 2007; Turner and Cornfield 2007). The North American Free Trade Agreement helped create some of these connections, as the Authentic Labor Front (FAT), an independent union in Mexico, reached out to progressive unions in the United States and Canada, forming coalitions to protect labor rights in all three countries (Hathaway 2000).

Another model for protecting worker rights is holding transnational corporations responsible for the working conditions in their subcontracting factories through codes of conduct, whereby companies can be "named and shamed" if they do not ensure minimum standards (Armbruster-Sandoval 2005; Esbenshade 2004). At the same time that women at Moctezuma were striking, women at the Kukdong factory in a nearby state were also contesting managerial abuses and forming an independent union. They also suffered repression, but unlike Moctezuma, they produced Reebok sweatshirts for U.S. universities. Having an identifiable consumer base—university students—organized through United Students Against Sweatshops, the Worker Rights Consortium, and the presence of a local worker support group, the Centro de Apoyo al Trabajador was critical in their ability to mobilize international support and force Reebok to demand improved working conditions. The transnational coalition then oversaw the branded manufacturer to make sure that, rather than running away from its responsibility, it instead strengthened the reconstruction of a dignified workplace (Juárez Nuñez 2003; Rodríguez Garavito 2008).

Not all products will have a visible pressure or institutional group that can be mobilized in support of worker movements, however. It would have been difficult to organize the isolated businessmen who wore suits made at Moctezuma. Moreover, the mere presence of codes of conduct, which Moctezuma had, does not secure better working conditions. Transnational consumer campaigns often use a broad human rights framework and focus on the most heinous labor abuses to mount successful media campaigns to force corporations to voluntarily comply with codes of conduct. These campaigns have the unintended consequences of portraying workers as helpless victims and focusing on northern consumers (Brooks 2007). Gay Seidman argues that a more successful route would be to build or reinforce more egalitarian transnational networks, based on the needs and proposals made by communities and workers in the South. This can then be a springboard to demand independent monitoring, organize consumer and shareholder pressure, and, importantly, strengthen national state regulatory capacities and the ability of workers to insist on the enforcement of their citizenship rights (2007).

Although in the end, the women and men from Moctezuma did not successfully defend their jobs, many experienced empowerment as they stood up to oppressive forces and asserted their dignity. As Vicki, the single mother with a small child, who lived with her father and sold food outside her front door every evening and weekend in addition to her job at Moctezuma, succinctly articulated, "The company forced us to go on strike. I'd rather lose my job than accept what they want to give us. We workers, not beggars."

# Appendix A
# The Workforce at Moctezuma

TABLE A.1

FEMALE WORKERS BY MARITAL STATUS AND NUMBER OF CHILDREN, 2001
(PERCENTAGES IN PARENTHESES)

| Women workers | Partnered | | Unpartnered | | | Unknown Marital Status | Total |
|---|---|---|---|---|---|---|---|
| | MARRIED | COHABITING (*UNION LIBRE*) | SINGLE | DIVORCED | WIDOWED | | |
| With children | 322(82) | 10(20) | 270(65) | 2(8) | 5(36) | 8(50) | 617(68) |
| Without children | 72(18) | 41(80) | 143(35) | 23(92) | 9(64) | 8(50) | 296(32) |
| Total number | 394 | 51 | 413 | 25 | 14 | 16 | 913 |

Source: Compiled by author from worker files provided by human resources. These data reflect the most complete database, provided by the company as an Excel file, on marital status. Categories were designated by human resources. Data for men were not recorded.

TABLE A.2

EDUCATION LEVEL BY GENDER, 2001

| Educational level | Women | | Men | | All Workers | |
|---|---|---|---|---|---|---|
| | NO. IN SAMPLE | % OF ALL WOMEN | NO. IN SAMPLE | % OF ALL MEN | TOTAL NUMBER BY GRADE LEVEL | % OF TOTAL SAMPLE |
| Grade school | 156 | 23 | 20 | 20 | 176 | 23 |
| Ninth grade | 375 | 56 | 48 | 49 | 423 | 55 |
| Twelfth grade | 63 | 9 | 23 | 23 | 86 | 11 |
| Technical degree | 74 | 11 | 7 | 7 | 81 | 10 |
| Missing data | 1 | 2 | 1 | 1 | 2 | 0 |
| Total number | 669 | 101 | 99 | 100 | 768 | 99 |
| % of total sample | 87 | | 13 | | | |

Source: Company file with educational attainment data for 768 workers provided to author.
Note: Percentages that do not sum to 100 are due to rounding.

## TABLE A.3

### PERCENTAGE OF WOMEN WORKERS HIRED BY AGE GROUP UNDER CHANGING WORK ORGANIZATION OVER TIME

| Age Groups (in Years) | Under Taylorism | | | Under Transition, January 1994–August 1996 | Under Teamwork, September 1996–March 2001 | Under Flexible Taylorism, April 2001–December 2001 | Under All Work Organizations |
|---|---|---|---|---|---|---|---|
| | 1970s | 1980s | 1990–1993 | | | | |
| **16–20** | | | | | | | |
| % hired | 0 | 3.0 | 37.7 | 27.6 | 22.1 | 16.7 | 21.4 |
| No. of cases | 0 | 1 | 43 | 48 | 80 | 16 | 188 |
| **21–25** | | | | | | | |
| % hired | 56.3 | 39.4 | 26.3 | 24.7 | 31.4 | 31.3 | 29.2 |
| No. of cases | 9 | 13 | 30 | 43 | 131 | 30 | 256 |
| **26–30** | | | | | | | |
| % hired | 6.3 | 15.2 | 16.7 | 21.8 | 19.6 | 15.8 | 20.5 |
| No. of cases | 1 | 5 | 19 | 38 | 102 | 15 | 180 |
| **31–35** | | | | | | | |
| % hired | 6.3 | 21.1 | 10.5 | 21.8 | 19.6 | 18.9 | 19.2 |
| No. of cases | 1 | 7 | 12 | 38 | 93 | 18 | 169 |

| | | | | | | | Total |
|---|---|---|---|---|---|---|---|
| **36–40** | | | | | | | |
| % hired | 31.3 | 21.1 | 8.8 | 4.0 | 7.4 | 9.4 | 8.4 |
| No. of cases | 5 | 7 | 10 | 7 | 36 | 9 | 74 |
| **41–45** | | | | | | | |
| % hired | 0 | 0 | 0 | 0 | 0.6 | 6.25 | 1.0 |
| No. of cases | 0 | 0 | 0 | 0 | 3 | 6 | 9 |
| **46–50** | | | | | | | |
| % hired | 0 | 0 | 0 | 0 | 0 | 1.04 | 0.1 |
| No. of cases | 0 | 0 | 0 | 0 | 0 | 1 | 1 |
| **51–55** | | | | | | | |
| % hired | 0 | 0 | 0 | 0 | 0 | 1.04 | 0.1 |
| No. of cases | 0 | 0 | 0 | 0 | 0 | 1 | 1 |
| **Total** | | | | | | | |
| % hired | 100.2 | 99.8 | 100 | 99.9 | 100.7 | 100.4 | 100.8 |
| No. of cases | 16 | 33 | 114 | 174 | 445 | 96 | 878 |

Source: Compiled by author from worker files; represents workers present August to December 2001.

Note: Percentages do not sum to 100 because of rounding.

TABLE A.4

PERCENTAGE OF MEN WORKERS HIRED BY AGE GROUP UNDER CHANGING WORK ORGANIZATION OVER TIME

| Age Groups (in Years) | Under Taylorism | | | Under Transition, January 1994–August 1996 | Under Teamwork, September 1996–March 2001 | Under Flexible Taylorism, April 2001–December 2001 | Under All Work Organization |
| | 1970s | 1980s | 1990–1993 | | | | |
|---|---|---|---|---|---|---|---|
| 16–20 | | | | | | | |
| % hired | 0 | 27.3 | 37.5 | 40.0 | 31.5 | 15.63 | 21.4 |
| No. of cases | 0 | 3 | 3 | 4 | 23 | 16 | 188 |
| 21–25 | | | | | | | |
| % hired | 0 | 27.3 | 37.5 | 30.0 | 34.2 | 31.25 | 29.1 |
| No. of cases | 0 | 3 | 3 | 3 | 25 | 30 | 256 |
| 26–30 | | | | | | | |
| % hired | 0 | 27.3 | 25.0 | 20.0 | 21.9 | 15.63 | 20.5 |
| No. of cases | 0 | 3 | 2 | 2 | 16 | 15 | 180 |

| | G | F | E | D | C | B | A |
|---|---|---|---|---|---|---|---|
| **31–35** | | | | | | | |
| % hired | 0 | 0 | 0 | 10.0 | 9.6 | 18.75 | 19.2 |
| No. of cases | 0 | 0 | 0 | 1 | 7 | 18 | 169 |
| **36–40** | | | | | | | |
| % hired | 0 | 9.1 | 0 | 0 | 2.7 | 9.38 | 8.4 |
| No. of cases | 0 | 1 | 0 | 0 | 2 | 9 | 74 |
| **41–45** | | | | | | | |
| % hired | 0 | 9.1 | 0 | 0 | 0 | 6.25 | 1.0 |
| No. of cases | 0 | 1 | 0 | 0 | 0 | 6 | 9 |
| **TOTAL** | | | | | | | |
| % hired | 0 | 100.1 | 100.0 | 100.0 | 99.9 | 100.1 | 100.1 |
| No. of cases | 0 | 11 | 8 | 10 | 73 | 26 | 128 |

Source: Compiled by author from worker files; represents workers present August to December 2001

Note: Percentages that do not sum to 100 are due to rounding.

# Appendix B
# Past Work Employment Classification Methods

Organizational researchers rarely have access to data on workers' past employment. Moctezuma provided me with unobstructed access to all worker files, so I was able to discern workers' employment histories. These data had to be organized so they could be compared across time and work organization at the company.

The data obtained from workers' files was in response to the job interviewer's question, "Where did you work before?" Answers reflected a range of employment situations, including responses like "factory work"; "at X company"; "sewing workshop"; "as a domestic worker"; "I was in the United States for a year." These answers do not neatly fit neatly into recognized occupational classifications. The U.S. 2000 Standard Occupational Classification System (from the U.S. Bureau of Labor Statistics) stresses the characteristics of work performed along with skills, training, and credentials required for different jobs (Levine, Salmon, and Weinberg 1999). European ISCO-88 codes (International Standard Classification of Occupations-[19]88), established by the International Labor Organization, are structured around levels of education and skills that are utilized in different professions and occupations (Elias and Birch 1994).

To facilitate international comparisons, the Mexican Classification of Occupations (CMO) adapted the ISCO-88 categories to Mexican employment relations, where many workers labor under precarious conditions in small workshops and micro establishments (INEGI 2007). Hence, jobs are distinguished both by training and skills required, as well as employment relations, and by technology and machinery used by in different types of establishment. For example, the CMO differentiates between production of materials using traditional artisan methods and small workshops (category 52), those that utilize machinery and/or are organized in large establishments (category 53), and those that assist workers in either of the previous two categories (category 54).

Since the majority of workers at Moctezuma have low levels of education (23 percent to sixth grade; 55 percent to ninth grade; 11 percent to twelfth grade; and 11 percent, technical degrees), using classifications based on training and educational level did not make sense. Only the CMO is organized around establishment types. Therefore, I consulted detailed work descriptions from the CMO and added categories for "no previous work outside the home," "previous immigration to the United States," and "homework" (sewing garment orders at home). While the last category does not exist in the CMO, it could theoretically fit under the classification that included artisan work or domestic work. However, given the relevance of homework for this study, I gave it its own grouping.

Limitations of the data include the fact that information is based on workers' self-reported last employment as collected by human resource interviewers. Since this was not a standardized survey instrument but, rather, a job interview, questions could have been asked in different ways, eliciting different answers. In the few cases in which more than one past employment situation was provided, I used the last one listed. When the answer was not readily apparent, it was coded as missing data.

Table B.1 includes the CMO classifications utilized, descriptions of their main characteristics, and examples of past employment found at Moctezuma. Table B.2 uses the CMO classifications and codes to show the percent of women hired by work category for previous employment from the 1970s until 2001.

TABLE B.1

MEXICAN CLASSIFICATION OF OCCUPATION (CMO) CODES AND
CATEGORIES FOR MOCTEZUMA'S WORKERS

| Code Number | CMO Category | Past Employment Examples found at Moctezuma |
| --- | --- | --- |
| 13 | Education workers | Elementary teacher, university professor |
| 14 | Entertainers | Musician |
| 21 | Public- and private-sector executives and officers | Judge, small businesses owner |
| 41 | Agricultural workers | Subsistence farmer, flower cultivator |
| 51 | Production supervisors | Quality supervisor |

(continued)

TABLE B.1

MEXICAN CLASSIFICATION OF OCCUPATION (CMO) CODES AND
CATEGORIES FOR MOCTEZUMA'S WORKERS (*continued*)

| Code Number | CMO Category | Past Employment Examples found at Moctezuma |
|---|---|---|
| 52 | Production by artisans, craft workers, and in workshops | |
| | Artisans | Jeweler |
| | Craft workers | Plumber, electrician, carpenter, mechanic, repair person (not industrial repair), welder |
| | Food preparation | In small and medium establishments, not factory |
| | Workshop | Sewing, ceramic products |
| | Construction | Construction worker |
| 53 | Production in factories | Production worker in medium-to-large establishments, use of specialized machinery |
| 54 | Assistants to other workers | Waiter, assistant cook, craft-worker assistant, factory assistant, construction assistant |
| 55 | Transportation workers | Taxi driver, long-distance transport driver |
| 61 | Administrative supervisors | Bank supervisor |
| 62 | Office and administration | Secretary, receptionist, data collector, cashier |
| 71 | Sales and related workers | Store attendant, delivery person, salesperson |
| 72 | Street vendors | Food and clothing vendor |
| 81 | Personal services | Child-care provider in school, nurse's aide, gardener, hotel chambermaid, door attendant |
| 82 | Domestic workers | Child-care provider in home, cleaning and laundry for individuals |
| 83 | Security and armed forces | Police, security guard, military |
| 97 | No previous work outside the home[a] | |
| 98 | Homework[a] | |
| 99 | Previous immigration to the United States[a] | |

Sources: INEGI Occupational Classification (2007) and author compilation.

[a]Author-added category and category numbers.

TABLE B.2

PERCENTAGE OF WOMEN HIRED BY MEXICAN CLASSIFICATION OF OCCUPATION (CMO) WORK CATEGORY
FOR PREVIOUS EMPLOYMENT, 1970s–2001

| Code | CMO category | 1970s | 1980s | 1990 | 1991 | 1992 | 1993 | 1994 | 1995 | 1996 | 1997 | 1998 | 1999 | 2000 | 2001[a] | (All Years) Total |
|---|---|---|---|---|---|---|---|---|---|---|---|---|---|---|---|---|
| 13 | Education workers | 0 (0) | 0 (0) | 0 (0) | 0 (0) | 0 (0) | 0 (0) | 0 (0) | 2.44 (1) | 0 (0) | 1.18 (1) | 0 (0) | 1.20 (1) | 0 (0) | 0.96 (1) | 0.44 (4) |
| 21 | Executives and officers | 0 (0) | 0 (0) | 0 (0) | 0 (0) | 0 (0) | 0 (0) | 0 (0) | 0 (0) | 0 (0) | 0 (0) | 0 (0) | 0 (0) | 0.64 (1) | 0 (0) | 0.11 (1) |
| 41 | Agricultural workers | 0 (0) | 0 (0) | 5.71 (2) | 0 (0) | 0 (0) | 0 (0) | 1.41 (1) | 0 (0) | 0 (0) | 0 (0) | 0 (0) | 0 (0) | 0 (0) | 0 (0) | 0.33 (3) |
| 51 | Production supervisors | 0 (0) | 0 (0) | 0 (0) | 0 (0) | 0 (0) | 0 (0) | 0 (0) | 0 (0) | 0 (0) | 0 (0) | 0 (0) | 1.20 (1) | 0.64 (1) | 1.92 (2) | 0.44 (4) |
| 52 | Craft workers | 0 (0) | 0 (0) | 0 (0) | 0 (0) | 0 (0) | 0 (0) | 0 (0) | 0 (0) | 0 (0) | 1.18 (1) | 0 (0) | 0 (0) | 1.27 (2) | 0.96 (1) | 0.44 (4) |
| 52 | Food preparation | 0 (0) | 0 (0) | 2.86 (1) | 8.67 (2) | 2.13 (1) | 0 (0) | 4.23 (3) | 0 (0) | 2.33 (3) | 1.18 (1) | 1.79 (1) | 1.20 (1) | 3.82 (6) | 1.92 (2) | 2.33 (21) |
| 52 | Production in workshops | 10.53 (2) | 9.09 (3) | 14.2 (5) | 0 (0) | 6.38 (3) | 10.53 (2) | 8.45 (6) | 0 (0) | 5.43 (7) | 3.53 (3) | 3.57 (2) | 0 (0) | 7.01 (11) | 1.92 (2) | 5.10 (46) |
| 53 | Production in factories | 31.58 (6) | 30.30 (10) | 28.57 (10) | 13.04 (3) | 29.79 (14) | 26.32 (5) | 25.35 (18) | 34.15 (14) | 36.43 (47) | 41.18 (35) | 37.5 (21) | 44.58 (37) | 31.85 (50) | 54.81 (57) | 36.25 (327) |

| | | 1 | 2 | 3 | 4 | 5 | 6 | 7 | 8 | 9 | 10 | 11 | 12 | 13 | 14 | 15 |
|---|---|---|---|---|---|---|---|---|---|---|---|---|---|---|---|---|
| 54 | Assistants to other workers | 5.26 (1) | 0 (0) | 0 (0) | 0 (0) | 0 (0) | 0 (0) | 4.23 (3) | 0 (0) | 2.33 (3) | 3.53 (3) | 1.79 (1) | 8.43 (7) | 0.64 (1) | 0.96 (1) | 2.11 (19) |
| 62 | Office and administrative | 5.26 (1) | 6.06 (2) | 5.71 (2) | 0 (0) | 8.51 (4) | 0 (0) | 2.82 (2) | 2.44 (1) | 6.20 (8) | 4.71 (4) | 3.57 (2) | 9.64 (8) | 10.19 (16) | 8.65 (9) | 6.54 (59) |
| 71 | Sales and related services | 0 (0) | 9.09 (3) | 8.57 (3) | 21.74 (5) | 19.15 (9) | 26.32 (5) | 14.08 (10) | 7.32 (3) | 10.08 (13) | 9.41 (8) | 14.29 (8) | 9.64 (8) | 12.74 (20) | 2.88 (3) | 10.86 (98) |
| 72 | Street vendors | 5.26 (1) | 3.03 (1) | 0 (0) | 0 (0) | 0 (0) | 0 (0) | 1.41 (1) | 0 (0) | 2.33 (3) | 0 (0) | 3.57 (2) | 0 (0) | 0.64 (1) | 1.92 (2) | 1.22 (11) |
| 81 | Personal services | 0 (0) | 0 (0) | 0 (0) | 4.35 (1) | 2.13 (1) | 0 (0) | 2.82 (2) | 2.44 (1) | 3.88 (5) | 4.71 (4) | 3.57 (2) | 1.2 (1) | 3.18 (5) | 1.92 (2) | 2.66 (24) |
| 82 | Domestic workers | 0 (0) | 3.03 (1) | 11.43 (4) | 17.39 (4) | 4.26 (2) | 5.26 (1) | 7.04 (5) | 2.44 (1) | 6.98 (9) | 11.76 (10) | 16.08 (9) | 4.82 (4) | 6.37 (10) | 0 (0) | 6.65 (60) |
| 83 | Security and armed forces | 0 (0) | 0 (0) | 0 (0) | 0 (0) | 0 (0) | 0 (0) | 0 (0) | 0 (0) | 0.78 (1) | 0 (0) | 0 (0) | 0 (0) | 0 (0) | 0.96 (1) | 0.22 (2) |
| 97 | No previous work outside the home | 21.05 (4) | 24.24 (8) | 17.14 (6) | 26.09 (6) | 19.15 (9) | 21.05 (4) | 19.72 (14) | 36.59 (15) | 14.73 (19) | 10.59 (9) | 8.93 (5) | 10.84 (9) | 15.29 (24) | 11.54 (12) | 15.96 (144) |
| 98 | Homework | 5.26 (1) | 9.09 (3) | 2.86 (1) | 0 (0) | 4.26 (2) | 0 (0) | 4.23 (3) | 0 (0) | 2.33 (3) | 2.35 (2) | 1.79 (1) | 3.61 (3) | 0 (0) | 0 (0) | 2.11 (19) |
| 99 | Previous immigration to the United States | 0 (0) | 3.03 (1) | 0 (0) | 0 (0) | 0 (0) | 0 (0) | 0 (0) | 2.44 (1) | 0.78 (1) | 1.18 (1) | 0 (0) | 0 (0) | 0 (0) | 0 (0) | 0.44 (4) |

(continued)

## TABLE B.2

### PERCENTAGE OF WOMEN HIRED BY MEXICAN CLASSIFICATION OF OCCUPATION (CMO) WORK CATEGORY FOR PREVIOUS EMPLOYMENT, 1970s–2001 (*continued*)

| Code | CMO category | 1970s | 1980s | 1990 | 1991 | 1992 | 1993 | 1994 | 1995 | 1996 | 1997 | 1998 | 1999 | 2000 | 2001[a] | (All Years) Total |
|---|---|---|---|---|---|---|---|---|---|---|---|---|---|---|---|---|
| | Missing data | 21.05 (4) | 3.03 (1) | 2.86 (1) | 8.70 (2) | 4.26 (2) | 10.53 (2) | 4.23 (3) | 9.75 (4) | 5.43 (7) | 3.53 (3) | 3.57 (2) | 3.61 (3) | 5.73 (9) | 8.65 (9) | 5.76 (52) |
| | Total percentage | 99.99 | 99.9 | 100 | 99.98 | 100.02 | 100.01 | 100.02 | 100.02 | 100.04 | 100.02 | 100.02 | 99.97 | 100.01 | 99.97 | 99.97 |
| | Total number of workers hired by year | 19 | 33 | 35 | 23 | 47 | 19 | 71 | 41 | 129 | 85 | 56 | 83 | 157 | 104 | 902 |

Source: Compiled by author from worker files.

Note: Number of cases are in parentheses. Percentages that do not sum to 100 are due to rounding.

[a]January–September 2001 only.

# Appendix C
# Reprimands in Worker Files, 1993–2001

These data were obtained from 1,046 individual worker files. Every time a worker received a reprimand from a supervisor, a form with the date and description of the reprimand was entered into the file. After reviewing all of the entries, I coded the types of infraction into five categories—absenteeism, low efficiency, poor quality, violation of work rules, and insubordination. When workers missed work without prior authorization or did not have a medical excuse, they received a reprimand for absenteeism. If a worker did not produce at 100 percent of volume (efficiency) or quality for a certified operation, he or she was liable to be reprimanded. Before 1996, such entries usually noted the percentage of volume at which the worker labored; after 1996, they noted volume and quality. It was unusual to be cited for anything above 80 percent of quota. Reprimands for violation of work rules (as set forth in the collective-bargaining agreement) included eating at one's machine, wearing jewelry, taking more than thirty minutes for lunch, and punching in someone else's timecard.

Technically, three reprimands for absenteeism, low efficiency, or poor quality in a month were grounds for automatic termination of employment. However, several workers fell in this category. As can be seen in the table C.1, the number of workers committing infractions per year (denoted by brackets) was always fewer than the reprimands, meaning that the same workers were responsible for multiple infractions. While some individuals may have been terminated for more than three infractions, others were not, demonstrating an uneven application of the rules.

The last category, insubordination, includes infractions that denote worker contestation, often noted in the files with specific examples of worker actions. In subordination is different from violation of work rules in that workers were acting outside the established factory regulations or reacting to management's violation of the collective-bargaining agreement. While not included in this table, the only other year where this type of infraction occurred was 1983, when,

TABLE C.1

NUMBER OF REPRIMANDS BY INFRACTION, 1993–2001

| Reprimand | 1993 | 1994 | 1995 | 1996 | 1997 | 1998 | 1999 | 2000 | 2001 |
|---|---|---|---|---|---|---|---|---|---|
| Absenteeism | 139 | 371 | 335 | 292 | 17 | 36 | 108 | 153 | 326 |
|  | [68] | [139] | [135] | [140] | [15] | [35] | [101] | [121] | [224] |
| Low efficiencies | 2 | 81 | 61 | 11 | 0 | 3 | 2 | 34 | 97 |
|  | [2] | [20] | [26] | [4] | [0] | [3] | [2] | [30] | [70] |
| Poor quality | 48 | 70 | 96 | 24 | 23 | 16 | 51 | 42 | 67 |
|  | [24] | [31] | [61] | [19] | [13] | [14] | [44] | [35] | [55] |
| Work-rule violation | 5 | 16 | 5 | 9 | 1 | 2 | 18 | 30 | 11 |
|  | [5] | [14] | [4] | [7] | [1] | [2] | [18] | [29] | [11] |
| Insubordination | 1 | 3 | 0 | 0 | 0 | 0 | 1 | 0 | 8 |
|  | [1] | [3] | [0] | [0] | [0] | [0] | [1] | [0] | [5] |
| Total | 195 | 541 | 497 | 336 | 41 | 57 | 180 | 259 | 509 |

Source: Compiled by author from worker files.

Note: Numbers in brackets indicate total number of workers committing infractions per year.

according to managers' written notes in worker files, workers "stayed inside factory for tumultuous demonstration." This phrase appeared in eight worker files. In 1993, the reprimand was for "staying in factory during factory protest that invaded offices." In 1994, the reprimands were for "insubordination" (*indisciplina*), and two for refusing to work extra hours when asked to come to work during the weekend. I code the latter as insubordination because workers were standing up to a managerial request that was outside the collective-bargaining agreement. The one reprimand in 1999 was given for leaving before 4:36 P.M. During this time, the workers, organized in self-managed teams, decided they could leave at 4:00 P.M. if they completed their production quotas early. Management fought this change in work hours but finally relented.

The majority of insubordination reprimands were given in 2001, after the strike. When I entered information from the workers' files, I found 135 case files that were not included on the master list given to me by one of the secretaries. When I asked her why those workers were not listed, I was told that these workers had either been fired or had quit voluntarily. Importantly, all the cases of insubordination for 2001 belonged to the fired-or-quit category. The handwritten entries read: "refused to sign because she said her union was not present"; "intercepted a note that read 'meet at the plaza to refuse union being imposed from DF' [Mexico City]"; "bad attitude"; and "insubordination."

This information on reprimands is suggestive in nature. The worker files constitute a snapshot of the factory workforce in late summer 2001. The reprimands per year are for those workers still at the factory in 2001, so this is not a longitudinal comparison. Moreover, uniform and constant managerial strategies cannot be assumed. Nevertheless, a few insights can be drawn by taking into account that new owners took over in early 1994 and that teams were gradually implemented from 1997 to 1999.

- There were significant increases in every type of infraction when the new ownership took over in 1994 and most likely imposed new rules.
- Both managers and workers interviewed described the period in which teams were put into effect as one of great turnover, which was caused by firing workers or their voluntary departure. The drop in the absenteeism, low-efficiency, poor-quality, and work-rule violations from 1997 to 1998 was probably due to the remaining workers adapting to team rules and new quality imperatives.
- The increase of infractions beginning in 1999 likely represents workers' attempts to make use of self-managed team rules in their favor. For example, in 1999, workers decided to change the end of the workday from 4:36 P.M. to 4 P.M. Given that the majority of the workforce was participating in this contestation of rules, it is possible that managers tried to reestablish control by citing workers for other individual infractions.
- Dramatic increases in all infractions—except work-rule violations from 2000 to 2001—likely represent worker contestation, managerial efforts to clamp down on worker mobilizations, and the introduction of many new workers as movement participants were fired or quit. After the March strike, workers participated in a 50-percent slowdown, which helps to explain the jump in low efficiencies but not poor quality since less work was done in same time.
- The fact that only five workers were cited for insubordination, while other infractions increased, likely represents workers finding other ways to protest.
- Last, the shared burden of participation (ratio of infractions per number of workers cited) demonstrates that there was widespread support for mobilizations and not just "a few bad apples," as claimed by management.

# Notes

1. The name of the firm and all persons interviewed are pseudonyms. The name *Moctezuma* captures the local nature of the firm, given its pride in being a top Mexican firm.

2. A maquiladora is an export assembly firm that imports materials and equipment duty-free as long as the finished goods are exported back to the country of origin. Moctezuma cut, sewed, and trimmed high-end men's suits and distributed them ready for market to national and international destinations. Thus it was considered a first-tier manufacturer, not a maquiladora.

3. *Compañeros/compañeras* are male and female forms of *companion*, or *workmate*.

4. I use Edwards and Scullion's definition of a strike as "a collective stoppage of work 'to express a grievance or enforce a demand' . . . [where] workers lost pay" (1982, 225). I prefer this definition because it highlights workers' actions rather than the politically charged practice of labor authorities declaring strikes legal, illegal, or nonexistent. Therefore, in the case of Moctezuma, the strike occurred even though the state arbiter refused to certify its legality.

5. The kinds of work available to men and women, however, differ. Historically, state protectionist policies, trade union exclusionary practices, and managerial gender ideologies restricted women's work activities to "protect" their procreative and moral health (Rose 1992). The effect was to fortify patriarchal norms of the male breadwinner and female homemaker, reinforce the separation between production (work) and reproduction (family), and establish gender-based segregated labor markets where men are concentrated in high-paying primary jobs in large bureaucratized organizations and women in low-paying, high-turnover jobs in the competitive secondary market (Gordon et al. 1982; Hartmann 1976). Once a job is marked as male or female, organizational inertia and management's gender ideologies tend to maintain sex typing, reproducing segregated labor markets and inequalities (Milkman 1987).

6. In this way, it is similar to Temma Kaplan's *female consciousness*, where women accept their societal role as protectors of the family. When the state (or in this case, management) do not provide the conditions to fulfill this role, women organize "to demand their rights as mothers and potential mothers" (1982, 551).

7. See Plankey-Videla (forthcoming) for a fuller discussion of issues of consent in this study.

8. While I note in text when I quote directly from taped interviews, the conversations I cite throughout the book from field notes are to be considered my best effort to convey the meaning of what was said, and not necessarily an objective repetition.

9. Descriptive statistics and chi-squares are available from me on request.

## CHAPTER 1 — CONTEXTUALIZING THE CASE OF MOCTEZUMA

1. In response to an organized effort by several women's groups, the 1927 Civil Code reform provided limited property rights for women; however, a husband could still deny his wife the right to work if it interfered with her ability to fulfill her domestic duties.

2. The law was later modified, allowing women to work overtime but at three times their usual pay. This discrepancy between women and men, who were paid time and a half for overtime, was cancelled in 1975 after the First Women's International Conference in Mexico City (Healy 2008).

3. For example, in 1973, foreign currency transactions were twice the level of international trade in manufactured goods and other services. By 1995 foreign exchange dwarfed world trade by a ratio of 70:1. Ninety percent of these financial trades are believed to have been speculative (Dicken 2007).

4. Pérez and his family, representing a group of investors that included high-level public officials, controlled 53 percent of shares, with the rest belonging to a newly privatized bank. In 1996, the bank in question was among the first to be bailed under the state rescue plan (Fernández 1999; Fernández-Vega 1999).

## CHAPTER 2 — "I LIKE PIECEWORK MORE . . . BECAUSE I WORK FOR MYSELF"

1. The history of the 1972 mobilization is reconstructed through interviews with workers as well as the following scholarly sources: Basurto (1989); García Quintanilla (2000); Martínez Cruz (2000); Rendón Galicia (2008); Roxborough (1984); and Sánchez Resendiz (2001).

2. A strike being declared inexistent means that it does not fulfill the requirement of "balancing the forces of production" as dictated by the Federal Labor Law.

3. To guard against nostalgia for past organizational forms of workers operating under teamwork, six interviews were conducted with women who labored at Italia and Moctezuma in the 1960s and 1970s in 2009. All participated in the 1972 strike. Of the six women workers interviewed, five were permanent workers, and three were movement leaders. Two of these women held posts in the independent union formed after the firing of the 110 temporary workers.

4. See Appendices A and B for a cross-sectional view of the characteristics of workers present at the factory from August to September 2001.

5. At the end of each December, the company provided workers with their last paychecks and end-of-year profit sharing (*aguinaldo*) and closed the books. When the workers came back in January, the company "lent" them money by giving them advances (*anticipos*) on their first two-week paychecks because the company knew that they would be tight for money after celebrating Christmas and Three Kings Day on January 6 (the traditional day in Mexico for gift giving.) The advance was deducted in small amounts from each paycheck.

6. The existence of gendered job ladders that result in women's concentration in dead-end jobs or reduced promotion chances—and men's ladders extending into higher levels,

with positions of authority—is a common characteristic of workplaces. See Padavic and Reskin (2002).

## CHAPTER 3 — FROM PIECEWORK TO TEAMWORK

1. Such requests were not unusual during this time given the concentration of power in the global apparel industry. See Bonacich and Appelbaum (2000), Collins (2003), and Rosen (2002) for more examples.

2. While there is variation in Japanese management practices and the implementation of lean production in that country, scholars have pointed to these three particular elements as the pillars of Japanese lean production (Cole 1979; Oliver and Wilkinson 1997).

3. One of the human resource managers kept her notes and documents from the period of lean production implementation in a binder entitled "American Consulting Teamwork Project at Moctezuma" (identifying names have been changed). Included were memos and reports from the implementation team to the company president and department representatives. The weekly memos included information on production and quality statistics and evaluation of individual supervisors and workers, as well as to-do lists.

4. For more on how the community of fate belief developed at Moctezuma, see Plankey Videla (2006b).

5. According to company documents, turnover had been lowered to 14 percent in 1998 and 10 percent in 1999. Absenteeism had also diminished from 12.4 percent in 1995 to 8 percent in 1998.

6. Quitting was preferable to dismissing workers because Article 48 of the Federal Labor Law provides that an employee fired without justification must be compensated in the amount equivalent to three-months salary plus seniority (equal to twelve days salary per year of employment), as well as the proportional vacation and yearly profit-sharing for that year (Bensusán 1998).

7. Under Mexican law, women are permitted twelve weeks of paid maternity leave (Colectivo Atabal 1994).

8. Acker and Van Houten (1974) show that gender inequality in organizations begins with recruitment policies that target women for positions with less authority. Regarding teams, Vallas (2003a) notes a similar process at paper pulp mills that selected workers based on attitudes toward teamwork.

9. All deaths, births, and marriages had to be validated with legal certificates to receive benefits. The term *concubine*, I believe, refers to common-law spouses since many couples cohabited rather than married.

10. Vallas (2003b) also found that the adoption of teams in the paper and pulp industry cut job ladders by stressing technical over tacit knowledge.

11. When a worker signed up for INFONAVIT, the firm automatically deducted a weekly amount from her pay to be deposited with the government toward a subsidized apartment or house.

12. He stressed how the complexity of pants (with a hundred and fifty operations) and jacket construction (over two hundred operations) did not allow for teams to produce the entire product but, rather, only a part of the final product.

13. The second shift worked shorter hours, from 5:00 P.M. to 1:30 A.M. since it was at night. They also had fewer pieces to complete per shift.

14. In 1999, women workers in self-managed teams decided that if they finished their quota by 4 P.M., they could leave early.

15. Company production data refute this claim; both quotas and production methods *had* changed.

16. The use of consultants to introduce organizational innovations is common. See Fantasia (1988); Grenier (1988); and Vallas (2003a).

17. According to neo-Fordists, managers secure consent through the ideological illusion that workers participate in decision-making processes, which when combined with increased monitoring by not only supervisors but also team members leads to work intensification. Thus, rather than a break with old managerial patterns, there is an intensification of capitalist control (Barker 1993; Besser 1996; Collins 2001; Graham 1995; Grenier 1988; Parker and Slaughter 1988). Neo-Taylorists hold that participative innovations have reverted to the principles of scientific management that reinforce control, increase workload, and intensify stress under worsening conditions of work (Crowley et al. 2010).

18. Poaching, the practice of luring managers or workers from one firm to another, did not occur until the firm was imploding during the summer of 2001. Several top managers were offered attractive packages at Moctezuma's competitors in nearby states. These top managers took midlevel managers with them. It was at this time that midlevel managers from the shuttered transnational corporation began working at Moctezuma.

### CHAPTER 4 — BECOMING A WORKER

1. I worked in two teams: team four in pants was considered one of the worst teams for its internal conflict and inability to complete work quota, and team six in the jackets one production line (J-1), was considered one of the best, consistently fulfilling its work orders. I draw on both teams to understand social relations on the shop floor. However, I cannot compare them to properly discern what accounted for one team's malfunction and the other's success. I worked in team four for only three months before the strike and in J-1 for one week before the strike, followed by another five months under worker mobilization.

2. Although still married, this woman considered herself single because she had not heard from him in years and had lost hope of him coming back. She used her wages and his remittances to build a nice cement house with running water and electricity but no sewage connection to the city. When I went to her house in a working-class neighborhood on the outskirts of town, we hung out in the courtyard; it had a small water fountain that was her pride and joy.

3. *Partnered* means that the women are married or cohabitating. Many couples live in common-law marriage. In the lower-economic sectors in Mexico, legal marriages and divorces are often cost prohibitive. Cohabiting and separating are thus common and widely accepted.

4. For more on the gendered contradiction of self-managed teams, see Plankey-Videla (2006a).

5. Company records did not include the operations workers performed so I cannot compare my impressions with the data. However, only 12 percent of workers were male. Since most of the cutting and final pressing departments were men, a very low percentage would be in the jackets or pants department.

6. In pants, several workers would not even speak to each other or receive each other's work because of fights emanating from poor quality.

7. Something similar occurred at Burawoy's machine parts factory (1979). Middle management went along with the game of "making out," although it broke company rules, because in the end workers produced more.

8. Cedric Herring defines *colorism* as "the discriminatory treatment of individuals falling within the same "racial" group on the basis of skin color. It operates both intraracially and interracially. Intraracial colorism occurs when members of a racial group make distinctions based upon skin color between members of their own race. Interracial colorism occurs when members of one racial group make distinctions based upon skin color between members of another racial groups" (2004, 3).

## CHAPTER 5 — LEAN DURING MEAN TIMES

1. It is possible that some complaints were made and I did not hear them or that workers chose not come forward to share concerns with me. However, by this point in the fieldwork, the team had accepted me as a member, and I was now friendly with most of the workers. Furthermore, working in such proximity, I think I would have heard conversations or surmised by body languages any contestation between workers.

2. The benefits frozen were the gift of three meters of cloth for marriages, $125 pesos (around U.S.$14) for births, Christmas gift baskets, T-shirts with the company logo used as uniforms, and a monthly bonus of towels, soap, and detergent.

3. According to the contract, human resources had to find a new team for an expelled member. If no team was willing to accept the worker, she or he would be dismissed.

4. I later found out this occurred on February 9, when management also informed the courts it was canceling the second shift.

5. For unions in Japan, see Cole (1979). For the changing character of unions in Mexico, see Bensusán and Cook (2003), Bouzas Ortiz and Gaitán Riveros (2001), and Ramírez Cuevas (2005).

6. The company proposed a guaranteed wage with fewer multiskilled levels, starting at $360 pesos for no operations (base wage), $500 pesos for two to three operations, $550 pesos (top level) for utility workers; biweekly food coupons of $50 pesos for everyone; vacation time calculated as 15 percent of wages, increasing by seniority; and end-of-year profit sharing equivalent to 15 days of work. The union proposed a guaranteed wage that started at $531 pesos for the base salary and ranged to the highest level for utility workers, from $796 to $938 pesos; food coupons of $250 pesos for everyone; vacation time calculated as 70 percent of wages across the board; and profit sharing equivalent to 30 days of work.

7. The union had informed the local conciliation and arbitration board and the company of its intent to call a strike (*emplazar a huelga*)—as required before any contract or salary revision.

8. Labor theorists would say that better-paid workers represent a *labor aristocracy*, content with their standard of living and thus unwilling to support mobilizations. While the term dates back to Marx and Engels, an important modern treatment of the concept can be found in Hobsbawm (1964).

## CHAPTER 6 — THE STRIKE

1. Lupe asked if she could take the digital recorder to tape what the factory owner told them. Her intention was to put him on the spot, to use the recording to further movement goals. I thought it was interesting that she considered this strategy. Unfortunately, in the end, Lupe had difficulty operating the device.

2. As it turns out, they had good reason to be distrustful of the union. I later spoke with the one of Moctezuma's major client's representative in Mexico. He told me the company had assured him—the day before the strike—that there would be no trouble; the union

had already signed the contract. As he was told, the union was paid good money to continue business as usual despite workers' discontent.

3. According to Mexican labor law, several unions can operate in one workplace (what is known as an open shop), but only one can legally represent workers. To contest representation (*titularidad*), a union must demand a recount (*recuento*) of workers' votes to show that they represent the majority of the workforce. Since there is no secret ballot requirement for recounts, votes often take place in public and in front of management, making intimidation all but certain. The LCAB must then certify the union (*tomar nota*) as the legal representative for workers. Certain legal requirements must be met in order to certify a union, including notarized copies of general assembly minutes showing where elections took place, names and addresses of union members, a copy of union statutes, and the name and address of the employer (Cook 2007; La Botz 1992; Middlebrook 1995).

4. Company records for the year 2001 show the percentages of production levels for Jackets-1 for weeks 11 to 19 to be 50.95, 44.42, 107.27, 65.20, 43.20, 53.56, 45.25, 75.79, and 66.11, respectively.

5. There was another meeting outside the factory the next day, which my coworkers wanted me to attend. Vicki and Ana (who were normally mortal enemies) came together with four other women from team four and offered to form a *bolita* (a circle) around me so that no one would bother me. I was touched by their gesture but declined.

6. While the previous chapters are mainly based on participant observation and interviews, portions of this chapter, recounting what occurred once the women were forced back to work, rely heavily on newspaper articles and interviews. This was necessary since I was only able to conduct participant observation on the shop floor until April 2001, although I continued to visit and roam the factory three to four times per week for the next five months, conducting interviews with workers and managers in the afternoon. Newspaper articles inform the analysis of follow-up interviews with workers and managers in 2003, 2004, 2006, and 2009, with a few telephone interviews in 2010 and 2011—all of which paint a complex and incomplete story of continued confrontations at the firm. I compiled a newspaper article database from 1999 to 2009 from two of the main regional newspapers. The newspaper I call *Major Regional Newspaper One* (*MRN1*) provides a center-left point of view, whereas the newspaper I call *Major Regional Newspaper Two* (*MRN2*) provides a center-right perspective and is considered to represent the business community. While both newspapers portrayed the case of Moctezuma as one of workers fighting government/firm complicity, *MRN1* was more likely to cover worker statements and include denunciatory editorials. *MRN2* was more likely to cover the development of the legal cases. A research assistant examined every copy of these daily newspapers, obtaining copies of any article that dealt with Moctezuma, the factory's parent company, subsidiaries of the parent company, labor reform, foreign direct investment in the local area, immigration from the area, and the local economic situation. The articles were coded with NVivo 8 software (QSR International Pty Ltd. 2008).

7. For this discussion, to differentiate between the two unions, I will use the terms *old, discredited,* or *deposed union* to denote the union that signed the controversial contract with management and *new, independent,* or *democratically elected union* when referring to the one chosen by workers after the strike.

8. Later documents showed that he was a member until at least September 2001.

9. All local newspapers covered the sit-in, as did TV news cameras. The reports in the left-leaning *MRN1* and the right-leaning *MRN2* differed slightly. First, while the *MRN1* claimed that nine hundred workers participated, *MRN2* calculated a thousand workers.

The official estimate by police was two hundred and fifty. Second, *MRN1* focused on the labor authorities' lack of response and trickery, while *MRN2* mentioned the same but highlighted the ways workers were not willing to negotiate. Furthermore, *MRN2* depicted the women as "allowing themselves to be swayed" by radical leaders from the 1970s— namely, the business agent.

10. "Civic Coalition" is a pseudonym for the coalition of NGOs, composed of environmental, human rights, independent labor, and women's groups.

11. Protection unions are also often called *protection contracts*. I use the term *protection union* to highlight how the contract legally implies the presence of a union. The protection union installed at Moctezuma, which I call Protejer (meaning *to protect*), belongs to one of the largest and most powerful protection union confederations, which holds thousands of union contracts in a wide array of industries. The confederation represents workers in transnational corporations (Frito-Lay, Unilever, McDonald's, Cinemex, Hewlett Packard, Daewoo, Nike, Xerox, Acumuladores Mexicanos LTH, Sony Music Entertainment, Evenflo), Mexican big business interests (Telcel, Centros de Integración Juvenil, Transportes Figuermex, Transter, Líneas Unidas del Sur), banks (Banco Unión, Banca Cremi), airlines (Aviacsa, Aerocaribe United, Northwest, Air Canada, Air France, KLM, British Airways, Aeroflot), and most port operations. Proteger also controls unions at universities (Del Valle de México, Latinoamericana, Femenina de México, Colegios La Salle), presses (Planeta, Bruguera, Gustavo Gili), and even a major newspaper (*El Universal*). See García Flores (2007).

12. For more on the function of the *titularidad*, see note 3.

13. The CTM and CTC used the media to make their case. The CTM state leader, who was also a state senator for the PRI, used the strongest workerist discourses to convince women to affiliate with them. The CTC leader clearly articulated its employer predisposition: "The way in which the governor acted against the women workers of Moctezuma is not the way to do it. However, it is a sign that they are trying to bring down the unionized working class. I am not against the protection of companies, but there has to be equity and strict application of the law" (Calvo Elmer 2001b).

14. Translation by author. *MRN1* (2002).

### CHAPTER 7 — "WE LOST CONTROL OF THE SHOP FLOOR"

1. See Appendices A and B for more information.

2. Vicki from the pants department filed suit with a law office that represented 180 workers from Moctezuma. They have met on the last Sunday of every month for ten years. Vicki mentioned that many workers have migrated north but send family representatives to the meetings.

3. A *precautionary embargo* meant that Moctezuma could not move any machinery, merchandise, or other assets until the bankruptcy case was settled.

4. Translation by the author.

5. Pacts have been signed between employer associations and official unions since 1996 (Cook 2007).

6. Worker citizenship actions entail efforts to enhance productivity and strengthen organizational cohesion beyond what is required (Hodson 2001, 45–46).

### CONCLUSION

1. Andrés Manuel López Obrador, a leftist politician, was mayor of Mexico City from 2000 to 2005 and was a presidential candidate in 2006. Some believe he won the 2006

presidential elections. He proclaimed himself the legitimate president and has since been building a national grassroots movement, MORENA (Movement for National Renovation), to combat the effects of neoliberalism and corruption in Mexico. Many believe he will run for president again in 2012.

2. Vicki was owed $200,000 pesos (around U.S.$22,000), including vacations, savings, and back pay, of which she received $75,000 pesos, or 38 percent, in 2010. From this money, she discounted 20 percent owed to the lawyers. In the end, she received 29 percent, or $58,000 pesos (around U.S.$6,400) of what Moctezuma legally owed her in compensation for unlawful firing.

3. All of these mills have since filed for Chapter 11 bankruptcy protection. Bair and Gereffi (2002) report that the mills also blame Asian currency devaluations and the strong U.S. dollar.

4. China's WTO Accession Agreement includes safeguards for apparel and textile, whereby WTO signatories can request consultations with China if their national industry is being hurt by Chinese imports (*just-style* 2005b).

5. For discussion on the labor law reforms, see Bensusán and Cook (2003); La Botz and Alexander (2003); and Cook (2007).

# Glossary

**abuelita:** Grandmother

**acosar:** To accost

**acoso sexual:** Sexual harassment

**anticipo:** Paycheck advance

**antojitos:** Snacks, usually Mexican delicacies like tacos

**aguinaldo:** End-of-year profit sharing

**caballito:** Attack of a worker by several people, bringing the worker to the floor to be hit and kicked

**canasta básica:** Basic food shopping basket

**compañeros/compañeras:** Male/female forms of *companions* or *workmates*

**contrato ley:** Master union contract

**economía:** Time-out feature in piece-rate work that allows workers to be off the clock

**emplazar a huelga:** Notification of the intent to strike

**empleados:** Administrative employees who have flexible hours and higher status than workers

**la escuelita:** The little school

**guardia:** Guard shifts

**jefes:** Bosses

**kaizen (Japanese):** Continuous improvement

**kanban (Japanese):** Visual markers that pull production through just-in-time inventory

**las mañanitas:** Traditional happy birthday song

**maquiladora:** In-bond assembly firm

**obrera:** Female factory worker

**permiso:** Permit to be absent or tardy

**poka-yoke (Japanese):** an *andon* cord pulled to stop the assembly line when there is a defective piece or errors

**posada:** Reenactment of Mary and Joseph seeking shelter at the inn

**práctica:** Internship

**presionar:** To pressure

**recuento:** Recount of union votes to decide who represents workers

**seiketsu (Japanese):** Progress

**seire (Japanese):** Selection

**seiso (Japanese):** Cleanliness

**seiton (Japanese):** Order

**shitsuke (Japanese):** Discipline

**titularidad:** Union representation through the collective-bargaining agreement

**tomar nota:** Certification of a union

**unión libre:** cohabitation

**viejas:** Old hags

# Bibliography

Abernathy, F. H., J. T. Dunlop, J. H. Hammond, and D. Weil. 1999. *A Stitch in Time: Lean Retailing and the Transformation of Manufacturing: Lessons from the Apparel and Textile Industries.* Oxford: Oxford University Press.

Abernathy, F. H., A. Volpe, and D. Weil. 2006. "The Future of the Apparel and Textile Industries: Prospects and Choices for Public and Private Actors." *Environment and Planning A* 38 (12):2207–2232.

Abrahamson, E. 1991. "Managerial Fads and Fashions: The Diffusion and Rejection of Innovations." *Academy of Management Review* 16 (3):586–612.

———. 1996. "Management Fashion." *Academy of Management Review* 21 (1):254–285.

Acker, J., and D. Van Houten. 1974. "Differential Recruitment and Control: The Sex Structuring of Organizations." *Administrative Science Quarterly* 19 (2):152–163.

Almeida, P. D. 2008. *Waves of Protest: Popular Struggle in El Salvador, 1925–2005.* Minneapolis: University of Minnesota Press.

Appadurai, A. 1996. *Modernity at Large: Cultural Dimensions of Globalization,* vol. 1. Minneapolis: University of Minnesota Press.

Appelbaum, E., T. Bailey, P. Berg, and A. L. Kalleberg. 2000. *Manufacturing Advantage: Why High Performance Work Systems Pay Off.* Ithaca, NY: Cornell University Press.

Appelbaum, R., and G. Gereffi. 1994. "Power and Profits in the Apparel Commodity Chain." In *Global Production: The Apparel Industry in the Pacific Rim,* ed. E. Bonacich, L. Cheng, N. Chinchilla, N. Hamilton, and P. Ong, 42–62. Philadelphia: Temple University Press.

Arias, P., and F. Wilson. 1997. *La aguja y el surco: Cambio regional, consumo y relaciones de género en la industria de la ropa en México.* Jalisco, Mexico: Universidad de Guadalajara and Center for Development Research.

Ariza, M., and O. de Oliveira. 2001. "Familias en transición y marcos conceptuales en redefinición." *Papeles de Población* 28:9–39.

Armbruster-Sandoval, R. 2005. *Globalization and Cross-Border Labor Solidarity in the Americas: The Anti-Sweatshop Movement and the Struggle for Social Justice.* New York: Routledge.

Arroyo Alejandre, J., and D. Rodríguez Álvarez. 2008. "Migración a Estados Unidos, remesas y desarrollo regional." *Papeles de Población* 58:41–72.

Arthur, J. B. 1994. "Effects of Human Resource Systems on Manufacturing Performance and Turnover." *Academy of Management Journal* 37:670–687.

Bailey, T. 1993. "Organizational Innovation in the Apparel Industry." *Industrial Relations* 32:30–48.

Bair, J., and E. Dussel Peters. 2006. "Global Commodity Chains and Endogenous Growth: Export Dynamism and Development in Mexico and Honduras." *World Development* 34 (2):203–221.

Bair, J., and G. Gereffi. 2002. "NAFTA and the Apparel Commodity Chain: Corporate Strategies, Interfirm Networks, and Industrial Upgrading." In *Free Trade and Uneven Development: The North American Apparel Industry after NAFTA*, ed. G. Gereffi, D. Spener, and J. Bair, 23–50. Philadelphia: Temple University Press.

———. 2003. "Upgrading, Uneven Development, and Jobs in the North American Apparel Industry." *Global Networks* 3 (2):143–169.

Babb, S. 2005. "The Social Consequences of Structural Adjustment: Recent Evidence and Current Debates." *Annual Review of Sociology* 31:199–222.

Barham, B., S. G. Bunker, and D. O'Hearn. 1994. *States, Firms, and Raw Materials: The World Economy and Ecology of Aluminum.* Madison: University of Wisconsin Press.

Barker, J. R. 1993. "Tightening the Iron Cage: Concertive Control in Self-Managing Teams." *Administrative Science Quarterly* 31:561–586.

Basurto, J. 1989. *La clase obrera en la historia de México: En el régimen de Echeverría rebelión e independencia.* 2nd ed. Mexico City: Siglo Veintiuno Editores.

Benería, L., and M. Roldán. 1987. *The Crossroads of Class and Gender: Industrial Homework, Subcontracting, and Household Dynamics in Mexico City.* Chicago: University of Chicago Press.

Bensusán, G. 1998. "Los determinantes institucionales de la flexibilidad laboral en México." In *¿Flexible y productivos? Estudios sobre la flexibilidad laboral en México,* ed. F. Zapata, 39–68. Mexico City: El Colegio de México.

———. 2008. "Los determinantes institucionales de los contratos de protección." In *Contratos colectivos de protección patronal ¿Tema imprescindible de la reforma laboral?* Mexico City: Fracción Parlamentaria del Partido de la Revolución Democrática/ Cámara de Diputados–Fundación Friedrich Ebert.

Bensusán, G., and M. L. Cook. 2003. "Political Transition and Labor Revitalization in Mexico." *Research in the Sociology of Work: Labor Revitalization: Global Perspectives and New Initiatives* 11:229–267.

Berensztein, S. 1996. "Rebuilding State Capacity in Contemporary Latin America: The Politics of Taxation in Argentina and Mexico." In *Latin America in the World-Economy,* ed. R. P. Korzeniewicz and W. C. Smith, 229–246. Westport, CT: Praeger.

Berg, P., E. Appelbaum, T. Bailey, and A. L. Kalleberg. 1996. "The Performance Effects of Modular Production in the Apparel Industry." *Industrial Relations* 35:356–373.

Besser, T. L. 1996. *Team Toyota: Transplanting the Toyota Culture to the Camry Plant in Kentucky.* Berkeley: University of California Press.

Bonacich, E., and R. P. Appelbaum. 2000. *Behind the Label: Inequality in the Los Angeles Apparel Industry.* Berkeley: University of California Press.

Bonilla-Silva, E. 2002. "We are all Americans! The Latin Americanization of Racial Stratification in the USA." *Race & Society* 5:3–16.

Bouzas Ortiz, J. A., and M. M. Gaitán Riveros. 2001. "Contratos colectivos de trabajo de protección." In *Democracia sindical,* ed. J. A. Bouzas Ortiz, 49–66. Mexico City: Universidad Autónoma Metropolitana/Universidad Nacional Autónoma de

México/Frente Auténtico del Trabajo/American Federation of Labor and Congress of Industrial Organizations.

Braverman, H. 1974. *Labor and Monopoly Capital: The Degradation of Work in the Twentieth Century*. New York: Monthly Review Press.

Bronfenbrenner, K. 1996. *Final Report: The Effects of Plant Closing or Threat of Plant Closing on the Right of Workers to Organize*. Report submitted to the Labor Secretariat of the North American Commission for Labor Cooperation, International Publications. Paper no. 1. Ithaca, NY: ILR/Cornell University Press. http:// digitalcommons.ilr.cornell.edu/intl/1.

Brooks, E. C. 2007. *Unraveling the Garment Industry: Transnational Organizing and Women's Work*. Minneapolis: University of Minnesota Press.

Bucio, N. 2001a. "El sindicalismo 'duro'contaminó el movimiento en Moctezuma-Italia, puntualizan empresarios." *MRN1*, May 10.

———. 2001b. "Denuncian obreras a Moctezuma-Italia ante el Secretario de Trabajo, Carlos Abascal Carranza." *MRN1*, June 7.

———. 2001c. "Retorno de migrantes colapsaría al estado: CCE." *MRN1*, October 5.

Burawoy, M. 1979. *Manufacturing Consent: Changes in the Labor Process under Monopoly Capitalism*. Chicago: University of Chicago Press.

———. 1985. *The Politics of Production: Factory Regimes under Capitalism and Socialism*. London: Verso.

*Business Wire*. 1997. "Business/Fashion Editors." August 23.

Callaghan, G., and P. Thompson. 2002. "'We Recruit Attitude': The Selection and Shaping of Routine Call Centre Labour." *Journal of Management Studies* 39 (2):233–234.

Calvo Elmer, M. 2001a. "Realizan nuevo plantón las obreras de Moctezuma en demanda de 'justicia laboral' al gobernador." *MRN1*, July 4.

———. 2001b."Anuncia la CTC que prepara una 'sorpresa' a favor de trabajadoras de la compañía Moctezuma." *MRN1*, July 30.

Camp, R. A. 1989. *Entrepreneurs and Politics in Twentieth-Century Mexico*. New York: Oxford University Press.

Caplan, B. 1998. "A House Built on Sand." *Euromoney*, July. http://www.euromoney .com/Article/1005538/A-house-built-on-sand.html.

Carney, L. S., and C. G. O'Kelley. 1990. "Women's Work and Women's Place in the Japanese Economic Miracle." In *Women Workers and Global Restructuring*, ed. K. Ward, 113–145. Ithaca, NY: ILR/Cornell University Press.

Carrillo, J. A. Hualde, and A. Almaraz. 2002. "Commodity Chains and Industrial Organization in the Apparel Industry in Monterrey and Ciudad Juárez." In *Free Trade and Uneven Development: The North American Apparel Industry after NAFTA*, ed. G. Gereffi, D. Spener, and J. Bair, 181–199. Philadelphia: Temple University Press.

Carrillo, J., A. Hualde, and C. Quintero Ramírez. 2005. "Recorrido por la historia de las maquiladoras en México." *Comercio Exterior* 55 (1):30–42.

Castells, M. 2000. *The Rise of Network Society*. Vol. 1, *The Information Age: Economy, Society, and Culture*. 2nd ed. Hoboken, NJ: Wiley-Blackwell.

CEREAL [Centro de Reflexión y Acción Laboral]. 2004. "Informe sobre la situación del derecho a la libertad sindical en México: Audiencia temática en el marco del 119° periodo ordinario de sesiones de la Comisión Interamericana de Derechos Humanos." http://www.fatmexico.org/actualidad/Informe%20Libertad%20Sindical.doc.

Chalmers, J. N. 1989. *Industrial Relations in Japan: The Peripheral Workforce*. London: Routledge.

Chant, S. 2007. *Gender, Generation and Poverty: Exploring the "Feminisation of Poverty" in Africa, Asia, and Latin America*. Cheltenham, UK: Edward Elgar.

Chun, J. J. 2009. *Organizing at the Margins: The Symbolic Politics of Labor in South Korea and the United States*. Ithaca, NY: Cornell University Press.

Cole, R. E. 1979. *Work, Mobility, and Participation: A Comparative Study of American and Japanese Industry*. Berkeley: University of California Press.

Colectivo Atabal. 1994. *El ABC de las trabajadoras domésticas: Cartilla sobre los derechos y las obligaciones laborales de las trabajadoras y trabajadores del servicio doméstico*. Mexico City: Colectivo Atabal, A.C.

Collier, R. B., and D. Collier. 1991. *Shaping the Political Arena*. Princeton, NJ: Princeton University Press.

Collins, J. L. 2001. "Flexible Specialization and the Garment Industry." *Competition and Change* 5 (2):165–200.

———. 2002. "Mapping a Global Labor Market: Gender and Skill in the Globalizing Garment Industry." *Gender and Society* 16 (5):921–940.

———. 2003. *Threads: Gender, Labor and Power in the Global Apparel Industry*. Chicago: University of Chicago Press.

Collinson, D. L. 2003. "Identities and Insecurities: Selves at Work." *Organization* 10 (3):527–547.

Cook, M. L. 1996. *Organizing Dissent: Unions, the State, and the Democratic Teachers' Movement in Mexico*. University Park: Pennsylvania State University Press.

———. 2007. *The Politics of Labor Reform in Latin America: Between Flexibility and Rights*. University Park: Pennsylvania State University Press.

Cravey, A. J. 1998. *Women and Work in Mexico's Maquiladora*. Lanham, MD: Rowman & Littlefield.

Crowley, M., D. Tope, L. J. Chamberlain, and R. Hodson. 2010. "Neo-Taylorism at Work: Occupational Change in the Post-Fordist Era." *Social Problems* 57 (3):421–447.

Cruz Campa, C. 2009. "Situación actual de la economía y de la industria del vestido." Mexico City: Cámara Nacional de la Industria del Vestido (CANAIVE).

Dahl, H. M., P. Stoltz, and R. Willig. 2004. "Recognition, Redistribution, and Representation in Capitalist Global Society: An Interview with Nancy Fraser." *Acta Sociologica* 47 (11):374–382.

Damanpour, F., and W. M. Evan. 1984. "Organizational Innovation and Performance: The Problem of 'Organizational Lag.'" *Administrative Science Quarterly* 29 (3):392–409.

De Coster, J. 2007. "Mexico Slow to Move from U.S. Supplier to Global Player." *just-style.com*, April 18. http://www.just-style.com/article.aspx?id=97055.

de la Garza Toledo, E., ed. 1998. *Estrategias de modernización empresarial en México, flexibilidad y control sobre el proceso de trabajo*. Mexico City: Fundación Friedrich Ebert.

———. 2003. "Estructura industrial y condiciones de trabajo en la manufactura." In *Situación del trabajo en México*, ed. E. de la Garza Toledo and C. Salas, 251–272. Mexico City: Plaza y Valdés-IET.

———. 2006. "Modelos de producción en la manufactura ¿Crisis del toyotismo precario?" In *La situación del trabajo en México*, ed. E. de la Garza Toledo and C. Salas, 55–87. Mexico City: Plaza y Valdés.

de la O, M. E. 2002. "La flexibilidad inflexible: Estudios de caso de plantas maquiladoras electrónicas en el norte de México." *Papeles de Población* 33:200–221.

DesMarteau, K. 1999. "Defining the Key Issues of 1999." *Bobbin* 41 (4):44–46.

Dicken, P. 2007. *Global Shift: Mapping the Changing Contours of the World Economy.* 5th ed. New York: Guilford Press.

DiMaggio, P. J., and W. W. Powell. 1983. "The Iron Cage Revisited: Institutional Isomorphism and Collective Rationality in Organizational Fields." *American Sociological Review* 48 (2):147–160.

Doeringer, P., and M. Piore. 1971. *Internal Labor Markets and Manpower Analysis.* Lexington, MA: D.C. Health.

Dohse, K., U. Jürgens, and T. Malsch. 1985. "From 'Fordism' to 'Toyotism'? The Social Organization of the Labor Process in the Japanese Automobile Industry." *Politics & Society* 14:115–146.

Domínguez-Villalobos, L., and F. Brown-Grossman. 2010. "Trade Liberalization and Gender Wage Inequality in Mexico." *Feminist Economics* 16 (4):53–79.

Dunlop, J. T., and D. Weil. 1996. "Diffusion and Performance of Modular Production in the U.S. Apparel Industry." *Industrial Relations* 35 (3):334–355.

Dussel Peters, E. 2005. "Economic Opportunities and Challenges Posed by China for Mexico and Central America." Study prepared for the German Development Institute. Bonn: German Development Institute.

———. 2008. "GCCs and Development: A Conceptual and Empirical Review." *Competition and Change* 12 (1):11–27.

Dussel Peters, E., C. Ruiz Durán, and M. J. Piore. 2002. "Learning and the Limits of Foreign Partners as Teachers." In *Free Trade and Uneven Development: The North American Apparel Industry after NAFTA,* ed. G. Gereffi, D. Spener, and J. Bair, 224–245. Philadelphia: Temple University Press.

Eckstein, S. 2002. "Globalization and Mobilization: Resistance to Neoliberalism in Latin America." In *The New Economic Sociology: Developments in an Emerging Field,* ed. M. F. Guillén, R. Collins, P. England, and M. Meyer, 330–368. New York: Russell Sage Foundation.

Edwards, P. K., and H. Scullion. 1982. *The Social Organization of Industrial Conflict: Control and Resistance in the Workplace.* Oxford: Basil Blackwell.

Edwards, R. 1979. *Contested Terrain: The Transformation of the Workplace in the Twentieth Century.* New York: Basic Books.

Edwards, R., and J. McCarthy. 2004. "Resources and Social Movement Mobilization." In *The Blackwell Companion to Social Movements,* ed. D. A. Snow, S. A. Soule, and H. Kriese, 116–124. London: Blackwell.

Elger, T., and C. Smith, eds. 1994. *Global Japanization? The Transnational Transformation of the Labour Process.* London: Routledge.

Elias, P., and M. Birch. 1994. "Establishment of Community-wide Occupational Statistics: ISCO 88 (COM), a Guide for Users." University of Warwick, Institute for Employment Research, Coventry. http://www2.warwick.ac.uk/fac/soc/ier/research/isco88/isco88.pdf.

Elson, D., and R. Pearson. 1986. "Third World Manufacturing." In *Waged Work: A Reader,* ed. *Feminist Review,* 67–92. London: Virago.

Epstein, G. A. 2005. *Financialization and the World Economy.* Cheltenham, UK: Edward Elgar.

Esbenshade, J. L. 2004. *Monitoring Sweatshops: Workers, Consumers, and the Global Apparel Industry.* Philadelphia: Temple University Press.

Escobar Latapí, A. 2003. "Men and Their Histories: Restructuring, Gender Inequality, and Life Transitions in Urban Mexico." In *Changing Men and Masculinities in Latin America,* ed. M. C. Gutmann, 84–114. Durham, NC: Duke University Press.

Evans, P. 2000. "Fighting Marginalization with Transnational Networks: Counter-hegemonic Globalization." *Contemporary Sociology* 29 (1):230–241.

———. 2008. "Is an Alternative Globalization Possible?" *Politics & Society* 36 (2):271–305.

Fantasia, R. 1988. *Cultures of Solidarity: Consciousness, Action and Contemporary American Workers*. Berkeley: University of California Press.

Fernández, J. 1999. "Inside Politics: Fobaproa's Belly." *Business Mexico* 9 (8):19.

Fernández-Kelly, M.P. 1984. *For We Are Sold, I and My People*. Albany: State University of New York Press.

Fernández-Vega, C. 1999. "Expediente FOBAPROA." *La Jornada*, August 2. http://www.jornada.unam.mx/1999/08/02/expediente.html.

Florida, R., and M. Kenney. 1991. "Transplanted Organizations: The Transfer of Japanese Industrial Organization to the U.S." *American Sociological Review* 56 (3):381–398.

Fraser, N. 1997. *Justice Interruptus: Critical Reflections on the "Postsocialist" Condition*. New York: Routledge.

Frausto Sánchez, M. 2000. "CONOCER: Consejo de Normalización y Certificación de Competencia Laboral." *Ingenierías* 3 (7):52–27. www.ingenierias.uanl.mx/7/pdf/7_Manuel_Fraustro_Conocer.pdf.

García Flores, L. 2001. "A dos meses de iniciado el movimiento en Moctezuma, la JLCA aún no ha entregado la toma de nota." *MRN1*, June 1.

———. 2007. "De Protección, 90 por ciento de los contratos laborales en el DF: Mirón." *MRN1*, May 7.

García Flores, L., and C. O. Morales. 2001. "Suman voces obreras y campesinos para exiger acabe política del garrote." *MRN1*, May 2.

García Quintanilla, J. 2000. "Las mujeres y los movimientos sociales en estado central." In *Las hojas de la comunidad*, ed. A. Chao Barona, 285–294. Temixco, Mexico: UNICEDES [Unidad Central de Estudios para el Desarrollo Social].

Garrido, C. 2000. "Entrepreneurial Strategies in Response to Structural Change in Mexico." In *Emerging Markets: Past and Present Experiences, and Future Prospects*, ed. S. Motamen-Samadian and C. Garrido, 55–72. London and New York: Macmillan.

Garrido, C., and C. Puga. 1990. "Transformaciones recientes del empresariado Mexicano." *Revista Mexicana de Sociología* 52 (2):43–61.

Garrido Noguera, C., and C. Ortiz Guerrero. 2009. "De crisis en crisis: La evolución reciente de las grandes empresas Mexicanas." *Problemas del Desarrollo* 40 (154): 47–75.

Gereffi, G. 1997. "Global Shifts, Regional Responses: Can North America Meet the Full-Package Challenge?" *Bobbin* 39 (3):16–31.

Gereffi, G., and M. Martinez. 1999. "Blue Jeans and Local Linkages: The Blue Jeans Boom in Torreón, Mexico." October. Background paper prepared for the *World Development Report 2000/2001 on Poverty and Development*. World Bank. http://siteresources.worldbank.org/INTPOVERTY/Resources/WDR/Background/gereffi.pdf.

Gereffi, G., M. Martinez, and J. Bair. 2002. "Torreón: The New Blue Jeans Capital of the World." In *Free Trade and Uneven Development: The North American Apparel Industry after NAFTA*, ed. G. Gereffi, D. Spener, and J. Bair, 203–223. Philadelphia: Temple University Press.

Gereffi, G., D. Spener, and J. Bair, eds. 2002. *Free Trade and Uneven Development: The North American Apparel Industry after NAFTA*. Philadelphia: Temple University Press.

Goodwin, J. 2001. *No Other Way Out.* Cambridge: Cambridge University Press.

González de la Rocha, M. 2006. "Vanishing Assets: Cumulative Disadvantage among the Rural Poor." In *Out of the Shadows: Political Action and the Informal Economy in Latin America,* ed. M. P. Fernández-Kelly and J. Shefner, 97–123. University Park: Pennsylvania State University Press.

González de la Rocha, M., and A. Escobar Latapí. 2008. "Choices or Constraints? Informality, Labour Market, and Poverty in Mexico." *IDS [Institute of Development Studies] Bulletin* 39 (2):37–47.

Gordon, D. M., R. Edwards, and M. Reich. 1982. *Segmented Work, Divided Workers: The Historical Transformation of Labor in the United States.* Cambridge: Cambridge University Press.

Graham, L. 1995. *On the Line at Subaru-Isuzu: The Japanese Model and the American Worker.* Ithaca, NY: ILR/Cornell University Press.

Gramsci, A. 1971. *Selections from the Prison Notebooks.* New York: International Publishers.

Grenier, G. J. 1988. *Inhuman Relations: Quality Circles and Anti-unionism in American Industry.* Philadelphia: Temple University Press.

Grupo Financiero Banamex Accival. 1996. *Mexico: Your Partner for Growth.* Mexico City: Mexican Investment Board.

Guerrero Ortíz, M. 2007. "Percepción de remesas de los hogares y condición migratoria en Zacatecas, 2000–2005." *Revista Electrónica Zacatecana sobre Población y Sociedad* 7 (31):1–20.

Guler, I., M. F. Guillén, J. M. Macpherson. 2002. "Global Competition, Institutions, and the Diffusion of Organizational Practices: The International Spread of ISO 9000 Quality Certificates." *Administrative Science Quarterly* 47 (2):207–232.

Hamilton, N. 1982. *The Limits of State Autonomy: Post-revolutionary Mexico.* Princeton, NJ: Princeton University Press.

Hannan, M. T., and J. H. Freeman. 1984. "Structural Inertia and Organizational Change." *American Sociological Review* 49:149–164.

Hanson, G. H. 1994. "Industrial Organization and Mexico-U.S. Free Trade: Evidence from the Mexican Garment Industry." In *Global Production: The Apparel Industry in the Pacific Rim,* ed. E. Bonacich, L. Cheng, N. Chinchilla, N. Hamilton, and P. Ong, 230–246. Philadelphia: Temple University Press.

Hartmann, H. 1976. "Capitalism, Patriarchy, and Job Segregation by Sex." *Signs* 1:137–169.

Harvey, D. 2005. *A Brief History of Neoliberalism.* Oxford: Oxford University Press.

Hathaway, D. 2000. *Allies across the Border.* Boston: South End Press.

Healy, T. 2008. *Gendered Struggles against Globalisation in Mexico.* Hampshire: Ashgate.

Herring, C. 2004. "Skin Deep: Race and Complexion in the 'Color-blind' Era." In *Skin Deep: How Race and Complexion Matter in the "Color-blind" Era,* ed. C. Herring, V. Keith, and H. Derrick Horton, 1–21. Urbana: University of Illinois Press.

Hirschman, A. O. 1970. *Exit, Voice, and Loyalty: Responses to Decline in Firms, Organizations, and States.* Cambridge, MA: Harvard University Press.

Hirst, P., and G. Thompson. 2001. *Globalization in Question: The International Economy and the Possibilities of Governance.* 2nd ed. Hoboken, NJ: Polity.

Hobsbawm, E. J. 1964. *Labouring Men: Studies in the History of Labour.* New York: Basic Books.

Hodson, R. 2001. *Dignity at Work.* Cambridge: Cambridge University Press.

Hodson, R., S. Creighton, C. S. Jamison, S. Rieble, and S. Welsh. 1994. "Loyalty to Whom? Workplace Participation and the Development of Consent." *Human Relations* 47:895–909.

Hodson, R., S. Rieble, S. Welsh, C. S. Jamison, and S. Creighton. 1993. "Is Worker Solidarity Undermined by Autonomy and Participation? Patterns from the Ethnographic Literature." *American Sociological Review* 58 (3):398–416.

Hossfeld, K. J. 1990. "'Their Logic against Them': Contradictions in Sex, Race, and Class in Silicon Valley." In *Women Workers and Global Restructuring*, ed. K. Ward, 149–178. Ithaca, NY: ILR Press.

ILO [International Labor Organization]. 2005. "Informe núm. 336 (México): Queja contra el gobierno de México presentada por el Sindicato Progresista de Trabajadores de las Industrias Maquiladoras de la República Mexicana (SPTIMRM)." http://www.ilo.org/ilolex/cgi-lex/pdconvs2.pl?host=status01&textbase=ilospa&document=1428&chapter=3&query=M%E9xico%40ref&highlight=&querytype=bool&context=0.

ILOGB [International Labor Office Governing Body]. 2009. "354th Report of the Committee on Freedom of Association." Geneva: International Labor Organization.

INEGI [Instituto Nacional de Estadística, Geografía e Informática]. 1999. "Características principales de las unidades económicas manufactureras, según rama de actividad y estratos de personal ocupado." XV Censo industrial industrias manufactureras subsector 32. Producción de textiles, prendas de vestir e industria del cuero, tabulados básicos censos económicos 1999, 21. Aguas Calientes, Mexico: INEGI. http://www.inegi.org.mx/sistemas/biblioteca/detalle.aspx?c=10345&upc=702825176020&s=est&tg=0&f=2&cl=0&pf=Eco.

———. 2001. Table: "Indicadores de distribución de la población." In *Indicadores sociodemográficos de México, 1930–2000*, 21. Aguas Calientes, Mexico: INEGI. http://www.inegi.gob.mx/prod_serv/contenidos/espanol/bvinegi/productos/integracion/sociodemografico/indisociodem/2001/indi2001.pdf.

———. 2002. *La industria textil y del vestido en México*. Aguas Calientes, Mexico: INEGI.http://www.inegi.org.mx/prod_serv/contenidos/espanol/bvinegi/productos/integracion/sociodemografico/Textil/2002/ITVM%202002.pdf.

———. 2007. *Clasificación Mexicana de ocupaciones (CMO), vols. 1 and 2*. Aguas Calientes, Mexico: INEGI. Vol. 1, http://www.inegi.gob.mx/est/contenidos/espanol/metodologias/clasificadores/Clasificaci%C3%B3n%20Mexicana%20de%20Ocupaciones,%20vol%20I.pdf. Vol. 2, http://www.inegi.gob.mx/est/contenidos/espanol/metodologias/clasificadores/Clasificaci%C3%B3n%20Mexicana%20de%20Ocupaciones,%20vol%20II.pdf.

Jacobs, B. A. 1998. "Mexico Promises to Remain No. 1 for Production Sharing." *Bobbin* 39:20–25.

Jefferson, L. R. 1996. "Mexico: No Guarantees, Sex Discrimination in Mexico's Maquiladora Sector." *Human Rights Watch (New York)*. http://www.unhcr.org/refworld/docid/3ae6a7f110.html.

Jiménez, B. 1999. "El crédito al consumo, 10.25 por ciento más caro que en latinoamérica." *El Financiero*, October 7.

Juárez Nuñez, H. 2003. *Rebelión en el greenfield*. Puebla, Mexico: Benemérita Universidad Autónoma de Puebla.

Juravich, T. 1985. *Chaos on the Shop Floor: A Worker's View of Quality, Productivity, and Management*. Philadelphia: Temple University Press.

*just-style.* 2005a. "Which Countries Will Win and Lose?" *just-style.com,* January 7. http://www.just-style.com/analysis/which-countries-will-win-and-lose_id92431 .aspx.

*just-style.* 2005b. "CHINA: US Textile Talks Fail, New Safeguards Announced." *just-style.com,* September 1. http://www.just-style.com/article.aspx?id=90503&lk=s.

*just-style.* 2007. "Central America's Textile Sector Could Woo $1bn Under CAFTA-DR." *just-style.com,* April 24. http://www.just-style.com/article.aspx?id=97109&lk=s.

*just-style.* 2010. "June 2010 Management Briefing: Mexico Clothing and Textile Sector Rides Boom and Bust." *Just-style.com,* June 21. http://www.just-style.com/ management-briefing/mexico-clothing-and-textile-sector-rides-boom-and-bust_ id108052. aspx?lk=dm.

Kaplan, T. 1982. "Female Consciousness and Collective Action: The Case of Barcelona, 1910–1918." *Signs 7* (3):545–566.

Kaplinsky, R., with A. Posthuma. 1994. *Easternisation: Spread of Japanese Management Techniques to Developing Countries.* Ilford, UK: Frank Cass.

Keck, M. E., and K. Sikkink. 1998. *Activists beyond Borders: Advocacy Networks in International Politics.* Ithaca, NY: Cornell University Press.

Kenney, M., and R. Florida. 1993. *Beyond Mass Production: The Japanese System and Its Transfer to the U.S.* New York: Oxford University Press.

Kessler, J. A. 1999. "New NAFTA Alliances Reshape Sourcing Scene." *Bobbin* 41 (3):45–55.

Kessler-Harris, A. 1982. *Out of Work: A History of Wage-Earning Women in the United States.* New York: Oxford University Press.

Klandermans, B., M. Roefs, and J. Olivier. 2001. "Grievance Formation in a Country in Transition: South Africa, 1994–1998." *Social Psychology Quarterly* 64 (1):41–54.

Knauss, J. 1998. "Modular Mass Production: High Performance on the Low Road." *Politics & Society* 26 (2):273–296.

Kopinak, K. 1996. *Desert Capitalism: Maquiladora's in North America's Western Industrial Corridor.* Tucson: University of Arizona Press.

Krippner, G. R. 2005. "The Financialization of the American Economy." *Socio-economic Review* 3:173–208.

Kucera, D. 1997. "Women and Labor Market Flexibility: The Cases of Japan and the Former West Germany in the Postwar Years." In *Gender and Political Economy: Incorporating Diversity into Theory and Policy,* ed. E. Murati, H. Boushey, and W. Fraher IV, 132–149. New York: M.E. Sharpe.

La Botz, D. 1992. *Mask of Democracy: Labor Suppression in Mexico Today.* Boston: South End Press.

———. 2005. "Mexico's Labor Movement in Transition." *Monthly Review* 57 (2). http://www.monthlyreview.org/0605labotz.htm.

La Botz, D., and R. Alexander. 2003. "Mexico's Labor Law Reform: Employers' Rights vs. Associational Rights." *Guild Practitioner* 60 (149):149–161.

Lamphere, L. 1985. "Bringing the Family to Work: Women's Culture on the Shop Floor." *Feminist Studies* 11(3):519–540.

———. 1987. *From Working Daughters to Working Mothers.* Ithaca, NY: Cornell University Press.

Laslavic, M. 1999. "The Mexican Apparel Industry." White Plains, NY: Gilbert Co. http://members.fortunecity.com/sgci1/foreign/mexapparel.html.

Lee, C. K. 1998. *Gender and the South China Miracle: Two Worlds of Factory Women.* Berkeley: University of California Press.

Levine, C., L. Salmon, and D. H. Weinberg, 1999. "Revising the Standard Occupational Classification System." *Monthly Labor Review* 122 (5):36–45.

Levy Orlick, N. 2006. "Nuevo comportamiento de los bancos y su efecto en países con mercados financieros débiles: El caso de México." *Problemas del Desarrollo: Revista Latino Americana de Economía* 36 (141):59–84.

Lichterman, P. 1996. *The Search for Political Community: American Activists Reinventing Commitment.* Cambridge: Cambridge University Press.

Lipietz, A. 1987. *Mirages and Miracles: The Crises of Global Fordism.* London: Verso.

Lozano Ascencio, F. 2001. "Características sociodemográficas de los hogares percep-tores de remesas en México: Los casos de Morelos y Zacatecas." Paper presented at the Latin American Studies Association, Washington, DC, September.

———. 2003. "Discursos oficiales, remesas y desarrollo en México." *Migración y Desarrollo* 1:1–15.

Lustig, N., and T. Rendón. 1979. "Female Employment, Occupational Status, and Socioeconomic Characteristics of the Family in Mexico." Translated by Ximena Bunster B. *Signs* 1 (5):143–153.

MacDuffie, J. P. 1995. "Human Resource Bundles and Manufacturing Performance: Organizational Logic and Flexible Production Systems in the World Auto Industry." *Industrial and Labor Relations Review* 48(2):197–221.

Mackin, Robert. 1995. "Explaining Independent Unionism in Mexico: The case of the *Frente Auténtico del Trabajo.*" Madison: University of Wisconsin, Sociology Department.

MacLeod, D. 2004. *Downsizing the State: Privatization and the Limits of Neoliberal Reform in Mexico.* University Park: Pennsylvania State University Press.

Mansbridge, J. 2001. "The Making of Oppositional Consciousness." In *Oppositional Consciousness: The Subjective Roots of Social Protest,* ed. J. Mansbridge and A. Morris, 1–19. Chicago: University of Chicago Press.

Maquila Solidarity Network. 2008. "Interviews with Apparel Brands about Trends in Global Sourcing." http://en.maquilasolidarity.org/en/node/824.

———. 2009. "The Crisis and Its Effect on Mexico's Textile and Apparel Industry." http://en.maquilasolidarity.org/node/906.

Maquila Solidarity Network and Human and Labour Rights Commission of the Tehuacán Valley. 2003. *Tehuacán: Blue Jeans, Blue Waters and Worker Rights.* Toronto: Maquila Solidarity Network. http://en.maquilasolidarity.org/sites/maquilasolidarity.org/files/MSN-Tehuacan-ENG-2003.pdf?SESS89c5db41a82abcd7da 7c9ac 60e04ca5f= unvlgtieu.

Martínez Cruz, J. 2000. "Quince años de lucha proletaria." In *Las hojas de la comunidad,* ed. A. Chao Barona, 151–172. Temixco, Mexico: UNICEDES [Unidad Central de Estudios para el Desarrollo Social].

Massey, D. S., and M. Sánchez R. 2010. *Brokered Boundaries: Creating Immigrant Identity in Anti-immigrant Times.* New York: Russell Sage Foundation.

Maxfield, S. 1990. *Governing Capital: International Finance and Mexican Politics.* Ithaca, NY: Cornell University Press.

Mayo, E. 1933. *The Human Problems of an Industrial Civilization.* New York: Macmillan.

McAdam, D. 1982. *Political Process and the Development of Black Insurgency, 1930–1970.* Chicago: University of Chicago Press.

McCarthy, J., and M. Zald. 2002. "The Enduring Vitality of Resource Mobilization Theory of Social Movements." In *Handbook of Sociological Theory,* ed. J. H. Turner, 533–565. New York: Kluwer Academic/Plenum.

McKay, S. C. 2006. *Satanic Mills or Silicon Islands? The Politics of High-Tech Production in the Philippines*. Ithaca, NY: Cornell University Press.

Meyer, D. S. 2004. "Protest and Political Opportunity." *Annual Review of Sociology* 30:125–145.

Middlebrook, K. J. 1995. *The Paradox of Revolution: Labor, the State, and Authoritarianism in Mexico*. Baltimore: Johns Hopkins University Press.

Mier Merelo, A. 2003. *Sujetos, luchas, procesos y movimientos sociales contemporáneos*. Temixco, Mexico: UAEM-UNICEDES [Universidad Autónoma del Estado de Morelos–Unidad Central de Estudios para el Desarrollo Social].

Milkman, R. 1987. *Gender at Work*. Urbana: University of Illinois Press.

———. 1997. *Farewell to the Factory: Auto Workers in the Late Twentieth Century*. Berkeley: University of California Press.

Mohanty, C. T., A. Russo, and L. Torres, eds. 1991. *Third World Women and the Politics of Feminism*. Bloomington: Indiana University Press.

Molyneux, M. 2000. "Twentieth Century State Formation in Latin America." In *Hidden Histories of Gender and the State in Latin America*, ed. E. Dore and M. Molyneux, 33–84. Durham, NC: Duke University Press.

Montaño, S., and V. Milosavljevic. 2010. "La crisis económica y financiera: Su impacto sobre la pobreza, el trabajo y el tiempo de las mujeres." In *Mujeres y desarrollo*, series. Santiago, Chile: UN Comisión Económica para América Latina [CEPAL], División de asuntos de género.

Moore, B Jr. 1978. *Injustice: The Social Basis of Obedience and Revolt*. White Plains, NY: M. E. Sharpe.

Morales, C. O. 2001a. "Gobierno, obreros y patrones firman pacto por una nueva cultura laboral." *MRN1*, September 18.

———. 2001b. "Insiste líder de CTM en hacer frente común en contra del desempleo." *MRN1*, September 15.

Morera Camacho, C. 1998. *El capital financiero en México y la globalización: Límites y contradicciones*. Mexico City: Ediciones Era.

Morgen, S., and A. Bookman. 1988. "Rethinking Women and Politics: An Introductory Essay." In *Women and the Politics of Empowerment*, ed. A. Bookman and S. Morgen, 3–29. Philadelphia: Temple University Press.

Motamen-Samadian, S. 2000. "Mexican Banking Crisis: Causes and Consequences." In *Emerging Markets: Past and Present Experiences and Future Prospects*, ed. S. Motamen-Samadian and C. Garrido, 3–29. New York: Macmillan.

*MRN1*. 2002. "Un año de dignidad en Moctezuma." March 25.

Muñoz Jumilla, A. R. 2004. "Evolución de las remesas familiares ante el crecimiento económico en México, 1950–2002." *Papeles de Población* 42:9–35.

Muñoz Jumilla, A. R., and L. E. del Moral Barrera. 2007. "Las remesas familiares frente la cuenta corriente en México, 1980–2006." *Papeles de Población* 54:163–190.

Naples, N. 2003. *Feminism and Method: Ethnography, Discourse Analysis, and Activist Research*. New York: Routledge.

Nehring, D. 2005. "Reflexiones sobre la construcción cultural de las relaciones de género en México." *Papeles de Población* 45:221–245.

Nolasco, M. 1977. "La familia mexicana." *Revista FEM* (2):14–19.

Oliver, N., and B. Wilkinson. 1989. "Japanese Manufacturing Techniques and Personnel and Industrial Relations Practice in Britain: Evidence and Implications." *British Journal of Industrial Relations* 27 (1):73–91.

————. 1997. *The Japanization of British Industry: New Development in the 1990s.* Cambridge: Blackwell.

Ong, A. 1987. *Spirits of Resistance and Capitalist Discipline: Factory Women in Malaysia.* Albany: State University of New York Press.

Ordoñez, S. 1997. "La reestructuración productiva industrial en México." *Papeles de Población* 14:59–70.

Padavic, I., and B. Reskin. 2002. *Women and Men at Work.* 2nd ed. Thousand Oaks, CA: Pine Forge.

Pangsapa, P. 2007. *Textures of Struggle: The Emergence of Resistance among Garment Workers in Thailand.* Ithaca, NY: Cornell University Press.

Parker, M., and J. Slaughter. 1988. *Choosing Sides: Unions and the Team Concept.* Boston: South End Press.

Pastor, M., and C. Wise. 2003. "A Long View of Mexico's Political Economy: What's Changed? What Are the Challenges?" In *Mexico's Politics and Society in Transition,* ed. J. S. Tulchin and A. D. Selee, 179–214. Boulder, CO: Lynne Rienner.

Pedrero Nieto, M. 2003. "Las condiciones de trabajo en los años noventa en México: Las mujeres y hombres: ¿Ganaron o perdieron?" *Revista Mexicana de Sociología* 65 (4):733–761.

Peimbert Frías, G. 2002. "Innovación tecnológica y cambio cultural en la empresa pública y privada en México (Estudio comparativo entre la filial mexicana de la empresa multinacional Nissan y Capufe, organismo público descentralizado del estado mexicano, a principios del siglo XXI)." PhD diss. en Ciencias Políticas y Sociales, Centro de Investigación y Docencia en Humanidades, Cuernavaca, Mexico.

Peña, D. 1997. *The Terror of the Machine: Technology, Work, Gender and Ecology on the U.S.-Mexican Border.* Austin: University of Texas Press.

Pil, F. K., and J. P. MacDuffie. 1996. "The Adoption of High-Involvement Work Practices." *Industrial Relations* 35 (3):423–455.

Plankey-Videla, N. 2006a. "Gendered Contradictions: Managers and Women Workers in Self-Managed Teams." *Research in the Sociology of Work* 16:85–116.

————. 2006b. "It Cuts Both Ways: Workers, Management and the Construction of a 'Community of Fate' on the Shop Floor in a Mexican Garment Factory." *Social Forces* 84 (4):2099–2120.

————. 2012. "Informed Consent as Process: Problematizing Informed Consent in Organizational Ethnographies." *Qualitative Sociology* 35 (2).

Pollert, A. 1996. "'Team Work' on the Assembly Line." In *The New Workplace and Trade Unionism,* ed. P. Ackers, C. Smith, and P. Smith, 178–209. London: Routledge.

Prechel, H. 1994. "Economic Crisis and the Centralization of Control over the Managerial Process: Corporate Restructuring and Neo-Fordist Decision-Making." *American Sociological Review* 59 (5):723–745.

————. 2000. *Big Business and the State: Historical Transitions and Corporate Transformation, 1880s–1990s.* Albany: State University of New York Press.

Preston, J., and S. Dillon. 2005. *Opening Mexico: The Making of a Democracy.* New York: Farrar, Straus & Giroux.

QSR International Pty Ltd. 2008. NVivo qualitative data analysis software, ver. 8.

Rabon, L. C., and O. G. West. 2000. "Mexico's Balancing Act: NAFTA, New Markets and Major Investments, Textile Industry Growth Initiatives." *Bobbin,* July. http://findarticles.com/p/articles/mi_m3638/is_11_41/ai_64705151.

Rendón Galicia, S. 2008. *El sindicalismo automotriz independiente en el México de los Setenta.* Mexico City: CONACULTA/PACMyC [Consejo Nacional para la Cultura y las Artes/Programa de Apoyo a las Culturas Municipales y Comunitarias].

Rodríguez Garavito, C. 2008. "Sewing Resistance: Transnational Organizing, Anti-sweatshop Activism, and Labor Rights in the US-Caribbean Basin Apparel Industry (1990–2005)." Center for Migration and Development Working Papers, Woodrow Wilson School of Public and International Affairs, Princeton University, NJ.

Roethlisberger, F. J., and W. J. Dickson. 1939. *Management and the Worker.* Cambridge, MA: Harvard University Press.

Román de Santos, G. N.d. "Como sobrevivir en tiempos de competitividad mundial y hacer que tu empresa siga adelante: AMMJE, Romansa." PowerPoint presentation. Mexico City.

Ramírez Cuevas, J. 2005. "El sindicalismo de negocios: Contratos a la carta." *La Jornada,* March 20.

Roscigno, V. J., and R. Hodson. 2004. "The Organizational and Social Foundations of Worker Resistance." *American Sociological Review* 69 (1):14–39.

Rose, S. 1992. *Limited Livelihoods: Gender and Class in Nineteenth-Century England.* Berkeley: University of California Press.

Rosen, E. I. 2002. *Making Sweatshops: The Globalization of the U.S. Apparel Industry.* Berkeley: University of California Press.

Roxborough, I. 1984. *Unions and Politics in Mexico: The Case of the Automobile Industry.* New York: Cambridge University Press.

Salzinger, L. 2003. *Genders in Production: Making Workers in Mexico's Global Factories.* Berkeley: University of California Press.

Sánchez Resendiz, V. H. 2001. "La Lagunilla: Una historia para recordar." In *Las hojas de la comunidad,* ed. A. Chao Barona, 135–149. Temixco, Mexico: UNICEDES [Unidad Central de Estudios para el Desarrollo Social].

Saragoza, A. M. 1988. *The Monterrey Elite and the Mexican State, 1880–1940.* Austin: University of Texas Press.

Sassen, S. 2001. *The Global City: New York, London, Tokyo.* 2nd ed. Princeton, NJ: Princeton University Press.

Schaeffer, R. K. 2009. *Understanding Globalization: The Social Consequences of Political Economic, and Environmental Change.* 4th ed. Lanham, MD: Rowman & Littlefield.

Schneider Ross, B. 2008. "Economic Liberalization and Corporate Governance: The Resilience of Business Groups in Latin America." *Comparatives Politics* 40 (4):379–397.

Schrank, A. 2008. "Homeward Bound? Interest, Identity, and Investor Behavior in a Third World Export Platform." *American Journal of Sociology* 114 (1):1–34.

Secretaría de Economía. 2001a. *Central State Development Plan, 1994–2000.*

———. 2001b. *Programa para Competitividad de la Cadena Fibras-Textil-Vestido.* N.p.: Secretaria de Economía.

Seidman, G. W. 2007. *Beyond the Boycott: Labor Rights, Human Rights, and Transnational Activism.* New York: Russell Sage Foundation.

Selby, H. A., A. D. Murphy, and S. A. Lorenzen with I. Cabrera, A. Castañeda, and I. Ruiz Love. 1990. *The Mexican Urban Household: Organizing for Self-Defense.* Austin: University of Texas Press.

Sen, A. 2002. "How to Judge Globalism." *American Prospect,* special suppl., "Globalism and Poverty," 13 (1):A5.

Shaiken, H. 1990. *Mexico in the Global Economy: High Technology and Work Organization in Export Industries*, Monograph Series no. 33. San Diego: Center for U.S.-Mexican Studies, University of California, San Diego.

Silver, B. 2003. *Forces of Labor: Workers' Movements and Globalization since 1870*. Cambridge: Cambridge University Press.

Sklair, L. 1993. *Assembling for Development: The Maquila Industry in Mexico and the United States*. San Diego: Center for U.S.-Mexican Studies, University of California, San Diego.

Smith, D. E. 1987. *The Everyday World as Problematic: A Feminist Sociology*. Boston: Northeastern University Press.

Smith, M. P. 2007. "The Two Faces of Transnational Citizenship." *Ethnic and Racial Studies* 30 (6):1096–1116.

Smith, V. 1990. *Managing in the Corporate Interest: Control and Resistance in an American Bank*. Berkeley: University of California Press.

———. 1997. "New Forms of Work Organization." *Annual Review of Sociology* 23 (1):315–339.

Spener, D., G. Gereffi, and J. Bair. 2002. "Introduction: The Apparel Industry and North American Economic Integration." In *Free Trade and Uneven Development: The North American Apparel Industry after NAFTA*, ed. G. Gereffi, D. Spener, and J. Bair, 3–22. Philadelphia: Temple University Press.

Staudt, K. 1987. "Programming Women's Empowerment: A Case from Northern Mexico." In *Women on the U.S.-Mexico Border*, ed. V. L. Ruiz and S. Tiano, 155–173. Boston: Allen &Unwin.

Stephen, L. 1997. *Women and Social Movements in Latin America: Power from Below*. Austin: University of Texas Press.

Suárez Aguilar, E., and M. A. Rivera Rios. 1994. *Pequeña empresa y modernización: Análisis de dos dimensiones*. Cuernavaca: Universidad Nacional Autónoma de México, Centro Regional de Investigaciones Multidisciplinarias [CRIM].

Sydow, J., G. Schreyögg, and J. Koch. 2009. "Organizational Path Dependence: Opening the Black Box." *Academy of Management Review* 34 (4):689–709.

Taplin, I. M. 1996. "Rethinking Flexibility: The Case of the Apparel Industry." *Review of Social Economy* 54 (2):191–220.

Taylor, F. W. [1911] 1947. *Scientific Management*. New York: Harper & Brothers.

Tello, M. P., and W. E. Greene. 1996. "U.S. Managerial Strategies and Applications for Retaining Personnel in Mexico." *International Journal of Manpower* 17 (8):54–95.

Thompson, E. P. 1978. "Eighteenth-Century English Society: Class Struggle without Class?" *Social History* May 3 (2):133–165.

Tiano, S. 1994. *Patriarchy on the Line: Labor, Gender and Ideology in the Mexican Maquila Industry*. Philadelphia: Temple University Press.

Tilly, C. 1995. "To Explain Political Processes." *American Journal of Sociology* 100 (6):1594–1610.

Tirado, R. 1998. "Mexico: From the Political Call for Collective Action to a Proposal for Free Market Economic Reform." In *Organized Business, Economic Change, Democracy in Latin America*, ed. F. Durand and E. Silva, 3–22. Miami: North-South Center Press.

Tsutsui, W. M. 2001. *Manufacturing Ideology: Scientific Management in Twentieth-Century Japan*. Princeton, NJ: Princeton University Press.

Tuirán Gutiérrez, R., J. Santibáñez Romellón, and R. Corona Vázquez. 2006. "El monto de las remesas familiares en México: ¿Mito o realidad?" *Papeles de Población* 50:147–169.

Turner, L., and D. B. Cornfield. 2007. *Labor in the Urban Battlegrounds: Local Solidarity in a Global Economy.* Ithaca, NY: Cornell University Press.

*Twin Plant News.* 1997. "Textile Boom: Mexico Top U.S. Trade Partner." June.

Vallas, S. P. 1987. "The Labor Process as a Source of Class Consciousness: A Critical Examination." *Sociological Forum* 2 (2):237–256.

———. 2003a. "The Adventures of Managerial Hegemony: Teamwork, Ideology, and Worker Resistance." *Social Problems* 50 (2):204–225.

———. 2003b. "Why Teamwork Fails: Obstacles to Workplace Change in Four Manufacturing Plants." *American Sociological Review* 68 (2):223–250.

———. 2006. "Empowerment Redux: Structure, Agency, and the Remaking of Managerial Authority." *American Journal of Sociology* 111 (6):1677–1717.

Vallas, S. P., W. Finlay, and A. S. Wharton. 2009. *The Sociology of Work: Structures and Inequalities.* New York: Oxford University Press.

Varley, A. 2000. "Women and the Home in Mexican Family Law." In *Hidden Histories of Gender and the State in Latin America,* ed. E. Dore and M. Molyneux, 238–261. Durham, NC: Duke University Press.

Vidal, M. 2007. "Manufacturing Empowerment? 'Employee Involvement' in the Labour Process after Fordism." *Socio-economic Review* 5 (2):197–232.

Westney, D. E. 1987. *Imitation and Innovation: The Transfer of Western Organizational Patterns in Meiji Japan.* Cambridge, MA: Harvard University Press.

Westwood, S. 1985. *All Day, Every Day: Factory and Family in the Making of Women's Lives.* Urbana and Chicago: University of Illinois Press.

Williams, H. 2001. "Of Free Trade and Debt Bondage: Fighting Banks and the State in Mexico." *Latin American Perspectives* 28 (119):30–51.

Williams, R. 1977. *Marxism and Literature.* Oxford: Oxford University Press.

Wolf, D. L. 1992. *Factory Daughters: Gender, Household Dynamics, and Rural Industrialization in Java.* Berkeley: University of California Press.

Young, G. 1987. "Gender, Identification, and Working Class Solidarity among Maquila Workers in Ciudad Juárez: Stereotypes and Realities." In *Women on the U.S.-Mexico Border,* ed. V. L. Ruiz and S. Tiano, 105–127. Boston: Allen &Unwin.

Zetka, J. R. Jr. 1992. "Mass-Production Automation and Work-Group Solidarity in the Post–World War II Automobile Industry." *Work & Occupations* 19 (3):255–288.

Zolberg, A. 1972. "Moments of Madness." *Politics & Society* 2 (2):183–207.

# Index

Note: 'n' indicates a note; 't' indicates a table; and 'f' indicates a figure.

# About the Author

Nancy Plankey-Videla is an assistant professor of sociology at Texas A&M University. She was born in Chile, grew up in Mexico, and attended college in the United States. Her next project examines the connection between precarious employment and health disparities among migrant sex workers and day laborers in Texas.

CPSIA information can be obtained at www.ICGtesting.com
Printed in the USA
BVOW040002220512

290733BV00003B/2/P